Additional Advance Praise for *Legacy of Honor*

"Whether you choose to become a teacher, a police officer, a doctor, or even the mayor of the greatest city in the world, your experiences as an Eagle Scout will prove invaluable. Alvin Townley's *Legacy of Honor* does justice to the proud history and bright future of the Eagle Scouts."

—MAYOR MICHAEL BLOOMBERG

"Scouting and conservation share respect for the natural world, so it always seemed natural to me that many of our staff and volunteer leaders would be Eagle Scouts. This book provides wonderful insights into all that Scouting offers and how it helps develop tomorrow's leaders."

—STEVEN J. McCORMICK, PRESIDENT AND CEO, THE NATURE CONSERVANCY

"In *Legacy of Honor*, we learn not only who many of these Eagle Scouts were, but the kind of leaders they have become and the enormous contributions they have made to their country and the world. In compiling these life stories, Alvin Townley has completed a picture of an extraordinary program and how its training has helped shape equally extraordinary lives."

—HON. CHRISTINE TODD WHITMAN, FORMER GOVERNOR OF NEW JERSEY AND ENVIRONMENTAL PROTECTION AGENCY ADMINISTRATOR

"Commitment and devotion to the bedrock principles of our country—optimism, fairness, determination, and preparedness—are inseparably intertwined with Scouting. Alvin Townley does a superb job of portraying how Eagle Scouting helps shape these everyday yet incredibly powerful values that serve our families and society so well."

—J. W. MARRIOTT, JR., CHAIRMAN AND CEO, MARRIOTT INTERNATIONAL INC.

"*Legacy of Honor* captures clearly the spirit of America's Eagle Scouts—their dedication to high ideals, self-discipline, and character. Eagle Scouts are not just leaders but particular kinds of leaders, guided by a sense of purpose and service to others. The profiles of outstanding individuals in Townley's book explain why. It is a reassuring story in a period of history that sometimes causes one to wonder whether the development of character has gone out of fashion."

—KENNETH P. RUSCIO, PRESIDENT, WASHINGTON AND LEE UNIVERSITY

LEGACY *of* HONOR

For Nathan -
Remember, it's a
lifelong trail...
Best,

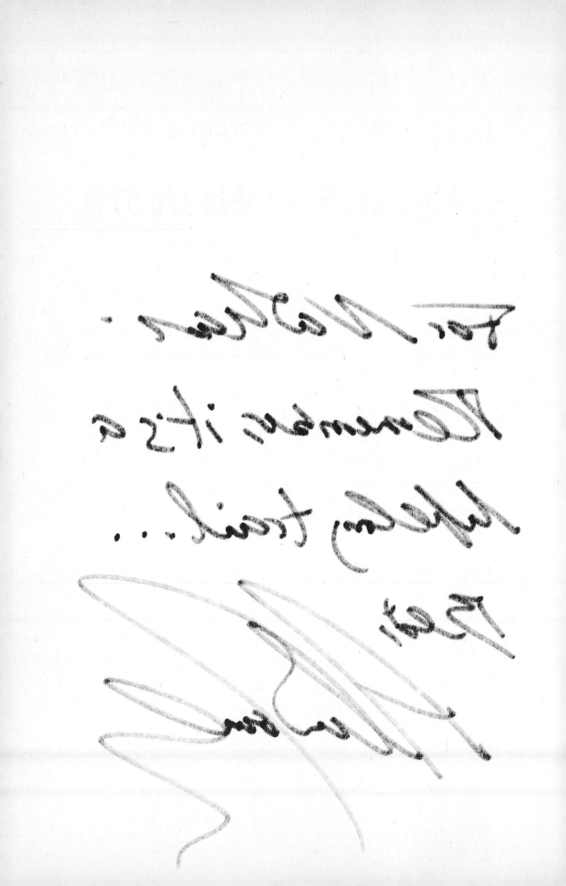

ALVIN TOWNLEY

LEGACY *of* HONOR

THE VALUES AND INFLUENCE OF
AMERICA'S EAGLE SCOUTS

THOMAS DUNNE BOOKS ST. MARTIN'S PRESS NEW YORK

THOMAS DUNNE BOOKS.
An imprint of St. Martin's Press.

www.thomasdunnebooks.com
www.stmartins.com

Book design by Jonathan Bennett

Library of Congress Cataloging-in-Publication Data

Townley, Alvin.
    Legacy of honor : the values and influence of America's Eagle Scouts / Alvin Townley.— 1st ed.
      p.   cm.
    Includes bibliographical reference and index.
    ISBN-13: 978-0-312-36653-7
    ISBN-10: 0-312-36653-1
    1. Eagle Scouts—United States—History.   2. Eagle Scouts—United States.   I. Title.

HS3313.Z7 T68   2007
369.43092'273—dc22

                                          2006051421

10 9 8

To all those who have devoted their lives to the service
of others—in work, in encouragement, and in time—
this book, with deep admiration, is dedicated.

CONTENTS

LEGACY *of* HONOR

INTRODUCTION

Like many Scouts, I finished the last requirements for the Eagle rank shortly before my eighteenth birthday, the last day a young man can achieve Scouting's highest award. As my mother pinned the silver Eagle badge to the chest pocket of my uniform, however, I neither fully understood nor bothered to contemplate how earning a badge at seventeen would have any lasting effect on my life. On that evening in 1993, I had no inkling that a decade later I would return to Scouting to consider that very question.

As I moved through that next decade, a journey slowly unfolded before me. Both the questions it posed and the answers it offered led me to uncover something about myself and, in a broader sense, my country. It eventually coaxed me down a path along which I began to capture the essence not only of an institution or a badge but of a code, a way, and a group of people who have truly shaped America.

It was during my college years on the carpeted aisle of a church in Lexington, Virginia, that I began my journey. I remember pressing through the dispersing congregation after the Sunday service and encountering an older gentleman who wore a silver Eagle Scout pin on the lapel of his suit. I caught the gentleman's eye and asked, "Oh, were you an Eagle Scout?" Since I'd already presupposed his answer, I added, "So was I."

"Well, son," he replied, "I still *am* an Eagle Scout," and with a grin he added, "And so are you."

The old gentleman, whose face I remember clearly but whose name I never learned, was right; you never cease being an Eagle Scout. Only three years had passed since I'd reached Eagle myself, and I had never considered his point. But during the years that followed, his words haunted me on occasion, and I began stumbling down this path, speaking with other Eagles and hearing their thoughts. I wondered what it meant to be an Eagle Scout after you shed your Scout uniform with its attendant patches and sashes. Further, how do the virtues represented by that small medal mark your adult life? Those were the questions I felt increasingly compelled to answer. Then another fellow Eagle turned those questions into a broader quest.

It happened over several slices of pizza with my longtime friend Sean O'Brien, who had just arrived home for Christmas from a semester spent pursuing his doctorate at Notre Dame. As we finished our last slices, Sean casually asked, "Oh, did I tell you I'm sending my Eagle badge back to the national office?"

"What," I asked, as if I hadn't heard him. He began explaining his decision. Sean disagreed with the national organization's stance on several difficult and contentious issues. For him, the very real challenges of the day had superseded the pride he held in his rank. He no longer considered himself an Eagle.

I thought differently. After all, we had stood side by side in the spring of 1993 as our mothers pinned our Eagle medals to our uniforms. To me, Sean has always embodied everything an Eagle should.

"I still *am* an Eagle Scout," I remembered the old gentleman telling me. But here was Sean, a friend I respect immensely, saying "I'm no longer an Eagle Scout. That rank no longer represents who I am."

It surprised me that Sean so quickly disavowed the rank he'd earned. Wasn't there something about being an Eagle Scout that far transcended the politics of the day? Weren't there a legacy and tradition to be proud of? I suddenly realized that I didn't know the answer.

As I first considered those questions, however, I began to glimpse their answers in the very person who prompted me to ask them in the first place. Outwardly, Sean and I are two very different people. He tends to favor Birkenstocks and progressive doctrine, while I wear polished wingtips far more often than I'd like and have moderate, middle-of-the-road views. Yet Sean and I are remarkably akin. We both live by the principles expressed in the pledge we recited together each Thursday night for six years at the meetings of Troop 103:

On my honor, I will do my best
To do my duty to God and my country
and to obey the Scout Law;
To help other people at all times;
To keep myself physically strong,
mentally awake, and morally straight.

In the Scout Oath, we found a set of common virtues that has defined us far more than our choice of footwear or political party. We share a code that will always guide the *way* we live our lives, even as the paths we follow may be entirely divergent.

Much like Sean and me, Scouting's nearly 2 million Eagle Scouts have had an incalculable number of differences: They are aged seventeen, thirty-four, and ninety-three. They descend from southern planters, western pioneers, great Indian chiefs, and newly arrived immigrants. They worship in mosques, cathedrals, and temples. They live in downtown Chicago, in the mansions of Old Greenwich, and in the sprawling suburbs of Los Angeles. They are astronauts and athletes, politicians and policemen. These men had the answers I sought, and I could wait no longer to meet them. I left a job I loved, sold a house I perhaps loved even more, and set out across the country. The ensuing year became an odyssey and a very personal journey during which I discovered as much about life as I did about Scouting.

I put Lexington, Virginia, in my rearview mirror in October 2004. In a Ford Explorer filled with clothes and gear, I headed south to find America's Eagle Scouts. The following night, I sat overlooking the South Carolina coast with two new friends, an Eagle and his wife, listening to stories of Scouting as it was in 1940. Shortly thereafter, I learned about Scouting as it is today, driving through the Florida Keys with a motley crew of camp counselors. Over the twelve months that followed, I traveled from coast to coast. I drove through a Seattle housing project with a former resident who had grown up to become a governor. I visited with the mayor of New York City before catching a train to Long Island, where a volunteer fire chief reminisced about Scouting until well past midnight. On Capitol Hill, senators spoke with me about camping trips. In Newport Beach, two California Scouts proudly walked me along the decks of *Del Mar* and *Argus*, the renowned ships their Scout unit cares for and sails. In summer, I suffered 100-degree heat at the National Jamboree with 35,000 Scouts; in winter, I shivered in 4-degree cold atop a Vermont peak with two others. On an emotional level, I looked for fulfillment in one place and found it in another. In the process I learned about what matters in life.

When the long journey finally ended, trains, planes, cars, and boats had carried me 40,000 miles throughout the country. Along the way, sometimes by plan, sometimes by happenstance, I found Eagles who were present at the events that marked our history. I spoke with Eagles who were part of the great movements that have swept our country. I met men who are molding our next generation, and I met those who *are* that next generation. Through the portraits of a few, I hoped to gain some understanding of them all. With their stories, I hoped to define how their common virtues have influenced American life.

In the accounts that follow, I have tried to emphasize the legacy of these Eagles. But in a larger sense, this story is not just about Eagle Scouts; it is also about timeless ideals and the contributions of great Americans. It delves into our country's heritage, and it gives us hope for the future. Through glimpses of these uncommon leaders, I hope we all come to understand how a common set of values makes us what we are as a nation.

THE EAGLE RANK

Thank you for listening, and God bless America," concluded Gary Locke, echoing the traditional closing line from the State of the Union address. With that, the camera lights were killed, and Washington's governor sat relieved, having just delivered his party's 2003 response to the president's annual message.

Three time zones away, camera lights in another studio flashed on, and a familiar voice replaced Governor Locke's on television screens across the nation. Venerable news anchor Tom Brokaw recapped, "Gary Locke, two-term governor of the State of Washington and chairman of the Democratic Governors' Conference, was chosen tonight to respond to the president's State of the Union message; Yale-educated, Eagle Scout." In one statement, Tom Brokaw told America volumes about Gary Locke.

Locke earned his Eagle Scout rank decades ago, before he could vote and long before he walked onto the political stage. Yet Brokaw chose *Eagle Scout*. The veteran anchor knew that upon hearing those two words, viewers in every household would immediately recognize something rare and admirable about Washington's governor. That recognition pays tribute to a long legacy, one nourished over the years by generations of Eagles and manifested in the marks they have left on our nation. It is a legacy born nearly a century ago from a mythic story.

The streetlamps of old London cast a dim glow along the path of an American businessman as he pushed his way through the thick fog that lay over the English capital. The clouds had rendered the midday sun helpless, so the city's gas lamps were lit before noon, and their weak glow was all William D. Boyce had to guide his way. Unfortunately for Boyce, the lamps were not enough, and he became lost in the fog-shrouded city. A young boy soon approached him and asked if he needed directions. Boyce answered affirmatively, so the boy guided him along London's misty streets, eventually delivering him to his destination. Once there, the well-meaning American pulled a coin from his pocket to tip his guide. The boy refused. "No thank you, sir," he said. "Not for doing a good turn."

Certain that an American boy would never have turned down a nickel, Boyce asked why this British boy refused.

"I'm a Scout," was the simple reply.

Boyce had never heard of a Scout and wanted to know more. The boy agreed to wait for him to finish his business and then take him to Scout headquarters in London. Soon, the two were again navigating foggy lanes en route to the Victoria Street headquarters of the Boy Scouts. They reached the door, but before Boyce could learn his guide's name, the British Scout disappeared into the haze and into history, having finished his good turn. The unknown Scout never knew how important that particular deed would become.

Inside Scout headquarters that day in 1909, William Boyce, a fifty-one-year-old newspaper and magazine publisher from Illinois, met Lieutenant General Robert S. S. Baden-Powell, a decorated British military hero and the founder of Britain's new youth movement. During a long conversation, the general's ideas for building character in British youth captivated Boyce and set history in motion: Scouting was coming to America.

When Britain's Lord Baden-Powell wrote *Scouting for Boys* in 1908 and began building the network of camps, troops, and leaders that would launch the Scouting movement, the United States was a case study in transition. Abroad, President Theodore Roosevelt announced America's emergence as a global military power by sending the Navy's Great White Fleet around the world, visiting foreign ports and inspecting America's new imperial territories. "The young giant of the West stands on a continent and clasps the crest of an ocean in either hand," Roosevelt proclaimed. "Our nation, glorious in youth and strength, looks into the future with eager eyes and rejoices as a strong man to run a race." Like the Imperial Britain that birthed Baden-Powell's Scouts, America needed well-trained, patriotic young men to realize the future Roosevelt envisioned.

At home, industrialization was busy changing American society in monumental ways. To grasp the evolving future, families knew their children would need a broader education. No longer did they send their boys directly into the fields to learn the skills and values of farming. Instead, they sent them to school in growing numbers, hoping they would gain the knowledge and experience this new America needed. At the same time, immigrants flooded cities, hastening urbanization and bringing children and youth into the labor force. Many feared that the physical health of the next generation would suffer, while others worried that familiarity with the outdoors, such a hallmark of American youth, would fade.

But perhaps most important, the nation's view of character and virtue began to change. The early twentieth century saw the dawn of the Progressive movement and suddenly people became concerned about the threats declining morality might pose to the still-young republic. The day's leading thinkers firmly believed that educating citizens for a democratic society would require instruction in ideals as well as practical skills. A preoccupation with values and morality marked the first decade of the 1900s, and the country's hunger to instill civic virtues in its youth opened the doorway for a new program that could build character in America's young men.

Into this receptive climate William D. Boyce introduced Britain's Boy Scout program. He brought together Ernest Thompson Seton of the Woodcraft Indians, Daniel Carter Beard of the Sons of Daniel Boone, and Edgar M. Robinson of the YMCA, who were already hard at work with their own independent youth organizations. Together, they established the Scouting movement in America. On February 8, 1910, they incorporated the Boy Scouts of America "to promote, through organization and cooperation with other agencies, the ability of boys to do things for themselves and others, to train them in Scoutcraft, and to teach them patriotism, courage, self-reliance, and kindred virtues using the methods which are now in common use by Boy Scouts." Following the philosophy of French observer Alexis de Tocqueville, Scouting would be a "school of democracy" that would develop the citizens this growing, aspiring nation would need in the decades ahead.

Once they firmly established the Boy Scouts of America, the founders took Baden-Powell's program and made it America's. Under the guidance of new Chief Scout Executive James E. West, they developed the Scout Oath and and the Scout Law, the creeds that still define Scouting's ideals. They also published a guidebook, the *Handbook for Boys*, which would become one of the best-selling books in history, and created a program of ranks and merit badges. Finally, the founders created one badge, one award to stand above all others, which would require the most time, dedication, and knowledge to achieve. It became Scouting's highest honor and a symbol of American character. The founders called it Eagle Scout.

The 1911 *Handbook for Boys* explained to its readers that the Eagle rank would "represent the all-around perfect Scout." By that description, the founders meant the type of person who best fit America's new vision of itself. They ensured that only the finest Scouts would attain the rank by designing a long trail of advancement. Before a boy reached the end, the Scouting program demanded that he master a broad array of skills, prove his character, and demonstrate his ability to lead others.

While working toward Eagle, a Scout progresses through the hierarchical ranks of Scout, Tenderfoot, Second Class, First Class, Star, and Life. As he achieves each of these successive ranks, he acquires a progressive set of skills, completes increasingly complex projects, and leads others within his troop and community. Advancement from one rank to the next also entails completing designated sets of merit badges. Eventually, a Scout must earn twenty-one of these small, circular patches to attain Eagle, and each badge requires him to master a new subject or skill. Merit badges resemble small academic courses and require boys to learn from older Scouts and adult experts. These seasoned counselors include local officials, doctors, businessmen, teachers, and other professionals who volunteer their time to give young Scouts firsthand exposure to new realms. Under the guidance of these mentors, Scouts organize projects and meet new intellectual and physical challenges in a dizzying array of areas.

Scouts earning Engineering merit badge, for example, must interview professional engineers and complete a detailed research project; those earning Aviation merit badge must explain the scientific principles behind flight and demonstrate how to control an airplane. Those earning Citizenship in the Nation learn as much about the basis of American government as many college students learn in an introductory government class.

The merit badges offered by Scouting represent the variety of new doors open to an Eagle Scout. Astronomy, Backpacking, Chemistry, Fish and Wildlife Management, Journalism, Medicine, Oceanography, Public Speaking, Rifle Shooting, Safety, Small Boat Sailing, Theater, Whitewater, and Wilderness Survival, to name several of the 120 subjects available to Scouts. To ensure that all Eagles share a common foundation, Scouting developed a list of required merit badges, which are sewn onto the merit badge sash of every Eagle Scout: Camping, Citizenship in the Community, Citizenship in the Nation, Citizenship in the World, Family Life, First Aid, Environmental Science, Personal Fitness, Personal Management, Cycling or Hiking or Swimming, and Lifesaving or Emergency Preparedness. These merit badges leave their recipients with lifelong interests in addition to practical knowledge they may use for years to come. Often, they challenge Scouts to venture into unfamiliar territory.

It seemed likely that Bill Bradley, a Rhodes Scholar, NBA and Olympic standout, and successful politician, might name Scholarship, Sports, and Citizenship in the Nation merit badges as those he valued most, but, when asked, this Eagle Scout from Crystal City, Missouri, replied: "Cooking merit badge. I still remember trying to build a fire and cook food over the fire in the backyard of the counselor overseeing whether I passed the requirements. And the others I valued most would be Lifesaving and First Aid. Those were the three memorable merit badges where I either got a skill, like Lifesaving, or did something that I didn't think I could do, like Cooking, or learned something that I needed to learn, which was First Aid."

In all its activities, Scouting reinforces the idea of leadership, and as boys near Eagle, their responsibilities increase. Sixteen-year-old Thomas Martin of Troop 74 is one example. For six months, Thomas had served as the troop's top nonadult leader: senior patrol leader. He bore responsibility for planning meetings, leading camping expeditions, and organizing the teams of Scouts within the troop, called patrols. He reported directly to the Scoutmaster, and all the troop's patrol leaders relied on his instructions. As soon as his fellow Scouts elected him senior patrol leader, Thomas ran Troop 74, but it took several months for him to become a true leader.

"I came in as SPL six months ago," confided Thomas. "For the first three months, I tried to lead by yelling at the guys. If they needed to do something, I'd try to make them do it or yell at them, or just yell louder. I finally learned that's not the way you lead. I realized you lead by taking them aside, one on one, and working with them, teaching them the 'whys' and 'hows.' You lead by example."

Once Scouts have honed their leadership abilities and earned the necessary merit badges, they face the Eagle Scout Service Project, the most infamous challenge on the climb to Eagle. In a very real sense, Eagles have left their mark on our nation by completing hundreds of thousands of projects across the country. Projects are very diverse and range from improving trails in wilderness areas and national parks to establishing lasting community programs that provide services to those in need. The diversity of projects—of which approximately 50,000 are completed in a single year—is as astounding as the number of Scouts and volunteers they involve.

One example is Dundalk, Maryland, where six Eagle Scouts from Troop 354 led projects that created artificial reefs to help restore fish and marine life populations in the Chesapeake Bay. Each Eagle recruited other Scouts to help manufacture hollow, concrete structures that now sit on the bottom of the bay, providing homes and shelter for aquatic life. In total, the reefs that Troop 354 made weigh over 19,000 pounds and required 2,500 hours of work from the Scouts and other volunteers. These Eagles, like Eagles across the country, identified a need, used their knowledge to design a plan, gained approval from local officials, recruited others, and managed their projects. Their preparation took months, but perhaps nothing challenged the Scouts more than convincing their friends to sacrifice several weekends for hard labor.

Once a Scout completes all the requirements for Eagle, he undergoes a review, during which a panel of Scout leaders tests his knowledge. Not everyone passes. "When I went before the board of review for the first time, I flunked it," remembers John Rainey, an Eagle Scout from Anderson, South Carolina. "This is 1955, and back then, you had to do semaphore signals [communicating with two flags]. I went before the board of review, and I can still see it; it's etched in my brain. It was in the First Baptist Church in a classroom, and three or four men were sitting at a table. I went up there, and

I don't remember all I messed up, but one of the things I got wrong was the semaphore signaling. And I didn't get Eagle. I had to come back and do it again. That was the first memorable failure in my life. I remember that one distinctly. I remember that I failed. I remember that I had to come back and try again. That has been one of life's great lessons because many times you fail, but if you just stick to it, if you just don't give up, if you just keep coming back and hitting it again and again, you'll make it."

Three decades later, John decided to repay Scouting by serving as Scoutmaster of Troop 1 in Spartanburg, where he helped his son and a number of other young men pass their own boards of review—hopefully on the first try— and become Eagle Scouts.

When all the attributes Scouting instills in an Eagle come together in later years, they make a very real difference. Admiral Bob McNitt offers a poignant example from his experience as executive officer of the U.S.S. *Barb*, one of World War II's most decorated submarines. He recalls rescuing Allied prisoners of war who had been afloat without food or water since the Japanese transport carrying them sank in the South Pacific.

"We got to the scene six days later," remembers this Eagle from Perth Amboy, New Jersey. "A few here and there on rafts seemed to be alive, and we would approach the raft, pass them a line, and one of these survivors would look up and hold the rope and not know what it meant. He'd be so far gone he couldn't understand what was happening. The only way to handle that was to go after them. So I put a line around myself, dove over the side, and swam out. I'd pick up a survivor with a cross chest carry and bring him back to the submarine and hoist him aboard. I did that until I was too tired to continue."

Sadly, only a handful of POWs survived the six-day ordeal and made it safely to the deck of the *Barb*. "Thirty-two out of 1,500," Admiral McNitt said quietly. "Awful situation."

"What did we learn from that?" he asked. "First, the value of being physically fit, which was Scouting's intent. We had learned how to swim strongly and knew the techniques of lifesaving. You learned to do what you have to do when it's necessary, and you jump in and do it. You don't tell someone to do it; *you* do it. I think these are all characteristics that Scouting develops."

Each of these Eagle Scouts belongs to a tradition begun in 1910. Almost a century later, the founders of the Boy Scouts would be proud of their legacy and the men it has produced. As Chief Scout Executive James West and his partners envisioned, only a small number of youth had the perseverance to reach Eagle: Of the 110 million boys who have joined the Scout movement, just shy of 2 million have reached its pinnacle. The group that did finish has made a tremendous mark on the world. As a result of their lives, the Eagle Scout has become an American icon, universally known as hard-working, successful, and honest, whether his silver medal hangs proudly on his khaki uniform or lies buried in his cluttered attic, unseen for fifty years.

"The Eagle rank means the same and requires the same across time and place," commented Pete Sessions, who earned his Eagle in 1970, many years before becoming a Scoutmaster and a U.S. congressman. "It means honor and respect. Eagle will be the one thing, the one constant, Scouts will carry from their youth throughout their whole life."

The consistent weight the rank carries through time stems from the record of other Eagles, as Gerald R. Ford noted. "Not only do you inherit this record of honor," observed Ford, the first Eagle to become president of the United States, "you also inherit the great obligation that goes with it. . . . Many Eagle Scouts have contributed to our country's greatness. You now have the opportunity, and the obligation, to help make her future still greater." Despite the changes time continually brings to American society, Eagles have forged this record by living out the same ideals, generation after generation.

In November 1910, Arthur R. Eldred joined a Scouting program with fewer than 60,000 members nationwide. Two years later, when he became the first Scout to earn the Eagle rank, women had yet to receive the right to vote and Henry Ford had just introduced the Model T to the public. Gerald Ford earned his Eagle on the brink of the Great Depression, a decade before he left home to fight the Second World War. Future generations made their way through Scouting, and boys earned their Eagles as Dr. Martin Luther King, Jr., told civil rights marchers in Washington about his dream and as astronauts came ever closer to the moon. When Alexander Holsinger earned the one-millionth Eagle Scout badge in 1982, America and Scouting had weathered the twin crises of Vietnam and Watergate. And the tens of thousands of Scouts who now attain Eagle each year become part of the newest generation in a movement that has become part of America. The country

Gerald R. Ford (far left) and Scouts from Troop 15, Grand Rapids, Michigan, 1929
COURTESY OF GERALD R. FORD LIBRARY

each of these Eagles knew in their youth has changed, but the phrase "Eagle Scout" still carries the same meaning as it did when it was first uttered in 1910. Throughout the past century, Eagle Scouts have lived the virtues of their rank, sustaining a great tradition and shaping American life.

PART I

The Legacy Through History

The 110 million young men who have worn the Scout uniform have left their marks on almost every major event in recent American history. Sometimes the organization itself helped to shape events. The Boy Scouts of America planned massive war bond drives during World War I and organized efforts to collect scrap metal during World War II. It launched early campaigns to prevent drug abuse during the 1970s and 1980s. Today, it regularly sponsors nationwide community service initiatives, mobilizing its 125,000 Boy Scout troops, Cub Scout packs, and other units.

Most important, however, Scouting has influenced America through its Eagle Scouts. As Scouts, not only did these young men learn skills, they also developed character. They learned to persevere as they climbed through the ranks. They learned about ethics as they followed the examples of their leaders. They developed a sense of duty to others as they served their communities, and they grew into true leaders, tested by experience on countless expeditions and projects. That combination of skills and character remained with them as they entered various arenas of adult life. And when they faced choices and challenges as soldiers and statesmen, teachers and parents, the virtues they exercised at critical junctures in our history shaped the nation for the better.

THE SECOND WORLD WAR

The first significant generation of Eagle Scouts earned the rank in the late 1920s and early 1930s. These young men belonged to a Scouting program that had finally become nationally established, having grown considerably from the time of its founding in 1910. Three decades into the twentieth century, the Boy Scouts of America had nearly 1 million members, with troops registered in every state. The Eagles of this generation were shaped not only by Scouting, but by the heady success of the Roaring Twenties and the wrenching uncertainty of the Great Depression. As they emerged from the dark years of scarcity that marked the 1930s, they began to steel themselves for the greater challenge that lay ahead.

Bill Kemp, an Eagle Scout and a Scoutmaster for seventeen years, was among the generation of Eagles who came of age during the Second World War. He was also among the last Scouts to see Scouting's founder, Lord Baden-Powell, and hear his message of peace. In 1937, Bill traveled to the Fifth World Scout Jamboree in the Netherlands where "B-P," as Baden-Powell was called, gave his farewell address to the boys he loved. The eighty-one-year-old "Chief Scout of the World" urged his audience to be brothers with Scouts of all faiths and backgrounds. He hoped they would keep their memories of the jamboree alive, saying "It will remind you of the many friends to whom you have held out the hand of friendship and so helped them through goodwill to bring about God's reign of peace among men." He hoped that somehow, the brotherhood of Scouting would avert the war he feared would come. Regrettably, it could not.

"That's the most vivid memory of my life," Bill recalled, himself eighty-one when we spoke. "He stood up at that bonfire with a Jacob's staff and he made a speech and said, 'You're my boys and before we meet again, we'll probably be at war. It's too bad the rest of the world can't get along like you can.'"

The storm clouds outside the World Jamboree continued to gather, and the days ahead would indeed be as dark as Baden-Powell feared. Sadly, he would not live to see the conflict's resolution, having died in 1941. Many of the 29,000 Scouts present at the jamboree also perished before peace was restored in 1945. But Baden-Powell's boys served well. A short decade after their mothers pinned the Eagle medal to their Scout uniform, America's Eagle Scouts led soldiers onto battlefields around the globe.

Steven Liscinsky of the Second Ranger Battalion traded his Scout pocket knife for an Army combat knife, which he jabbed into the rocky cliffs of Normandy as he scaled Pointe du Hoc before dawn on D-Day, June 6, 1944. On the Pacific outposts of Guadalcanal and Roi Namur, Mitchel Paige and Jimmie Dyess—one an enlisted sergeant, one a commissioned captain—earned

The founder of the worldwide Scouting movement, Lord Robert Baden-Powell, with Scouts from around the globe COURTESY OF BOY SCOUTS OF AMERICA

Congressional Medals of Honor as they rallied their fellow U.S. Marines against enemy lines. Nearby on the beaches of Tarawa, Corpsman Ken Rook used the skills he learned in First Aid merit badge to help wounded soldiers until a Japanese bullet found his shoulder, making him one of the 3,300 casualties of the infamously vicious four-day battle. With thousands of deeds like these, this generation of Eagle Scouts began to create a true legacy as the collective virtues of their youth carried the nation through the Second World War.

ROBERT L. SCOTT, JR.

TROOP 23, MACON, GEORGIA

EAGLE SCOUT, 1923

On the afternoon of December 26, 1942, the planes of the Twenty-third Fighter Group were spread across an airfield in southeastern China. Combat and the elements had weathered the planes' green paint, but the blazing eyes and hungry jaws emblazoned on their fuselages still marked each as a legendary Flying Tiger. The leader of this increasingly famous unit, Colonel Robert L. Scott, Jr., surveyed his command proudly. Since his boyhood, he had dreamed of becoming a pilot. Gazing across the sunny field, he saw his dreams realized.

Soon, he also recognized a serious problem. His eighteen P-40 fighters lay scattered across the wide airfield to confound any Japanese pilots who made their way through the base's defenses, as they had days earlier. Unfortunately, the primitive radar system gave the American pilots scant minutes to respond to an attack. On this day, Scott could find no Jeeps available to deliver his pilots to their far-flung planes quickly enough to defend the base in the event of an attack.

Clerks paid little attention to his requests for transportation, instead referring him up the chain of command again and again. Worried that a flight of hostile bombers could find the base wholly unprepared and incensed by the lack of cooperation, Scott made his case for transportation to the major in charge of the airfield. Rebuffed again, Colonel Scott pulled rank and commandeered the vehicles his men needed. He stormed out of the office under a hail of court-martial threats.

As it turned out, the Flying Tigers got this necessary transportation just before air raid sirens began to sound. They piled into the Jeeps and sped to their planes as the sirens wailed. The squadron rolled down the runway, rose into the sky, and followed their commander as he winged toward their prey.

Scott always led his pilots into combat with supreme confidence. Thousands of training hours had prepared him for this very moment, and he always approached battle with a sense of serenity and purpose. His confidence spread among his men and filled them with the assurance that helped the unit become one of the most famous and successful squadrons of World War II.

That day, the perpetually outnumbered Tigers took their usual position relative to their targets, between the enemy and the bright China sun. As the twenty-seven Japanese bombers approached, Scott's fighters fell upon them from above. The American pilots quickly sent several victims spiraling downward, smoke billowing behind them. The remaining bombers jettisoned their payloads in the futile hope of gaining enough agility to escape the quick P-40s. Within minutes, however, the Flying Tigers downed the entire squadron of Japanese planes. Scott alone claimed four.

Confident that they owned the sky—as Scott later phrased it—the Twenty-third Fighter Group flew home. Scott's men returned to relax and recount stories of the battle, but Scott went straight to headquarters to find his commanding officer and personal mentor, Major General Claire Lee Chennault. Scott knew he needed to answer for the Jeeps he commandeered. He reached headquarters after dark and found Chennault waiting.

"How'd you do Scotty," Chennault asked.

"We shot them all down, sir."

"Well, that's good," Chennault replied patiently. "And the bad news?"

"Well, I had to commandeer all the base traffic."

"In that case," Chennault sighed, "General Stillwell will be raising Cain. You better go to Chungking with me tomorrow."

The next day, they walked into General Stillwell's office and found him hastily drawing up court-martial charges against Scott. Chennault asked Scott to leave. As he walked out the door, Scott overheard his mentor saying, "Now listen you so-and-so. You tear those up. If he *hadn't* done what he did, *I* would be court-martialing him!"

Scott's actions occasionally put Chennault on the spot, but Scott became a son to the general. Several years later, Chennault wrote of Scott: "His story is a record of persistence, determination, and courage from early boyhood.

Having determined early in life that he had to fly, he overcame all obstacles in the way to the attainment of his ambition. This story alone should be an inspiration to every American boy."

Flight always fascinated Bob Scott, and in Troop 23 he began to explore his future. As his fellow Scouts set about earning the Aviation merit badge, Scott dutifully helped them ferret pieces of wood, fabric, and rubber from basements and scrap piles around his hometown of Macon, Georgia. As the boys began building model airplanes from their harvest of materials, Scott could feel their enthusiasm, but he didn't quite share it. The sandy-haired twelve-year-old had other plans.

The Scoutmaster had asked each Scout to build a model airplane, and while most Scouts conquered their task by building miniature models, Bob Scott had little desire to be like "most Scouts." Instead, he built a full-size glider, a contraption that dwarfed the rubber-band–powered models pieced together by his friends. Scott wouldn't consider his glider a success unless it could fly—that is, fly with him in it—so he took his quest to the dusty streets that marked many southern towns of the early 1920s.

"I would run along the ground in Macon, and I could feel the wings trying to lift the glider upward, but of course, you couldn't run fast enough to take off," Scott explained eighty years later. "So then I had it towed behind our $25 Model T Ford, but the police ran me off the road. So I figured the thing I needed was altitude."

To escape both the police and the bounds of gravity, the young Scout turned his sights to Mrs. Viola Napier, who owned the tallest house in town. Mrs. Napier agreed to let Scott fly his glider from her roof after he promised to avoid her cherished flowers. "She must have thought it was one of those little old things with rubber bands," he recalled with a not-so-innocent grin.

With the help of his fellow Scouts, Scott hoisted the glider to the rooftop. Then with their cheers egging him on, he ran down the roof and launched himself and his glider into the sky. He felt the wings lifting him upward and found himself flying, peering down on Mrs. Napier's garden nearly three stories below. Unfortunately for both Scott and Mrs. Napier's flowers, however, a sickening crack announced that the wing had broken, and he suddenly found himself *in* Mrs. Napier's garden.

As his friends picked him out of the quagmire of thorns, wood, and canvas that his crash had created, Scott was scratched but even more resolute. Loving nothing more than a challenge, he decided he would become a fighter pilot—and an ace.

I first met General Scott nearly eight decades after he ruined Mrs. Napier's roses. I had discovered that his 1908 birth date ranked him among the nation's oldest living Eagles and soon learned that he also ranked among her most interesting.

On a chilly February morning, I drove through the small town of Warner Robins, Georgia, and found the Museum of Aviation, a complex of buildings and hangars guarded by a number of decommissioned planes from various periods of military aviation. I parked beneath a mounted Vietnam-era fighter and walked into the museum where a volunteer kindly pointed me toward the office of the general, the chairman of the museum's capital campaign and its living legend in residence. On my way to the stairs, I confronted a dark green P-40 with thirteen Japanese victory flags painted on its fuselage. It bore the eyes, mouth, and teeth of the Flying Tigers, and inscribed just to the right of the flags, I saw the former pilot's name, "Col. Scott." Before me was a replica of the plane with which then-Colonel Scott introduced his name into aviation history.

I found the plane's retired pilot upstairs in a simple sky-blue corner office. He was leaning back in an old swivel chair behind a desk only slightly less cluttered than the surrounding shelves and tables. Evidently, the general had been neglecting paperwork and cleaning in favor of golf. At the moment, he was discussing his new glasses with someone on the phone. As I overheard, he'd recently gotten his first pair, ever, but only so he could see better on the golf course.

He warmly welcomed me into his office, offering me one of the chairs in front of his desk. My subject quickly bridged the sixty-seven-year age gap between us, and soon we were laughing together as he recounted the tale of his quest for an Aviation merit badge, which his Scoutmaster awarded him for his effort—if not complete success—in flying the glider. He then arrived at a larger point about merit badges.

"Just about every single thing I did in Scouting—all those merit badges—

was a new profession," he explained. "You can find people who know flowers, but they don't know birds. You can find those who can mix cement, but they couldn't take a hammer and a nail and hit the nail. You learn all of that in Scouting. I mean, you're even a little bit of a doctor. Every one of those merit badges makes you able to do different things. I had all the merit badges except three: Music, Interpreting, and Sculpture—and I couldn't get those now!

"One of the other main things the Boy Scouts teaches you is to be prepared, be prepared for anything," he continued. "And I knew that someday, I was going to meet somebody in the sky who loved his country as much as I loved mine. He might be better-looking, taller, stronger, or more agile, but he never was going to have the experience I had. And I bet you the first Japanese pilot I shot down was eighteen years old. He had two hundred hours at a maximum. I had ten thousand and was thirty-three."

Scott spent his younger years training incessantly to make sure he'd be ready when the call came. "I became what's known in the Air Force as a time hog," he said. "I flew every day and every single time that I was grounded, and I was grounded several times for flying too much. . . . God *un*grounded me."

"For instance, I came to Mitchel Field. I was a second lieutenant, and it was the first time I had a plane with my own name on it. I flew it every day. At the end of the week, the commanding officer sent for me and said, 'I've finally found out who's waking me up every morning. Scott, how many hours have you flown since you got here?'

"I said, 'Eighty-eight, sir,' really proud of myself." I imagined the look of pride and feigned innocence Scott probably gave the officer. As he well knew, eighty-eight hours far exceeded the official ration of flight time. So, with a cold glare, the CO shot back his reply, "Scott, you're grounded until April!"

"And this was only October," added Scott, a trace of irritation still detectable all these years later.

Scott of course, didn't stay grounded for long. He was soon flying again and getting in trouble again. Out came a second illustration of how, in his opinion, his superiors frequently did *their* best to foil him in doing *his* best. He remembered another commanding officer reprimanding him and saying, "You know Scott, you've burned up enough gasoline to fuel a battleship!"

Knowing that his superior had recently crashed a plane, Scott cockily replied, "Yes, sir. But *I* never crashed."

In the years before World War II erupted, this 1932 West Point graduate spent much of his time training young pilots, all the while hoping for the chance to join a fighter wing. When Japanese planes attacked Pearl Harbor on December 7, 1941, he thought that his chance to fly in combat for his country and to realize his boyhood dream had come, but, as Scott put it, "No one called."

He spent hours furiously writing letters to every ally he had in the Army Air Corps, hoping for a transfer from his training assignment to an active fighter wing, with no luck. In truth, no one called because, according to Army standards, Scott was too old and too high-ranking for combat. His commanding officer, General Henry Harms, finally heard of his efforts and sat down with the dejected thirty-three-year-old flight instructor. Scott recalled, "He put a fatherly arm over my shoulder and said, 'Scott, you *were* a fighter pilot. Why son, you're thirty-three years old. Go on back down there and run that flying school and be patient. You might be the youngest general in the army.'"

"I wasn't patient," quipped Scott. In March 1942 he finagled an assignment to a squadron of B-17 bombers bound for the Far East. Unfortunately, Scott arrived in India only to discover that his original mission had been scrubbed, and he soon began flying transport missions over the infamous "Hump," the Himalayas. Never one to give up easily, Scott was determined to make his way into a fighter cockpit.

He knew of General Claire Chennault's reputation for bucking the military system and hoped the general might offer him a chance to fly in combat. For weeks, he sought a chance to meet his future mentor without success. Then his commanders scheduled him to fly a transport into a tiny airstrip crudely carved from the dense Burma jungle. At that base, Scott learned, was Chennault.

There, in his office, the veteran pilot described landing his heavily laden plane on the short runway, which was covered in even proportions by steel planking and dank tropical mud. As his props spun to a halt, he saw Chennault riding tall in a Jeep, racing toward the transport. Scott immediately planned to reveal his boyhood dream of becoming a fighter pilot and was certain that Chennault would grant his wish.

Instead, Scott recalled the general shouting, "Get out of here! The Japanese will be here any minute. Get your airplane off the field; that's the first thing they'll see!"

Scott's plane was 2,000 pounds overloaded and couldn't take off on the short runway without unloading, so he leaped out of the cockpit, wove his way through scrambling pilots and personnel, and chased Chennault into a sandbagged bunker. As he slid into the bunker alongside Chennault, he spotted a lone P-40 fighter that was still on the ground. Scott grabbed the general's elbow and said, "That's the first thing they'll hit, the P-40. Let me have it!"

Chennault gave a withering look at the colonel's eagles on Scott's collar and said, "You're too high ranking and in the wrong-color uniform. Don't you see what that ship is? It's a Chinese airplane!"

In the early days of the war, the original Flying Tigers (also called the American Volunteer Group or AVG) were volunteers for the Chinese military and flew Chinese-owned P-40s, planes strictly off-limits to U.S. personnel. Of course, rules never discouraged Scott, so he repeated his plea. Chennault relented, and Scott sprinted toward the P-40.

General Scott paused in his story to enlighten me on starting a fighter. He methodically walked me through the six steps required to start a P-40 as if he'd just explained it to a new pilot yesterday. If I harbored any illusions of my young mind being sharper than his, he dispelled them. After the lesson, he veered back to his story.

"I don't remember doing any of those six things," he explained, "but the plane started . . . We'll say God started it. I finally got it off the ground, turned around, and looked for the Flying Tigers. Then when I couldn't find the Flying Tigers, I started looking for the Japanese with one airplane! Now that all sounds stupid, but that's what you have to do to win a war."

Chennault gradually welcomed this newcomer into the fighter group; with Scott's persistence, he had little choice. In June 1942, the "Old Man," as Scott called Chennault, gave "Scotty" command of the Flying Tigers. From that time forward, the Tigers would be part of the Twenty-Third Fighter Group, which became the pursuit wing of the new Fourteenth U.S. Air Force, but the group's nickname stuck. In his new post, Colonel Scott saw his work and determination pay off: His thirteen victories made him a double ace and one of the best-known pilots in the war.

I didn't realize how well known Scott was until I found the August 1942 issue of *Life* magazine. Introducing the issue's feature article on the war in China was a half-page glamour photograph of Scott, who looked more like a movie star than a pilot. This was patriotic journalism at its finest, and the caption below the picture called him a "one-man air force." The article itself read, "Colonel Robert L. Scott, commander of pursuits, is probably the most romantic American in China today. . . . Reckless, flashing, romantic, he is likely to become the D'Artagnan of the air in the Far East."

Regardless of how reckless or flashy his persona may have seemed, he does not attribute his leadership ability to these glamorous characteristics. Although he was thousands of miles and many years removed from Macon's Troop 23, he found the skills he learned in Scouting gave him the ability to lead his men into combat.

"An Eagle Scout has a general education as a boy," he said, "and they [*sic*] can do about anything that they're given pretty well. That's what I found out in China. I used to wonder what the common denominator was among all my squadron commanders, and they were all Boy Scouts, all Eagle Scouts."

He credits much of his success in the war to having been a good Scout: being able to earn the trust and respect of his men, lead different types of people, and understand a variety of disciplines. He bristles when he hears people today disparage the ethics that are part of Scouting. "Some people say, 'He acted like a Boy Scout.' And that means something bad," he lamented, leaning back in his chair and throwing up his long, slender arms. "I just hate for somebody to cast off and say, 'Don't be a Boy Scout.' The greatest thing you can be is a good Boy Scout."

Months after I first met General Scott, I visited him on a rainy afternoon at his modest home near the museum. Walking into his living room, I entered a trove of memorabilia. Scott introduced a leopard skin rug in the corner as a trophy from an African safari. Next to the unfortunate leopard sat a number of Chinese artifacts, some notably older than others. He quickly explained the distinction between items he collected during World War II and those he brought back from his latest trip to China, a ninety-day, solo odyssey along the Great Wall in 1980 at age seventy-two. Nobody had ever attempted a similar trek, and Scott relentlessly battled Chinese and American diplomats for years before winning permission. He trekked through the wilds of China armed with food, clothes, and a sand wedge for protection: "I could kill any-body with a sand wedge," he deadpanned. By this time, I'd learned that such feats and quips were quintessentially Scott.

As we moved out of the living room, I came to a shelf that held a row of fourteen neatly arranged books, all of which he wrote. Scott's 1943 autobiog-raphy, *God Is My Co-Pilot*, anchored the left side of the shelf. His latest book, a 1988 release titled *The Day I Owned the Sky*, anchored the right. The first book's cover carried a photograph of the thirty-three-year-old colonel in his propeller-driven P-40 Tomahawk, and the latter showed the seventy-six-year-old Air Force general perched triumphantly atop a modern F-16 Fal-con. "My wife Katherine always told me to have an airplane in the picture with me," he joked. "She said it made me look better."

As I picked up his last book, he proudly told me about the exemption he'd earned (or more accurately, one for which he fought tooth and nail) that allowed him to fly the F-16 and a host of other modern Air Force jets. The waiver let him sidestep the fact that his age placed him decades above the of-ficial age limit for pilots. As if I needed further convincing that he had never acknowledged his age, Scott pointed to a nearby photograph of him running with the Olympic torch as it made its way to the 1996 Centennial Games in Atlanta. At the time, he was eighty-eight years old.

I shelved the book, and we walked toward the rustic back porch, where Scott gestured to a plaque that hung above the door frame. It contrasted starkly with the sharply framed aviation and military prints covering his walls, and its character and simplicity immediately struck me. The weath-ered wood of the plaque was a perfect reflection of the man at my side.

In a Georgia accent roughened by over nine decades of living, he read aloud his favorite quote, a passage taken from Ecclesiastes: "Whatsoever thy hand findeth to do, do it with all thy might."

Considering our mutual interest in Scouting, Scott segued smoothly from Ecclesiastes to the Scout Oath, which he repeated so often in his younger days. "That first line, 'On my honor, I will do my best,' I've always figured that," he said. "And doing *your* best is what gets you in trouble with those people who don't do *their* best. Doing your best isn't trying to show off, but it's just your own way."

Then I understood, not just about the glider incident or his other es-capades but about him, what drove him to accomplish so much and to have so many adventures. The daring spirit of a young Scout who came of age in the early twentieth century never left Scott throughout his life. At the nucleus of that spirit burned two passions: a love of aviation and a penchant for excellence. He always prepared himself to do his best and achieve his own high measure of success. Looking back on our time together, these passions are unmistakable and ever-present, true hallmarks of his long, rich life.

Eventually we ended the day's conversation, drifted slowly out the kitchen door, and walked beneath the pine trees that line his driveway. As we reached my car and said good-bye, the sun at last broke through the clouds and began drying the beads of water on General Scott's Ford Thunderbird, which he reportedly drove as fast as he flew his old P-40. We both looked up at the clearing sky and glimpsed a gray jet taking off from Robins Air Force Base, which lay just a few miles away. Even though he didn't comment, I was sure the general wished he were in the pilot's seat.

Brig. Gen. Robert Lee Scott, Jr., USAF (Ret.)
COURTESY OF MUSEUM OF AVIATION

With that thought, I asked this steely-eyed pilot about the last time he exercised the Scott exemption and flew with the Air Force. "I haven't asked yet this year," he answered, "but I'll probably be tempted before long." That lifelong passion for flight and adventure forever burned warmly inside him. Well into his nineties, he continued doing what he loved, living life his way, according to his own definition of *best*.

As I drove home from what would sadly be our final visit together, I found myself chuckling at one of the last things General Scott told me: "If a song were ever meant for my life, it was Sinatra's 'My Way.'" He certainly trained, fought, and lived the way he wanted up until his death at age ninety-seven in 2006.

Then I considered a larger point: Certainly neither he nor his Flying Tigers won the war by themselves. No one person or group could make that claim. Ultimately, the collective acts of millions of servicemen and -women achieved the Allied victory. Many of those men had been shaped by Scouting and had developed the same virtues that guided General Scott. They were prepared. They took the initiative, sometimes audaciously. They knew how to lead. They also knew how to survive, and in World War II, the outdoor skills Scouting taught became particularly important, perhaps moreso than at any time since. The former Scouts who fought in Pacific jungles, African deserts, and European villages already had the experience of living in tents, cooking their own meals, and surviving far from home.

Taken together, *all* the traits Scouting aimed to instill in its boys helped America's youth gain a victory over nations whose young men may have learned the discipline of a military system but were unfamiliar with those attributes so important to America's free-thinking citizen-soldiers.

Thankfully, like General Scott, these soldiers didn't leave their virtues on the battlefield. I experienced the landings at Normandy as I walked an Atlantic beach with a veteran of D-Day, then learned how that ordeal, along with his Scout training, led to his choice of a career in medicine. I pored over memories with a husband and wife near the California coast and heard how a young medic from Missouri became a Scoutmaster in Pasadena. As I continued to meet these veterans, I realized that the Scout Oath and Scout Law guided their lives long after they had returned home from battle.

Toward the end of my journey, I discovered a eulogy that captured the essence of these World War II Eagles. My chance to meet this particular Eagle had passed, but I found his example important. Shortly before his death, in an interview with journalist David Gergen, Eagle Scout Terry Sanford recalled, "[Scouting] probably saved my life in the war. Boys who had been Scouts or had been in the CCC [the Civilian Conservation Corps of Franklin D. Roosevelt] knew how to look after themselves in the woods. . . . What I learned in the Scouts sustained me all my life; it helped me make decisions about what was best."

In the Second World War, Terry Sanford parachuted into occupied

France and helped defeat Nazi Germany. He then returned to his home state and faced many difficult decisions as he guided North Carolina through the civil rights struggle, fighting for understanding and progress amidst hatred. He became one of the state's most revered governors and later, one of Duke University's most beloved presidents.

At Sanford's 1998 funeral in Duke Chapel, childhood friend Dickson Philips eulogized this Eagle from Troop 20 in the town of Laurinburg. To the assembled crowd, he eloquently said, "[Terry Sanford] took an oath when he was twelve years old and kept it. It started out, 'On my honor, I will do my best to do my duty to God and my country,' and included such things as 'help other people at all times.' He believed it: He was the eternal Boy Scout."

THE BABY BOOM GENERATION

Hugh Morton grew up in the small, textile town of West Point, Georgia, whose local mill employed most of the adults in the isolated city and whose Troop 5 enrolled many of their sons. Hugh joined the troop and, like many boys of the Baby Boom generation, learned about new horizons. Decades after he reached Eagle, Hugh reflected on his former Scouting buddies, saying "They went on to very good jobs and supported their families and went to college. Coming from our background, they could've claimed all sorts of obstacles to prosperity or achieving goals, but in Scouts, they learned that if you work hard and achieve set goals, you'll succeed. I can't think of a single one of the guys who reached the rank of First Class that didn't wind up going on to college. When you look at our mill-town background it wouldn't have fostered that. Scouting was a tremendous influence."

The America of the 1950s and 1960s remained largely rural, with few television channels to bring the urban world into the heartland. Scouting became the only entrée to the broader world for thousands of young men. Hugh and his friends traveled outside the South for the first time when Troop 5 visited the 1957 National Jamboree in Valley Forge, Pennsylvania. These trips were expensive for boys from working-class families, and they each worked hard for an entire year to raise the money they needed. Hugh observed, "We learned that we could work and raise money and see and do and be part of the real world. It was a real broadening experience for kids who might not otherwise have ever left that area."

Hugh learned about new horizons and gained the skills that would carry him to new summits, literally in his case. As we hiked together along a trail near the crest of Kennesaw Mountain, this now-accomplished mountaineer observed, "You know, I don't think I would have ever become a climber if it weren't for Scouting. It didn't lead to it directly—I didn't learn to climb there—but it taught me to set goals and to love hiking and the outdoors. The rest grew from there."

As to where it went, Hugh had recently joined the handful of people who have reached the world's Seven Summits, the tallest points on each of the seven continents, three of which rise more than 20,000 feet above sea level. He scaled Kilimanjaro in Africa, Mt. McKinley in Alaska, Aconcagua in Argentina, Europe's Mt. Elbrus, Australia's Kosciusko, Antarctica's Vinson Massif, and the 29,035-foot Mount Everest.

"You get to Eagle one step at a time, and that's the same way you get to the summit of Everest," he said. He stopped on the trail and demonstrated what one step was like on the world's tallest mountain. He took a high step forward, took two deep breaths, then brought his other leg forward. Two more deep breaths followed, then another step. That was the best an expert climber could muster at the top of the world.

"Now, your Everest might not be a mountain," he continued. "It might be becoming a doctor, building a business, becoming a professor, or whatever else, but you get there the same way you got to Eagle: one step at a time."

Scouting helped millions of boys in Hugh Morton's generation set goals and develop the skills to reach them. The program likely influenced the Baby Boom generation more than any generation before or since. Scouting became a cornerstone of the traditional community as troops proliferated in the days before competitive sports leagues and modern media began competing for boys' attention. At the end of the Second World War, just shy of 2 million boys were Scouts, but as the first Baby Boomers began joining the movement in the 1950s, membership doubled. By 1960, Scouting had 5 million registered youths. Five years later, the Boy Scouts of America awarded the 500,000th Eagle Scout badge. Scout membership soon rose above 6 million. Nearly 800,000 boys attended Boy Scout camps each summer, and well over 2 million readers subscribed to *Boys' Life*, Scouting's flagship magazine. Consequently, many members of this new generation grew up expecting more of themselves and understanding more about their world.

In this era, artist Norman Rockwell created canvases that forever linked Scouting with American life. He portrayed the idyllic suburban atmosphere of the day in such paintings as *A Scout Is Loyal*, *On My Honor*, and *The Scoutmaster*. He helped instill the Scout program with the sense of tradition and security that seemed to mark the times. Not all Baby Boomers related to Rockwell's images, however. Young men from less fortunate families and minority groups often held very different views of mid-century America. Their Scouting experiences were something different and perhaps more powerful.

GARY LOCKE

The building that housed Seattle, Washington's First Chinese Baptist Church had scarcely changed since the days when Gary Locke made the three-quarter-mile walk there each Tuesday night for the meetings of Troop 254. The church building still sat on a hill just east of Chinatown, and its brick exterior showed only the wear that accompanies the passing of time. As our car pulled up beside the church, Gary reached across the seat to point out the door that led to the basement where he met his fellow Scouts during the 1960s. Through that door, this son of hard-working Chinese parents found new opportunities. In the church basement, the future governor of Washington found the experiences and leaders that would shape his life forever.

As Gary gave me my first tour of downtown Seattle, the state troopers to which he had grown accustomed in his two terms as governor did not accompany us. Nor did we ride in a state-owned limousine. The driver was Governor Locke himself, and the car was the Locke family's maroon Honda station wagon, slightly cluttered with car seats and other reminders of their three children, Emily, Dylan, and Madeline. Just three weeks earlier, he had retired happily after serving eight years as chief executive of the 6-million-person state. Today he was simply Gary Locke, an Eagle Scout from Troop 254 who still understands the value of those Tuesday night meetings.

"Those adult leaders were almost my extended family," Gary observed. "Lots of parents were working, so the few dedicated adult leaders that we had really became true surrogate parents for us. They were engineers at Boeing, they were postal workers, they were people who worked at the police department, but all were Chinese and spoke Chinese and a lot of the kids like myself didn't learn English until we went to school or kindergarten. The meetings were in half Chinese and half English."

The troop was composed wholly of Chinese boys and leaders, although it was not segregated; the group's all-Chinese composition stemmed from the ethnic make-up of the neighborhood and the sponsoring church. The boys of 254 took great pride in their heritage, and before each meeting, they donned neckerchiefs embroidered with Chinese characters. Gary still has his neckerchief.

Like many Eagles, he holds particularly warm memories of summer camp. In his case, that would be Camp Omache, in the rugged northern Cascades. He recalled the competitions at camp fondly, smiling as he told of winning whittling contests against other Scouts. He also worked with his troop as they competed against others in a variety of events, in the process of which he learned important lessons.

"You participate in competitions where you have to do things that you've never really done before," Gary explained. "It's a competition that involves teamwork, whether lashing together poles for a signal tower or relays with compasses or orienteering or things like that—swimming relays, canoeing, boating—a lot of these are activities that kids in the inner cities don't have much exposure to. It's fun, it's new, but it also has that team-building effect."

After learning about collaboration and the outdoors as a camper, Gary returned to Omache to teach those same skills as a counselor. While other camps in the Pacific Northwest had dining halls for their Scouts, Omache did not. The Scouts cooked their own meals, and the staff ate meals prepared by the troops in camp. Staff members assigned to the waterfront or commissary could accept dinner invitations from any troop, so they wisely dined with troops who earned reputations for having well-prepared meals, *well-prepared* being a relative term, considering the cooks were all teenaged Scouts.

Gary usually found himself assigned full-time to particular troops, and his lot fell with theirs. "I was assigned these troops that were kind of greenhorn, problem troops or young troops, and so there was many a night that I never got dinner," he explained. "Camp would shut down at five, dinner was at six, and camp would resume operations at seven. Oftentimes our kids were still trying to build a fire or having a difficult time boiling their water—so many times I didn't have dinner!"

Occasional missed dinners aside, he enjoyed helping the green Scouts build their skills and as so often happens in the course of doing something less-than-pleasant, he learned a lesson. He explained, "You couldn't build the fire for them, you couldn't take over for them, you could only give suggestions and try to help them feel like they were learning on their own. I was assigned troops who oftentimes didn't have the most active adult leadership or very young troops. They had a lot of problems, and we were trying to give as much help as possible without taking over, because you're only there with them for a week and you're only there with them a few hours a day around the time they're making their meals. You're checking in on them, trying to help develop their Scout leadership, their young leaders."

In the process, Gary learned even greater lessons in leadership. He explained, "Number one, a leader is not a dictator. To be an effective leader, you can't be a dictator. You can shout and rant and rave, but you won't get the respect of the Scouts or the people working with you. And when you're a camp counselor, the most effective way of helping kids isn't by doing it for them but really trying to teach them. And teaching isn't shouting and yelling and isn't just taking over but in some ways demonstration and in some ways subtle suggestions. Sometimes you can be especially good at teaching, but you can be a *more* effective teacher if they think they came up with the ideas on their own. If you kind of walk them through it but they're doing it with you helping them, they'll remember more than if you simply did it for them and said, 'Remember? Now *you* go do it.'"

Years later, as a public servant, Gary applied these same principles When he brought agendas or ideas to legislators, he never presented them with a *fait accompli*. "These are the parameters that you're working with," he would say upon presenting a piece of legislation. "What are your suggestions and how do you think we should approach it?" He would always leave funds unallocated and certain details undetermined to allow room for negotiation. Gary observed, "If it's all done for them, what are they, just a rubber stamp?"

The Honda soon arrived at Yesler Terrace, the Seattle public housing development where the Locke family lived during Gary's youth. There, the former governor showed me the small unit where he spent his childhood. It was a clean area, and the row houses and apartments were neat and modest. It was to these buildings that Gary's father returned to start a family after landing at

Utah Beach in Normandy and serving under General George Patton during World War II. He returned to an Asian community that had been shattered during the war as thousands of Japanese families were relocated and confined to government-run internment camps.

As his thoughts drifted back to that injustice, Gary hit the accelerator slightly harder than usual as we sped around a turn. He still remembered hearing accounts of the devastated businesses and lost homes to which many of his parents' fellow Asian neighbors returned. Worse, he added, was that the U.S. Army's 442nd Regimental Combat Team, composed of Japanese-American soldiers, became one of the most decorated units of the war, receiving 7 Presidential Unit Citations and 18,000 individual decorations, including 20 Congressional Medals of Honor. "The Army recruited these soldiers *directly* from the internment camps," he said, visibly irritated.

In 1950, Gary Locke was born into an America that discriminated heavily against Asians, although Seattle's strong Chinese community insulated its young children from those forces as best it could. As he grew older and entered public school, however, he began to struggle with his identity.

"It was a very tough cultural experience for me because in those days the TV shows were *Ozzie and Harriet* or *Father Knows Best*," he remembered. "You'd see all these moms on TV vacuuming the floor in dresses and high heels with pearl necklaces and dads eating dinner with the kids with a coat and tie." He recalled thinking at the time, "That's not how we do things in our family!" Gary's parents worked long hours at their grocery store, and Locke family life had little in common with the popular images on their television.

He also remembered his third-grade teacher monitoring what her students were eating for breakfast. Several times a week, she would ask the students about their morning meal. "If it wasn't a traditional American breakfast—ham and eggs, bacon and eggs, or pancakes—we had our hand slapped," Gary recalled. Children from Japanese, Chinese, and Filipino families made up the class, and sadly many grew ashamed of their heritage as they were pressured to hide their roots and traditions in order to fit neatly into the traditional American lifestyle. "It was a real guilt trip for us," he said. "A lot of us were somewhat embarrassed or ashamed of our parents and our culture. That was exacerbated when Mom and Dad couldn't come to the PTA meetings or open houses or meetings where parents could see what the kids were doing in school. That's why Scouting was even more important. Here, I had a surrogate family and kids I could relate to. We also had adults who tried to instill in us some pride in our culture while at the same time helping us understand American society."

As Gary moved through high school, other adults took an interest in him as well. He remains grateful for the high school counselors who encouraged him to explore where his potential could take him. The same discipline and optimism that led him to Eagle drove him to set his sights on a top school, and after he graduated from high school, Gary Locke traveled 3,000 miles to New Haven, Connecticut, where he spent four years at Yale. He laughed as he remembered using his Scouting knots to tie his luggage together when he packed for his cross-country trips. He continued chuckling as he admitted he'd been tying bowlines just weeks earlier when his family moved out of the Governor's Mansion.

After Yale, Gary earned his Juris Doctorate at Boston College and returned to Washington, serving as a public prosecutor and an attorney with the city of Seattle's Human Rights Office. Then he began thinking about his future and how he could make a difference. He thought back to his Scouting days and remembered: "Scouting says you should leave a campsite better than you found it, and for me in public service, that's how I've tried to approach things."

The young attorney entered public service and spent ten years in Washington's House of Representatives before becoming the chief executive of King County, which includes the city of Seattle. We had only driven several blocks from the Yesler Terrace housing project when Gary again reached over the seat to point out the office he occupied as county executive. From that office he attained the governorship of a state with an Asian population of 5 percent. His ethnicity never mattered. He shared the same values and love of Washington as citizens who had grown up in households more closely resembling those on the television shows he watched as a boy. He filled the post of governor for eight years, receiving praise from people of both parties inside and outside Washington. Studies consistently ranked his government among the most effective in the nation, and nobody criticized the ethics of the Locke Administration.

Throughout his terms, this Democratic governor spent time working with Republicans as well as, admittedly, fighting them, but he always tried to focus on issues, not parties. "Most issues in our state have nothing to do with

Democratic versus Republican politics," he said. "Fixing roads, trying to find dollars to improve the highway system or mass transit is not a Democratic or Republican issue. Improving schools is not a Democratic or Republican issue. Public safety or lowering the cost of incarcerating criminals to beefing up the penalties for people who commit crimes is not a Democratic or Republican issue. So I really try to work with people who are interested in those issues, be they Democrats or Republicans, and bring coalitions together."

When he took office in 1997, the technology boom had brought prosperity to western Washington but not to farmers in other regions of the state. By working with people of both parties and by serving as a trade representative for the United States, Gary helped open world markets for Washington's farmers. "We've been very, very successful in opening markets for Washington's agriculture outputs," he reflected, before noting how times quickly changed early in his second term. "And of course when the dot-com bubble burst and Puget Sound was in difficult times, rural Washington was actually in better shape than the Seattle area! Then we spent a lot of time trying to improve the business climate for the urban areas, and that meant meeting with a lot of businesspeople *and* labor, trying to forge compromises. If people are out of work, there's no quality of life. They can't support their families, they can't pay for college educations for their kids, they can't plan for their retirements, and that hurts *everyone*."

As governor, Gary attended several Eagle Courts of Honor, the often elaborate ceremonies in which Scouts receive their Eagle badge. At one Court of Honor I attended, the father joked that since he had no daughters, his son's Court of Honor had become his family's first wedding. Invitations to Washington's governor ran thirty to forty each month, and Gary regretted that he couldn't make time for most of them. One he did attend was for Sam Roe, who suffered from cerebral palsy but had persevered to earn his Eagle. Sam earned the rank without special help, even hiking up Washington's Monte Cristo in the snow. "He was the last one back to the car," Gary explained, "but he made it on his own!"

On becoming an Eagle, Sam had two wishes: (1) to have his Court of Honor aboard the aircraft carrier *Abraham Lincoln*, based in Everett, Washington, and (2) to have Governor Locke present the Eagle badge. "I heard of this story and of his incredible courage and his triumphs over all his disabilities," Gary remembered. "Our office would normally decline on this, but they showed it to me—they show me all the invitations they decline—and I said, 'No, we're going to do this one.'"

Aboard the *Abraham Lincoln* that day in 2004, the governor told Sam what he has told many young men who have earned that silver badge: "You say that you're an Eagle, and automatically people expect more from you. And that will continue throughout your life. Eagles are special. They've already shown perseverance, they've shown leadership qualities, and they've shown the ability to get things done, to accomplish things. So it doesn't matter what they do later on in life, whether it's as a movie director or an astronaut or a politician or a businessperson or an athlete, people have higher expectations for a person who has become an Eagle, who *is* an Eagle."

Governor Locke concluded that this broad recognition led Tom Brokaw to use the phrase "Eagle Scout" after his response to the president's State of the Union address. "The Eagle award symbolizes all of those qualities of leadership, of perseverance, of ability, whether it's lifesaving or swimming or first aid. People know that it represents significant skill, accomplishment, and leadership. So it becomes a great summary."

The award represents more than just broad public recognition. Gary told Sam that earning Eagle entails obligation as well. "I said, 'Please stay involved in Scouting and pay back. Share your knowledge with the younger Scouts because those younger Scouts look up to the Eagles,'" he continued. "I also tell Eagles that they'll have a lot more fun in Scouting once they've become an Eagle. . . . Older teens can really appreciate some of the great adventures available through the Explorer program, Order of the Arrow, being a counselor, being a junior leader."

As part of *his* obligation to give something back to Scouting, Gary Locke has remained active in the Chief Seattle Council as a camp counselor in his college days and as a volunteer today. "I don't know how I can ever separate my Scouting experience from who I am today," he reflected. "It's just a part of me—great memories, great fun, great friendships—but also great values, values that have become part of me." That, he says, has kept him active in Scouting through the years. In the adults of Troop 254, he witnessed the indispensable role strong adult leadership plays in a young man's life, and he has always remembered and applied that verity. When we met, he had recently volunteered with the council's campaign to bolster Seattle's inner-city Scouting program so boys growing up in Yesler Terrace and other city neighborhoods can enjoy the same benefits he did decades ago.

"I think Scouting is so much more important than ever before," he said. "Especially in the urban settings with all the temptations and distractions that kids can get into that are so serious with huge life implications for those kids." Recalling his younger days, Gary admitted, "Yeah, we could've gotten in trouble, but that trouble pales in comparison to the consequences to the troubles kids can get into today: gang shootings, drugs, and things like that. That's why it's really important to have good wholesome activities for kids to be engaged in, especially with responsible adult leaders who can guide and nurture them. . . . The value of adult leadership and role models are [sic] more important than ever before."

Gary Locke with his wife, Mona, and children, Dylan, Emily, and Madeline
COURTESY OF GARY LOCKE

Gary considers his wife Mona and himself as the most important role models for his own children. Amidst Scouting, state business, and a governor's busy schedule, he diligently defended his role as a father and a husband, leaving a legacy to his family, not just his state. He remembered the long hours his parents worked at their mom-and-pop grocery store—seven days a week, fourteen hours a day—and he promised himself he would be at home more for his family.

"My parents never closed down on Christmas, New Year's, or other holidays, and as a result my dad never went to any of our Scouting events, barely went to a Court of Honor—maybe [to] my Eagle Court of Honor—

never went on camping trips or outings with us. Nor could they come to things at school. I really felt kind of shortchanged by that. Upon getting older, I realized what they were doing: They were just sacrificing to make sure there was food on the table, enough money to buy those Scout uniforms, to send us off to college and pay for books and supplies. I really appreciate what they've done, but at the same time, as a kid, I would've liked more time with them. And so as governor, I really tried to carve out time for my family."

At a new governors' forum, he remembered hearing from his more experienced counterparts, "You'll be governor for a few years, but if you have a family, the title of 'dad' is forever." They explained, and Gary soon realized, that as governor, he would receive invitations to several events each night. "You need to set limits," Gary stressed, "because in the blink of an eye, you'll be out of office, and what will you have remembered? Going to a banquet, being there for fifteen to twenty minutes for some group? Or will you have the memory of your son and daughter taking their first walk, their first recital, their first game of T-ball?"

Gary and Mona Locke set limits on evening events to guard their time together as a family, and they developed a ritual of reading and singing to their children every night before Dylan, Emily, and baby Madeline fell asleep. "That became a routine we'd look forward to, and sometimes I'd go before a group and say, "I have to leave. I can't stay for the whole evening because I have to get back home to read to our kids." He still won reelection.

As three o'clock approached, our time together ran short, and Gary drove us toward the Washington State Ferry Terminal on the edge of Puget Sound. There, he left me with strict instructions to take the ferry to Bainbridge Island so I could enjoy a view of the Olympic Mountains and of snow-capped Mount Rainer rising proudly above his hometown. I stepped out of the Honda onto the corner. With a quick wave, Gary Locke turned toward his new neighborhood on Queen Anne Hill, where Dylan and Emily would find him waiting with the other parents when school let out.

———

Gary Locke showed me the value of adult leaders. His experience also exemplified the role Scouting could play in the lives of urban or disadvantaged youth. Too often, I associated Scouting with the middle-class lifestyle Norman Rockwell captured. As the miles went by, however, I began to realize that those in more challenging situations often reap the greatest rewards from the program.

Several months after I left Seattle, I met Frank Ramírez, whose story reminded me of Gary Locke. The American dream of *Father Knows Best* also eluded Frank's family, which emigrated from Mexico to Pueblo, Colorado, in the 1950s. His father, who had suffered a crippling injury, and his mother, who was blind, wanted a better life for their children, but, as Frank put it, "We lived so far below the poverty line that we didn't show up."

When a local Scoutmaster asked Frank to join Troop 49, Frank's parents said, "No." They couldn't afford dues and uniforms, let alone camping equipment.

"Don't worry about dues, and we have plenty of equipment he can borrow," Scoutmaster Robertson had assured them. "I just want the boy."

That one event changed his life forever, Frank told me. He earned Eagle and soon found himself in Washington, D.C., delivering the Boy Scouts of America's Annual Report to Congress. Afterward, newswoman Barbara Walters shared Frank's story with the nation. When he returned home to Colorado, the stack of college applications awaiting him opened his eyes. High school counselors never mentioned college to Frank; they assumed he would work in the local steel plant to support his family.

Frank now holds undergraduate and business degrees from Stanford University and a law degree from the University of California, Berkeley. During his career, he has founded several successful businesses that aim to build communities as well as equity. Between business commitments, he volunteers with the Boy Scouts, fostering Scouting in Hispanic communities throughout the West. He feels that he owes that much to Scouting and to the Scoutmaster who changed his life.

"What has Scouting been?" he asked. "For me, everything. For my family, transformational. For the communities I've been able to help, absolutely disruptive to the cycle of poverty. It helps ensure that young boys have an opportunity to pursue the American dream."

In the examples of Gary Locke and Frank Ramírez, I saw how adult leaders, through Scouting, changed the course of a generation. For Baby Boomers of more modest means, Scouting provided an entrée to new worlds. Millions of Scouts from less fortunate backgrounds had the chance to excel as boys and to make a difference in their country's life as men.

THE STRUGGLE FOR CIVIL RIGHTS

When Gary Locke was born, the government was busy disassembling the internment camps of which he spoke as we drove through Seattle. Southeast of Washington, in the state of Wyoming, lay one such camp: Hart Mountain. Hart Mountain War Relocation Camp held thousands of the nearly 120,000 Americans of Japanese descent who were interned during World War II. Barbed-wire fences and guard towers bound the world of the families there, but Scouting happened nevertheless.

Eagle Scout Art Okuno, in his young twenties at the time, formed Troop 343 for the boys inside the camp and became their Scoutmaster. The rules and facilities of the camp forced him to organize his program differently than he would have liked—camping trips outside the base were nearly impossible to arrange—but the troop made do and even met with a local Wyoming Scout troop. During those visits, Wyoming Scout Alan Simpson dug drainage ditches and tied knots with a Japanese-American Scout named Norm Mineta. Decades later, the two friends reunited in Washington, D.C., one as a Senator from Wyoming, the other as a cabinet member for Presidents Bill Clinton and George W. Bush.

Throughout time, Scouting has mirrored American society, for better or worse. During World War II and for decades before and after, Scouting reflected the discrimination that marked America, having separate troops for black Scouts and white Scouts. The first African-American Scout troop reportedly was formed in 1911 in Elizabeth City, North Carolina, but a black troop was not officially recognized until 1916: Troop 75 in Louisville, Kentucky. In the 1920s, the Boy Scouts of America organized the Inter-Racial

Service to help councils establish separate black troops, and while no official record of the first minority Eagle Scout exists, many believe Edgar Cunningham of Waterloo, Iowa, became the first African-American Eagle in June 1926. Arkansan Turner Denard became the first African-American Eagle of record in the South in 1929. In the following decades, the Scouting program gradually began to reflect the changes the civil rights movement was bringing to the country, and the era of segregated Scouting ended. The organization continued encouraging minority membership in the program, launching efforts to form troops in Native American, Hispanic, and immigrant communities across the country. Eventually, Scouting also carried these programs to inner-city youth.

While Scouts of different races may not have camped in the same troops during much of the twentieth century, they did recite the same codes and learn the same lessons. Thus, many of the young men who experienced discrimination as Scouts came through the program with a focused vision and, importantly, a set of skills and values that helped them bring change to the Scouting program and the larger world.

PERCY SUTTON

TROOP 72, SAN ANTONIO, TEXAS

EAGLE SCOUT, 1936

In 1961, Percy Sutton climbed into the bus that patiently awaited its riders at the bus depot in Atlanta, Georgia. The driver issued the smartly dressed black man a suspicious and condescending look but said nothing. Relieved, Percy turned past the driver and sat in the front row of the bus. He placed his briefcase, emblazoned with "NAACP," at his feet. He breathed deeply then turned to note the other blacks seated in the back as custom dictated. He breathed deeply again. Soon, the brakes hissed and the bus pulled into the street, carrying its cargo of Freedom Riders southward toward the crucible of the raging civil rights struggle.

"As we drove along," the long-time civil rights activist recalled, "people would drive by and harass us. By the time we got to LaGrange, Georgia, four or five people had been beating on the side of the bus because they saw my face in the window in the front of the bus. Well, the bus driver finally said we had to stop. See, they'd burned a bus the day before in Montgomery and maimed a few of the whites on there.

"As we approached Montgomery, other cars joined in harassing the bus: 'Stop the bus, get the nigger off!' By the time we were coming into Montgomery, people were yelling at us, 'No Freedom Riders here!'

"When we pulled into the station, the veins in my temple were so large, I massaged them and they felt as if they'd explode. My mouth was dry, and I thought, 'If they set this bus on fire, I'll burn up.' And the blacks in the back said, 'Come on back, don't do this.' They were electing to comply with the laws to stay alive."

Once the bus reached Montgomery, police and state troopers awaited the

Freedom Riders and held back the surging crowds gathered to jeer them. The Riders waded through the mass of vitriolic insults and hatred before reaching their destination, a soda shop.

"We went to the counter and they said, 'What do you want, nigger?'

"I said, 'or-or-or-orange ju-ju-juice please.' I could barely get the words out. And they slid the OJ down the counter so it splashed on me, but it was the best orange juice I ever had!

"Then we left and met the people in the city, who were really brave because they actually *lived* there. Next, we flew into Jackson, Mississippi, and I was finally arrested in a 'whites only' bathroom, literally, while I was going to the bathroom! My crime? Disturbing the peace. For that, they took me to Parchman Penitentiary!"

Several seconds of silence filled his office in Harlem. His dark eyes sparkled beneath his now-white eyebrows. He grinned unexpectedly. "The reason I can smile," he explained, "is that there is nothing like overcoming anger. There's nothing like being competitive and going up against the people who segregated you and doing better than they've done. It's funny; you can smile so easily when you're put in competition."

He concluded with a laugh that underscores his outlook on his life and struggles. From talking with him, one wouldn't think his battles were as monumental and difficult as they were. He treats them all with a sense of humor, but that's because he won.

Percy Ellis Sutton became the final addition to his San Antonio family when he arrived into the care of his mother, father, and fourteen older siblings in 1920. The Suttons were determined that Percy's skin color would never stifle his dreams or his ability to reach them. They sent him to school, and by the time he graduated Phillis Wheatley High School at age fifteen, his parents and six siblings had taught him in the classroom.

At home, the Suttons hosted a parade of civil rights leaders, including George Washington Carver, so Percy found himself in the struggle against segregation at an early age. "I was in the civil rights movement when I was six years old," he remembered. "Mine was a family of revolutionaries. I went to jail for the first time when I was nine years of age, and I've been to jail sixteen times. When I was nine, I tripped on a policeman's foot, he slapped me, and unfortunately, I instinctively kicked him. I didn't intend to kick him, I was just falling backward. I stayed in jail until eleven p.m. at night. That was terribly vivid; it bloodied my nose. But I must tell you that none of those things made us dislike whites. Mother and Father made sure we never grew up with an antiwhite attitude, just an anti-injustice attitude, and that has permitted me to relate so well to so many different groups in New York and elsewhere."

Mr. Sutton tried to shield his youngest son from the realities of injustice, and in the process, he almost cost Percy his Eagle. Percy remembers his father not allowing his brothers to join the Boy Scouts, which was segregated in the days before the Supreme Court's *Brown v. Board of Education* decision and its accompanying social changes. African-American Scouts often found second-rate Scouting experiences. For those reasons, Mr. Sutton kept his boys from Scouting and the discrimination that tainted it. By the time Percy and his brother Buster were of age, however, their father relented and let them join Troop 74, an all-black unit in San Antonio. He remembered his troop never being invited to Jamborees and many other Scouting events, and his most vivid memory was one that gave him a taste of the bitterness of segregation.

On a typically blazing Texas summer day, Percy and his brother set out in a family car for a Scout camp on the Guadeloupe River outside of San Antonio. They had taken the car to avoid the insult of riding in the back of the public bus, as all blacks were required to do. When they were nearly halfway on the thirty-two-mile journey, however, their engine failed. Determined not to arrive at camp on a segregated bus, the two boys set out on foot. Finally, tired, hot, and thirsty—and still a long hike from camp—they boarded a public bus. With his sparkling laugh, Mr. Sutton explained, "Yes, I'll never forget going to that Scout camp. It was the first time we ever rode on the back of the bus!"

As a Scout, Sutton also discovered aviation, and though he knew his skin color would bar him from becoming an army pilot, he nevertheless learned to fly. A neighbor volunteered to serve as his instructor, and Percy Sutton took the controls of a plane for the first time at age fourteen. He trained as if his dreams were boundless. Then, to his surprise, he received the chance he thought would never come: He traveled to Alabama and entered a U.S. Army flight training program.

Moton Field in Tuskegee, Alabama, was the birthplace of the Tuskegee

Airmen, the famed 332nd Fighter Group. First Lady Eleanor Roosevelt played an important role in forming the all-black unit, and when the first classes began to graduate flight school, Mrs. Roosevelt pressed the army to deploy the men on the front lines of World War II so they could prove themselves. Soon, these black airmen were flying through the thick flack above Nazi-controlled Europe, amassing a reputation that rivaled that of Bob Scott's Flying Tigers. But the Tuskegee Airmen remained a segregated group.

"When we went into combat in Italy, we were segregated," Sutton remembered sadly, and I could still hear in his voice how crestfallen he was upon realizing that segregation didn't end when he put on the U.S. Army Air Corps uniform he'd trained so hard to wear. "When we got into the war, they still thought of us as black people, not military men, not Americans.

"While we were in Italy and Sardinia, we never had a break from segregation, yet my group, the Tuskegee Airmen, is saluted today as an outstanding group. My group lost no planes—we were a fighter group and protected bombers flying into Italy, Germany, France—and we never lost a bomber. We were good."

In 1,578 missions and 15,552 sorties, the Tuskegee Airmen lost 66 men, downed or damaged 409 enemy planes, and received 100 Distinguished Flying Crosses. They never lost a single bomber under their escort.

By all rights a hero, this Tuskegee Airman returned home to find little had changed. He discovered that the service he and other blacks had rendered to their country was virtually meaningless. Segregation and prejudice still reigned in the United States. But Sutton had beaten the Germans; he believed he could beat the forces of American injustice as well.

As we sat across from one another that wintry day in New York, I asked the smiling eighty-year-old veteran to help me understand how it felt to sit on the back of a bus or be cursed for sitting in the front. How did it feel to return from World War II and face a nation that allowed a former German soldier to sit at the front of a bus but barred a decorated American officer from doing the same?

Over the quiet hiss of the heater in his office, he responded with a story that helped me understand something I never truly could. He told me about taking his new bride home to Texas to visit his family. On the train from New

York, the newly married couple had walked into the dining car one evening and there, his story began.

"I was a young captain," he remembered, "and I decided to sit at the table—I really thought I could do it—with a young white major . . . and I sat at his table. He didn't say anything, didn't speak to me. I said, 'Good morning, Major.' And my wife touched my knee. I knew she was upset. Again, I said, 'Good morning, Major.'" Still no response.

"He got up for a minute, said, 'Excuse me,' then the next thing I knew, he sat down again. . . . But he came back, and a young man—a private [from the military police]—came in. He said I had to get out. Now I had a .45 on my side, I've got my wife there who I wanted to respect me and take pride in me, and I had to decide. And I said, 'What have I done?'

"He said, 'The Major doesn't want you here.'"

"Major, are you suggesting that I should not sit at the table with you," asked Sutton. "Why?

"He said, 'I don't want you here.'

"Well, I'm not going to leave," Sutton replied. "I hope you can still digest your food.

"The next thing I knew the private had his hand on my shoulder and said, 'You'll have to leave.' He didn't pull his gun, but I stood up and put my hand on my gun, and my wife began to cry. She said, 'Please let's go, please let's go,' and they slowed the train down to put me off, just because I was sitting at the table."

As his anger resurfaced nearly six decades later, this distinguished veteran said, "I couldn't stand someone putting his hand on my shoulder, telling me I had to leave the table because of a guy with *no* medals on him. I'm sitting here with my medals; this major had apparently not served overseas.

"So you want to know about how I felt coming back? They put me off the train. I felt utterly humiliated." He paused. "It took me years to overcome that. Think about what it feels like to be utterly humiliated in front of your wife.

"But it helped me that I could overcome that as well," he said, his anger subsiding. "When people would do things to me later, say bar me from their restaurant, I'd put a picket line up. Bar me from housing, I'd put a picket line up. I'd do whatever was necessary." He chuckled, recovering the sparkle that rarely leaves his eyes. "And we certainly made some changes!"

He motioned across his old, cluttered desk to a framed sign that hung from the wall of his office. "I *AM* A MAN," read a slightly yellowed three-by-two-foot poster, a relic from the protests of the 1960s. Activists wore these signs as placards while they walked the picket lines of the civil rights struggle during that decade.

"We were picketing the city of Memphis in front of the mayor's office," his explanation began. "We were picketing to give equal pay to the black san-itation workers because we were treated so badly and job opportunities were poor. Their pay was so poor, I thought it'd be nice to have a sign that says 'I *am* a man.' If you were a black man, you knew how you were treated. I put that sign up there because I wanted my children to know about the struggle.

"But what does all this have to do with the Boy Scouts of America?" he asked. "It has to do with the climate that produced me: Scouts and family. I took from the Scout Oath much information that impacts my life," he said. Then he added with some satisfaction, "Still."

I asked him about how those values influenced him later in life as legal counsel to Malcolm X, president of the Borough of Manhattan for eleven years,

Percy Sutton, Tuskegee Airman, civil rights activist, business and political leader
COURTESY OF PERCY SUTTON

producer of the television series *It's Showtime at the Apollo*, and founder of Inner City Broadcasting, the city's first black-owned radio company, which eventually owned stations from coast to coast. He responded forcefully, "You should not, in business or politics, be morally wrong. Why? You don't have to be. I remember when I was president of the Borough of Manhattan, a person who didn't know me well tried to leave money for me in cash—a large sum—in an envelope. My office was across the street from City Hall. That person would come to City Hall, and I was helpful to him as long as the causes he'd bring were good. Then he left this envelope with this money. I thought, 'My God, no. Is that what he thinks of me?' I ran across the street, found him, and said, 'Friend, I can't help you anymore because I see what you thought of me. That's the wrong Percy Sutton!' So my childhood and the Boy Scouts have helped me all along.

"It even helps you learn as an adult," he observed over the muffled sounds of the 125th Street traffic two stories below. "I've gone to camps here in New York and taught merit badges. I've learned so many things . . . I was trying to find all the merit badges I've earned before we talked but couldn't find a list, but as the years have passed it's knot tying and taxidermy I remember best."

He moved to another point, noting how he continues to learn from Scouting as an adult. Local councils regularly invite the respected octogenarian to help teach merit badge courses and to share his knowledge with a new generation. While he gladly donates his time, he admits his donations are not entirely altruistic: "I always pick a course that I don't know anything about and read about it so I learn something myself!"

He discussed his lingering fascination with knots, and then shared with me what he tells those youths with whom he works, often youths from New York's underserved neighborhoods who need their sights raised.

"First, believe in yourself," he answered. "Believe you can make a difference, be willing to sacrifice—and I've made many sacrifices. I've lost elections many times. I've gone through lots of lean periods, and, even if I didn't have the money, I'd keep going. And second, if you lose and fall on your face, get up, wipe yourself off, and go at it again." This coming from a man who has been jailed sixteen times for his activism and who now owns a diversified communications firm that operates in a world where Mr. Sutton dines at any lunch counter he chooses.

After suffering for so long—as a Scout in a segregated troop, as a serviceman in a segregated army, and as a black citizen in the civil rights struggle at home—I thought that he surely must hold some grudge. He doesn't.

"To be an Eagle Scout means to me that in spite of everything I went through in that period, except for that Scouting experience, I might have been a very angry, bitter person," he said. "That's what that badge means to me. Even though it was segregated, within the cocoon of Troop 72, I, through my merit badge work in the period between Life and Eagle, explored the world and learned what it could be.

"Scouting played a very large role in my development," he concluded. "It gave me access; it helped me dream. I dreamed that I could go anywhere in the Boy Scouts."

Through his Scout work, schoolwork, and the extra reading assignments that came from his parents, he learned about the good in the world, about justice. He explored who he was and adopted the values of his troop and his family. He saw an America beyond the segregation that affected every facet of his daily life, and he willingly fought for his country's true ideals at home and abroad. So when he faced the demons of our society later in life, he never considered an option other than confronting his challenges head on, persevering, and making right that which was wrong.

After Mr. Sutton and I met, I went to see the place where he trained for his first battle against segregation. I realized that I could never truly understand how he suffered—nor could I understand how he mustered such courage and perseverance—but I thought visiting Tuskegee might help.

A kind park ranger unlocked the gates of the hangar complex, and I walked across old concrete slabs, grass and weeds growing from ever-spreading cracks. I stood alone under a blue sky blown clear by the cold breeze rushing over the open Alabama fields around me. The quiet scene was almost eerie. The brick hangars were in some disrepair, and it appeared that little had changed since Percy Sutton landed with his fellow pilots on the nearby airstrip during the 1940s. Outside the gates of Moton Field, however, *much* had changed. The veterans of the 332nd had changed America with their spirit and their refusal to give up. Laws, customs, power, and money aligned against their cause, but they never relented and never lost faith.

Eventually, all the Tuskegee Airmen who had those dreams of equality will be gone; after them, the Freedom Riders will pass. Memories of their battles will likewise fade, so it becomes important to remember what they accomplished because their war has not ended, as much as I once thought the last shots had been fired.

Before I set out on this journey, I generally confined myself to corporate and university circles, more by happenstance than by any conscious choice. Those were my communities, my realities, and it remained easy to believe the struggles recorded in history books were just that—history. Once I left my familiar circles, however, I could not ignore the discrepancies that still remain. Traveling across the country, I found that struggles continue, although the arenas may have changed. Thankfully, I found Eagle Scouts of all varieties carrying the banner of pioneers like the Tuskegee Airmen and Freedom Riders. In meeting one such Eagle, I finally understood how these historical struggles will ultimately find resolution.

"There have been lots of heroes in the struggle for civil rights, particularly during the 1950s and 1960s," Stephen Breyer explained in his Washington, D.C., office. "And there will *still* be places where we need heroes and pioneers. The efforts to make real the promises of equality are far from over. This court is involved in those efforts every day."

Several hours earlier, I had walked into the Supreme Court of the United States. The marble classic Corinthian building gleamed in the spring sunlight, and I felt consumed by the building itself as I walked up the flowing stairs and passed into the shadows of the massive portico, supported by two rows of eight towering columns. I walked along marble hallways and passed busts and stately oil painting of former justices: John Marshall, Oliver Wendell Holmes, Jr., Earl Warren, Thurgood Marshall. Presidents have appointed, and Congress has confirmed, only 110 justices to the Court since 1789, and soon I found myself with one of them, an Eagle Scout from San Francisco, California.

In his chambers, Associate Justice Stephen Breyer explained the legal issues underlying the cases we would both hear later that morning in the courtroom, one related to the death penalty, the other to racketeering. He was relaxed, coat off. Even as ten a.m. approached, he continued the lesson, apparently unconcerned that in several minutes' time, he would take his seat on the bench and hear two one-hour arguments about cases that would settle important points of constitutional law. Just before we both left for the courtroom, I asked him how he remained so calm.

"Well, before the arguments, I've already read the briefs," he explained. "A typical stack is about this thick." He stretched out his hand, making a large C to indicate the sheer volume of paper he had to digest for each case. "I've read them, my law clerks have read them, we've discussed them, then reviewed them again, so I'm pretty prepared for this. But it's not too late to persuade me. I'm keeping myself open. I'll go into oral arguments thinking one side is probably going to win. But the difference between 'decided' and 'tentative' is night and day. I'll have a tentative view, but I'm always thinking it might be wrong. In a significant number of instances, the arguments will change my view. When that happens, it's not a bad thing; rather, it's a great thing!"

Minutes later, I stood as Justice Breyer and the eight other justices of the Supreme Court took their seats in the palatial courtroom. From the gracefully curved bench, placed before a soaring backdrop of red curtains, the justices listened as lawyers argued their cases. They interrupted often, questioning the attorneys with a frequency, persistence, and sometimes pointed humor that surprised me. As the arguments continued, I thought about the history that had been made—and was still to be made—in that particular chamber. It struck me that Percy Sutton's struggle had reached its culmination in this very place.

Later that day, I rejoined Justice Breyer in his chambers. Foremost in my mind was the sacred responsibility discharged in that intimidating courtroom: interpreting the Constitution of the United States with consequences both personal and sweeping. I asked the Justice what I'd wanted to know since the morning's arguments began: How did that duty weigh on him?

"*Brown v. Board of Education* was decided right in that very room," he said. "I still try to pause and remember things like that. There are many difficult issues that come before us, and deciding each of them is a responsibility that members of the Court take very seriously. The most you can do is devote all your efforts and time to getting it right. You have to spend time considering the cases and reach each decision carefully. Once you—or we—come to a conclusion, you can't hesitate to decide because the job *is* deciding. That's our job and our purpose. You can't go back. You can't revisit those decision once you make them. It's the nature of the job."

Many years ago, Justice Breyer made a decision himself. He and his younger brother Charles, also an Eagle and now a judge, grew up as Jewish boys in California with two parents who stressed the values of equality and service. In his community, he saw opportunities often withheld from women and people of different religions and races; he decided to commit himself to public service and the movement for civil rights.

"People my age and younger began to question why this discrimination was so," the justice reflected. "There was no legal basis or moral association for these laws and practices. Two years after I earned Eagle—1954—the Court decided *Brown v. Board of Education*. It took many years to remove the legal structure supporting segregation. It required the efforts of many, many people. The issue of legal segregation has shifted, but the question remains: How do people of different races, religions, and viewpoints live together in the United States? The Court has provided me, from my position on the bench, the chance to see people from the full demographic spectrum argue causes. What is important is that they've all decided to resolve their differences through the law. It comes back to a basic respect for human beings. That's a basic principle.

"It's an ongoing experiment in whether we can make real that promise of equality," he continued. "Can we get our society to work? That's one of the fundamental questions of the Constitution itself. It's like a project on which you continually have to work. Segregation in many senses has gone, but we face problems like poverty, opportunity, race, the environment, access—wherever you look there are problems, and it takes a continual response to address them. That can be a response from a court, this Court, or an individual. James Madison, one of our nation's founders, made the point that law and liberty are not dictated from on high in this country. Law and liberty are created by the people, and our system only works when you get a great deal of participation."

I realized that Percy Sutton participated as he signed up for the 332nd Fighter Group. He participated as he boarded a bus bound for Montgomery. Likewise, Stephen Breyer participates in what he dubs "active liberty" by serving as a justice, and he encourages others to do the same, each in their own way.

Before our day ended, Justice Breyer had repeatedly gone back to his boyhood in explaining his life's course and the larger issues of justice and society. I found his lessons about civil rights tremendously enlightening. I found his observations about Scouting equally fascinating. Most of all, becoming an Eagle Scout taught him about participating in our democracy. "In Scouting, it's taken for granted that you're part of a community," he explained. "We were *part* of San Francisco. When you leave a campsite, you don't leave it a mess; that'd be being a bad citizen! Now apply the same principle to a city or town. You learn to participate by participating: at a campsite, earning a civics merit badge, or through a project in your community. Then you pass it on to the other guys in the troop and hopefully, to everyone you meet later in life.

"Scouting also tries to make a boy understand others have to look up to him—or her if you're talking about the Girl Scouts—because he merits it. To merit it doesn't mean you go around acting like you're holier than thou. You behave in a way that's considerate of others. I'm thinking back to our patrols in Troop 14. The patrol leader has to pay attention to what others think. If you want the patrol to win a competition—whether it's in a relay race, collecting old clothes to donate, building a fire, policing campsites, or whatever the challenge is—you have to get boys to cooperate, and you can't do anything but suggest and persuade.

"The lesson becomes how you get a group of people to act together. That's important to the individual and to the country. It takes all types of people to run the United States. And it takes trust: We need to be *worthy* of each other's trust because the way we work is to persuade. There are 300 million of us, so the differences are astounding, but we have to work together and *participate* together to make our democracy work. I see it from the bench every day. It's so valuable to work with others so you can begin to understand how others think.

"The underlying value behind civil rights is treating people on their merits," he continued. "To do that, people need to understand one another."

I learned something about Justice Breyer's concept of understanding along my trail. I found communities where affluent circles and less-fortunate circles never meet, immigrants and natives do not know one another, and youth from one side of the railroad tracks have no understanding of their counterparts on the other. Children cannot choose into what family they're born. Life quite arbitrarily deals each new child a hand of cards, but I observed that it instills in these children the same dreams. People want a chance to prove themselves. They want to provide for their families and create opportunities for their children. Rarely is this easy, particularly when life deals a difficult hand.

I came to realize that everyone struggles to reach his or her aspirations and that some must struggle harder than others. As I grasped that, the importance of the civil rights movement became all the more clear. People fight desperately for their dreams; they don't need unfair laws or practices, un-kindness, or prejudices making their struggles even more difficult. Justice Breyer helps these people from the Supreme Court of the United States. Percy Sutton led them on the streets of Montgomery and Memphis. As for me, I re-solved to understand better those with different circumstances and back-grounds. Spending time among the tremendously diverse Scouting family helped me toward that end, just as Scouting helped Justice Breyer years ago.

"In San Francisco, through Troop 14, we met people from different places, backgrounds, races, and points of view," the justice said as we neared the end of our conversation. "You lose a few prejudices that way. You learn to appreciate people for who they are, and I think *that*, writ large, is what the civil rights movement has been about: treating people on their merits. It starts on a personal level, and if that's not clear from Scouting, I don't know what is."

VIETNAM

Craig Honaman's Bell UH-1 "Huey" helicopter skimmed the canopy of the Vietnamese jungle as it responded to a call for help. American soldiers deep inside South Vietnam were in trouble, and the infantrymen listened intently for the sound of help: the unmistakable pulse of a Huey's rotors cutting through the thick air. Soon, they felt the breeze of the rotors as a dusty green helicopter with red crosses painted on its nose and doors appeared overhead.

"The enemy was in the treeline off to the far side, and we had the casualties at the point furthest from them, but it was still in their line of fire," Craig explained, recalling one of the 650 missions he flew during his tour of duty in Vietnam. "So, we came in down the treeline opposite of where the enemy was and we got to the casualty pickup point and we couldn't land; there were tree stumps and the ground was just not suitable to put the aircraft down. So we had to hover right above these tree stumps and turn the aircraft so the tail pointed toward the enemy; that way, when we started taking fire, at least it'd have to go through a lot of stuff before it got to us!"

Then the crew encountered a problem in addition to the Soviet-made rifles pointed at their helicopter. Enemy fire had the infantry pinned down, so Craig broke policy and ordered his crew out of the Huey. "I said, 'Go get 'em,'" the former fifty-seventh Medical Detachment pilot recalled. "They unhooked from the aircraft while we hovered there, and they went over and got the patients. The bullets were flying. They loaded the patients, we got our crew back on, and flew out. We ended up doing it again. They'd taken more casualties, and we came back to the same place, same situation! So we came in, got out again, loaded up, took more casualties out. And we had to do it a third time and we had to do it at night—and they were *still* taking fire. We took fire too and boy, it's mighty hard to make yourself small in that pilot's seat!"

This Eagle Scout from Troop 5 in Glenridge, New Jersey, did his job and kept his promise to the troops: If they were hurt, they knew the pilots of the Fifty-seventh were coming to get them. For those three missions, First Lieutenant J. Craig Honaman received the blue ribbon and bronze propeller of the Distinguished Flying Cross. In receiving the award, he joined the ranks of aviation heroes Charles Lindbergh, Richard Byrd, George McGovern, George H. W. Bush, and others who have shown "heroism or extraordinary achievement while participating in aerial flight." Twenty-five years later, that medal watched our conversation from its modest place on the wall of Craig Honaman's home.

He sat before a cluttered desk stacked with folders that chronicled seven decades of family involvement in Scouting. "The legacy in my case started with my grandfather, who was in Scouting and was a member-at-large of the National Council starting in 1935 and continued into the 1970s," Craig explained. "He was very active in a leadership role, but he was a Scout before the Eagle rank was really attainable in his area. Then my dad achieved Eagle and set the pace for my older brother and me." Craig then set the pace for his son, Justin, who earned his Eagle in 1988.

From one of the folders, Craig produced a speech given by James E. West, the first Chief Scout Executive. West delivered the speech in 1940, but it could have been 1917, 1965, or 2007.

"The preservation of liberty rests on the affirmation of the dignity of the individual and the acceptance of individual responsibility by every member of the democracy," it read. "The Scouting program is being intensified to meet the challenge brought on by world conditions, and the Scout organization will make every effort to instill in the boys of America the character and courage necessary to solve the problems confronting the nation."

Craig continued, quoting West, "We, as Americans, solemnly pledge ourselves to . . . be vigilant and courageous in maintaining human sympathy and respect for the rights to others; to beware of the enemies of democracy, whatever their passwords or places of birth, and wherever they may be found; to stand united with all lovers of freedom, whatever their tongue or origin; and to keep our nation strong in valor and confident in freedom. . . ."

"That's what the BSA was targeting," Craig observed. "Leadership, democratic values, and being able to instill democracy through the Boy Scout movement, which I thought fascinating. When one thinks about the foundation of those thoughts and ideals, one can begin to understand that through World War II and beyond, for boys who came across that philosophy and had that instilled in them, maintaining our way of life was very prominent in how they looked at the country. Here, we're being told that this situation in Vietnam could be a threat to our way of life. We were going to fight it, and we were going to fight it over there."

Yet another generation of young Eagle Scouts found itself facing war, and when Saigon fell in 1975, nearly 3.5 million men and women had served in Southeast Asia. Fifty-eight thousand never returned. Three hundred thousand were wounded. The mounting deaths of Vietnamese citizens and American servicemen pulled hard at the fabric of the nation, and as the politics driving the war became increasingly uncertain and complicated, the issue became a flashpoint.

Protest marches and stark news reports marked the times, and in the ensuing years, many hoped to forget Vietnam. Consequently, many forgot about the millions of soldiers who served honorably. Only in more recent years has the nation finally begun to comprehend what happened in Southeast Asia and to learn about personal accounts no less moving than those of the World War II generation. And in the Vietnam War, as in the Second World War, Eagle Scouts carried the virtues of their youth into battle and sustained their legacy of service.

GEORGE COKER

TROOP 32, LINDEN, NEW JERSEY

EAGLE SCOUT, 1959

On the fifth night, they were ready. Chip by chip, they had slowly and me-thodically whittled away the soft wood surrounding the hinges of their cell doors and now the doors were hanging precariously in their frames, although their captors never noticed. Nor did their captors realize these two American aviators had learned to unlock their handcuffs and leg shackles. The final mistake the North Vietnamese guards made was underestimating the inge-nuity and sheer audacity of their prisoners of war.

The beatings meted out by their Vietnamese interrogators had grown worse in the preceding days, and on October 12, 1967, Navy Lieutenant George Coker and Air Force Captain George McKnight made their decision, perhaps out of desperation as much as opportunity. Luckily, the guards had allowed McKnight outside the compound, and with his observations of nearby landmarks these two POWs fixed their exact position in Hanoi.

"It was maybe the only time that we were there that a POW knew where he was," a retired Commander Coker recalled. "At no other time did a guy know where he was. You might be climbing out of your compound into a cage of circus lions for all you knew or the ministry of defense. You'd have no idea if you'd be climbing into a cage that was harder to get out of. I don't think any-body ever knew what was outside of that big wall they wanted to climb over." But McKnight and Coker did. With nothing else to occupy their minds in their tiny solitary confinement cells, they plotted their escape.

Minutes after the guards completed their evening round on October 12, the servicemen pushed the cell doors open and carefully returned them to their frames. "As soon as they did [their round]," Coker recalled, "we were gone. Fifteen minutes later, the guards came back, the door was firm, and it looked like we were asleep under the mosquito net in the corner. We had moved our stuff to the far corner so it'd be as dark as possible and as far away as possible, so when we rolled up our trash under the mosquito netting, it looked like a body was there."

Together, the Americans crept through the dim hallways of the prison and climbed onto the rooftop, where they moved stealthily toward the wall separating the POW compound from the deserted streets of northern Hanoi and, more important, the Red River. After creeping through darkened roads to the riverbank, the pilots rushed across the low-lying marshes at the river's edge, tied their wrists together, and became two small heads bobbing south with the main current toward the Gulf of Tonkin and the American fleet.

"The idea," Coker explained, "was to get into the river. Then we were going to go downriver to the Gulf of Tonkin . . . and there, the game plan was to steal a little sailboat—they have a bunch of little fishing sailboats all over the delta—and the idea was to steal one of those and sail it to the fleet. It seemed like a plausible idea. It might have been far-fetched but what the heck. I think I was looking at forty or fifty miles . . . and the first day we got about fifteen, and we didn't get into the water until midnight."

Dawn began to break around five a.m., and McKnight and Coker had to find a hiding place to spend the day, safe from the eyes of the thousands of Vietnamese who traveled the river. They found a muddy spot on the river-bank and buried themselves. Only someone looking directly down into their hiding place could have seen them, George explained. Unfortunately, some-one looked.

"I'm guessing about nine o'clock a little old fisherman with a cane pole was going down the bank," he continued. "And he happened to stop right above us and he looked down and there were two white guys down there, and that was the beginning of the end. He was more frightened than we were. He ran away and within two or three minutes, hundreds of people were running toward the bank. The great escape was over."

The concluding chuckle he gave me decades later belied the emotions he felt in 1967. The two fugitives were returning to life as POWs, and they knew exactly what awaited them.

The cigar smoke swirled around Commander George Coker, USN (Ret.), as he unfolded the story of the escape in his Virginia home, where I had arrived that morning. In his early sixties, sitting before me in his favorite rocking chair, he was serene and comfortable. From time to time, I noticed his cigar shaking in his burly hand as the most difficult memories returned and he again became the young man in the story: a twenty-five-year-old officer, desperate, scared, and a long way from his New Jersey boyhood.

Coker served as a navigator aboard an A-6 Intruder attached to the aircraft carrier *Constellation* and had logged fifty-five successful missions over North Vietnam. On his fifty-sixth sortie, his luck changed as an antiaircraft shell neatly dismembered the wing of his Intruder. Thus, in August 1966, less than one month after his twenty-third birthday, George Coker was spiraling out of control toward the fields of North Vietnam. He would not return home until March of 1973.

"They were basically waiting with open arms," he said of the North Vietnamese militiamen who captured him. "They grabbed me immediately when I came down. I went to release my parachute fittings and my hands were grabbed before I could even reach my fittings."

So began six and one-half years of captivity—2,382 days—where on average, Coker spent just fifteen minutes per day outside his cell. His captors confined him, along with other POWs such as James Stockdale, John McCain, and Robbie Risner, to several prisons in North Vietnam, remnants of the French colonial penal system. American inmates dubbed their jails with such names as Alcatraz, Dirty Bird, the Hanoi Hilton, and Heartbreak Hotel. The men rarely saw one another before 1970, and an elaborate code system became their only means of communication and moral support. The system related letters to a complex code of taps. The prisoners called it "tap code."

	1	2	3	4	5
1	A	B	C	D	E
2	F	G	H	I	J
3	L	M	N	O	P
4	Q	R	S	T	U
5	V	W	X	Y	Z

To communicate the word *by*, for example, Coker would tap once, then twice. He followed that with five taps, then four more. Often, two prisoners would spend months or years tapping in code to one another through their cell walls without ever seeing each other's faces. Conversations in tap code often became the only personal exchanges Coker and other prisoners would have for months on end, aside from sessions with interrogators, which could begin at any time; the prisoners lived in constant fear.

For sustenance, Coker had only rice and an assortment of watery vegetable soups. To this day, he can't eat anything made with pumpkins. And while others his age married and started families, he spent his twenties languishing in solitary-confinement cells, enduring excruciating torture and unfathomable loneliness.

Decades later, those wartime experiences put the Coker children at a distinct disadvantage; they never had license to complain. "It's always his trump card," Coker's daughter, Teresa, told me as we ate lunch with her parents around their kitchen table. "If we ever complain about our food, there's a good chance Dad will say, 'I've had worse!'" Teresa giggled. Her father shrugged defensively and grinned.

Shortly after becoming POW #123 of the Vietnam conflict, Lieutenant Coker learned about the treatment he would receive when he was recaptured after his twelve hours and fifteen miles of freedom. The North Vietnamese officers planned to extract information or propaganda statements from the 766 Americans they captured during the course of the conflict. To that end, they provided powerful incentives that eventually brought worldwide condemnation crashing down upon the North's Communist government, but that reprobation and the resulting changes did nothing for George Coker during his first years of captivity. To this day, two particular incentives still haunt him. First, he told me about "the ropes."

In a detached voice marked only by the New Jersey accent he acquired as a boy, Commander Coker explained what he endured. "They would strap your arms behind your back and they would 'figure-eight' [a rope around your arms] and put their foot in your back and pull on it until basically your arms were touching from your elbows to about here," he said, pointing to his upper arms. "Your shoulders were almost touching in the back. They'd just put their foot against you and keep pulling, an inch at a time while you're screaming your head off. The thing that stopped them would be when your shoulders touched and your elbows are touching, the ropes had tightened up and you just couldn't pull them any closer together.

"Then what they'd often do was they'd pull your arms up over your head, and so now you're really getting pulled out of your shoulder sockets. And they could either hang you like that from a hook in the ceiling, or they'd bring the rope over and double up your legs and pull you up so you're being twisted up like a pretzel, and it hurt like hell, that's all there is to it, just unbelievable pain. Every joint in your body was screaming pain."

The worst ordeal Coker endured, however, involved less intense pain but, over time, brought even greater agony. Today, he seems genuinely amazed he survived "the wall." For two months, guards awakened him around five a.m. and stood him against a concrete wall with his hands raised above his head. He regularly refused their demands for information and political statements, so he remained standing until six p.m. with his arms raised. Thirteen hours a day, every day, for two months. If his arms dropped, they beat him.

"For one day it becomes a monumental effort," he explained. "At two months, it kinda becomes unbelievable. I just don't know how you do it physically—you do strange things under duress—but the real battle wasn't physical, it was mental.

"Part of you drifts away, thinks about something else to buy you time, but no matter how good you get, when your mind came back to the present it would hurt like hell." He trained himself to focus on prayers, family, memories, anything to help him escape the pain, loneliness, exhaustion, and hopelessness of torture. As the weeks progressed, he continued to refuse writing statements against the United States, but long hours on the wall taxed his brain and body heavily. He felt his mind slipping away and knew that keeping some positive memory offered the only hope for escaping—although only temporarily—the pain and sheer longevity of the wall. Toward the last weeks, he felt as if he'd completed a marathon but was forced to run another block, then another, and yet another with no end in sight.

"As time goes on, it gets more and more difficult to do this," he explained. "You're having to make the decision more and more often. It becomes a vicious cycle because you can't get away for 5 or 10 minutes, much less an hour. At the end I was living second by second. Sometimes you try to pass time by counting: You'd count to 120. At the end I couldn't count to 60. I couldn't get there. I could barely remember who I was. I could barely remember my family: If you'd asked me family names I couldn't have told you. The brain was shutting down, it wasn't functioning. The very last thing I could consciously hold onto was the Scout Oath. By the end, I could only get out the first verse: 'On my honor I will do my best.' That forced my brain to function and say 'I *will* do this again. I *will not* do what they want me to do.'

"Nobody ever pictures themselves saying the last thing they could hold onto was Scouting, but that's what happened in Hanoi. When I say, 'I owe Scouting my life,' that's a true statement."

I just sat there at his desk, overwhelmed by images of Vietnam. He thought I had another question waiting for him; uncharacteristically, I did not. I couldn't even begin to formulate one. The commander used my silence to clarify one more point: "This was really a character battle, and I would not have been the same person if it hadn't been for Scouting."

George Coker first dabbled in Scouting at age ten, lost interest, and then rejoined when he was thirteen. From there, he earned Eagle in three years, becoming the only one of the four Coker brothers to rise above the rank of Life. His brothers did not enjoy the same peer group that he did. A group of twelve boys George refers to as "the Dozen" joined together and made achieving Eagle a collective project. "We all moved along in the Scouting ranks and also went into Explorers and Sea Scouts together," he recalled. "We kind of pushed and pulled each other in a group effort."

The suburbs and cityscapes of New Jersey marked George's youth, but he found an escape on the waters surrounding Staten Island, where, as a Sea Scout, he learned the seamanship that led him into the Navy. During the summers, he found yet another escape. Troop 32 would leave Linden, which lay ten miles south of New York City, and travel into the country, another world entirely. The Scouts found themselves on their own, expected to buy their own provisions, plan their own trips, and make sure they had the supplies they would need, things they never had to do in the city. They learned independence.

Explaining the skills they developed on those trips, George recalled, "You need to know how to make a fire, you need to know how to pitch a tent, you need to know where to pitch the tent and where to make the fire. You need to know how to cook on wood fires. In order to pitch tents you need to know knots and ropes and lines. Then you had to understand pioneering, compass work, and map orientation because sometimes you did want to go on treks." Nodding to modern realities, he added, "Of course now you can't go anywhere that isn't on a path. You can go off but there's a sign saying NO TRES-PASSING!"

New Eagle Scout George Coker with his parents
COURTESY OF GEORGE COKER

George eventually served as a counselor at Camp Winnebago in northern New Jersey and became involved with the Order of the Arrow, Scouting's honor society, in addition to Explorers and Sea Scouts. In all those places, he was exposed to skills, opportunities, and careers he never would have been otherwise.

"Everything I've learned in Scouting I've used in my life in one little way or another. A rope, a knot, a compass, first aid, Architecture merit badge, Pioneering merit badge, all the aquatic skills—I've actually used those during my life a lot before I became a POW, some not until I got back."

When he finally returned from his ordeal in Vietnam, he met his wife Pam, began a family, and immersed himself in the military. When his son Thomas neared Scouting age, he decided he needed to repay an old debt. He signed on as a Cub Scout leader, and seven of the eight boys in his charge received the Arrow of Light, the highest award available in the Cub Scouting program, which serves boys ages seven to ten. Then he followed the boys to Troop 62, where he joked that the leaders quickly made the "new guy" Scoutmaster. He genuinely loved the job and watched all seven of those former Cub Scouts reach the rank of Life. He saw Thomas and three others earn Eagle. In his eight years as Scoutmaster, he helped twelve boys reach Scouting's pinnacle.

During those eight years, he learned the great trick of Scouting. He called it "the world's greatest bait and switch." Hiking, canoeing, rock climbing, and camping become the bait, disguising the lessons on character and leadership lurking at the program's core.

"I don't think people entirely understand what Scouting is sometimes," said Coker. "It's not even an organization. It's a *program* designed to try to develop character and leadership within a fun context, and the fun is outdoor camping or the outdoors in general. In that respect, Scouting skills in the philosophical sense are not really a fundamental part of the Scouting program, that's the vehicle. The real heart of the program is teaching character and leadership."

The bait-and-switch technique also applies to parents, who often provide the volunteer leadership on which the program relies. As volunteers, parents serve as chaperones on local campouts and long backpacking treks, often learning new skills themselves. They serve as merit badge counselors for badges that correspond to their profession, they reinforce the Scout Oath at home, and they often encourage their sons to master the next skill and reach the next rank. Along the way, something rubs off.

"Scouting brings parents back into that fold and that ideal. It gives them something to continue looking up to," Coker said. "You presume they had that at one time—whether in Scouts or not—but it's character building for the parents in a certain respect. Going through that program, the process of teaching kids skills, taking them camping, going to the Scout meetings—I think it really helps them be better parents."

Scouting teaches leadership in many ways, but the true foundation of the program lies in Baden-Powell's original patrol method. In England, the revered general divided his Scouts into units of five boys, with a senior boy as patrol leader of each. B-P placed full responsibility for the boys on the shoulders of each patrol leader. The Boy Scouts of America adopted the patrol method and made it the heart of every troop. Within their patrols— usually ranging from five to ten boys—Scouts learn, lead, and plain grow up. Scoutmaster Coker explained B-P's method as he saw it in Virginia Beach's Troop 62, saying "You go into a troop as a Scout and you're an eleven-year-old. When you're twelve or thirteen you may be an assistant patrol leader or patrol leader. Well, you're not leading a giant corporation, but the twelve-year-old is in fact in charge of seven other boys in his patrol. He learns that being in charge is not being the boss but being the *leader*. His job is to guide and teach these boys skills he already knows. So right off the bat at a very young age, you're taught to lead and to teach. Leading is teaching by example; it's not giving orders."

Often Scouts learn from their own example; that is, they learn by failing. "One of the beauties of Scouting," George Coker reflected, "is that it's the last organization where you're allowed to make mistakes. Say you try to make a fire and you make a mess of it. Well, try again. Explain what you did wrong and try it again. But it's not like the only objective is that you must make a perfect campfire, otherwise you get kicked off the team. You learn how to make a campfire and who's teaching you how to do this? A kid that's a year or two older than you, not the Scoutmaster."

The boys teach; the Scoutmaster tests. Before a Scout can advance to the next rank, he undergoes a Scoutmaster's conference. The conference becomes both a test and a counseling session. The Scoutmaster ensures the young man has learned the requisite skills, and then he talks with the Scout about his hopes, goals, and concerns. With relish, George recalled his Scoutmaster conference.

"I had a reputation as a Scoutmaster that you didn't get through my Scoutmaster conferences easily," he recalled with a laugh. "I grilled the kids, and you did not get through until you knew it. Sometimes, they'd get bent out of shape, but it was clear-cut: There was no mischief; I wasn't going to ask you a single thing that wasn't right in the requirements."

Coker also discovered that many Scouts approached his conference like school: They learned the material for a single test, then promptly forgot all they had learned. That strategy failed in Troop 62. "For Tenderfoot, that's fine, that's all I ask you," he said. "You make Second Class, it's Second Class

Veteran POW Scoutmaster George Coker BARBARA J. WOERNER/
THE VIRGINIAN-PILOT

plus anything left over from Tenderfoot, and for First Class, it's everything under First Aid merit badge, everything from Pioneering, everything from ropes and knots, everything in Safety, everything in the water sports that are required. If you don't know one of them, the conference is over. This was absolutely crystal clear to the kids, and they learned it.

"A strange thing happened," he continued with mock surprise. "The boys *accepted* those standards! They're not out arguing about trying to change the standards or saying 'Isn't that good enough?' They know the standards, and they strive to meet those standards."

Then he turned his thoughts to helping me along my journey and reflected upon Scouting's mark. He observed, "I think it's helped develop a cadre of good citizens and skilled leaders who've gone into every conceivable profession and endeavor we have. You look around, you see Eagle Scouts everywhere. One of them is an astronaut who walked on the moon. One Eagle Scout ended up in a prison camp. Leaders of industry, guys working the coal mines—they're everywhere. And I think if you found *all* your Eagle Scouts, you'd probably find a very large majority are exhibiting leadership skills somewhere. They may be poor, they may be so-called common labor, but I'd be willing to bet you that wherever they are, they're exhibiting leadership skills whether it's in a coal mine, a union, their church, a local civic league. If nothing else, they're helping people."

My conversations and travels were beginning to show exactly that: Eagles help others. Sometimes, they might teach a Scout to build a fire so he can cook his dinner on a campout. Other times, they instill something in a young mind, the real value of which only emerges years later. And undoubtedly, older Eagles in Troop 32 helped a young Scout named George Coker develop the skills and character he needed to survive 2,382 days as a prisoner in Vietnam.

Prior to this trek, I had never spoken with a Vietnam veteran about his service in Southeast Asia. Many of my parents' friends had served, but I never approached them about the subject. I wondered if they were bitter, sad, or proud. I was never sure how to view the difficult conflict and the men and women who served in it. My uncertainty about Vietnam grew as the last decade poured forth movies, books, and television specials about the World War II generation. The troubling images from Oliver Stone's *Platoon* were quickly replaced by epics such as *Saving Private Ryan* and *Band of Brothers*, while the World War II publishing blitz of Stephen Ambrose crowded books on Vietnam off store shelves. The legacy of Vietnam remains complicated, but along these miles, I encountered an Eagle who helped me understand.

I found Lieutenant Colonel Bob Baird by accident. A documentary on Vietnam drew me to a film festival one Sunday evening, and shortly before *In the Shadow of the Blade* was to begin, a silver-haired gentleman in an olive flight suit strode up to the theater's stage. His upright carriage immediately marked him as a military man, and I easily imagined him walking across helicopter-filled tarmacs as a pilot for the 283rd Medical Detachment and the 101st Airborne, the insignia of which still garnished the shoulders of his flight suit. Bob was one of the forces behind the documentary, and in a strong voice eerily reminiscent of Tom Brokaw, he explained that the film was more a healing experience than a documentary. After a brief talk, Bob left the stage, the lights dimmed, and the dark theater filled with the sound of Vietnam: the deep, unmistakable thwap of a UH-1 helicopter's pulsating rotor.

For the next two hours, I watched a team of veterans fly a restored Huey 10,000 miles across the United States, from landing zone to landing zone, reuniting those affected by Vietnam. When the helicopter touched down, Bob would gently hop out of the Huey and lumber up to the waiting veterans. He embraced them and welcomed them home with his easy grin.

The film told the stories of Vietnam and alternately filled its audience with feelings of great joy and deep sadness. Listening to the stories was like standing before the Vietnam Wall and hearing each of the names carved into the polished black granite speak. The stories overwhelm you, but that's part of the healing and understanding. Since leaving that theater, I've had a new appreciation for the men I occasionally see wearing olive jackets covered with military patches embroidered with names of distant places such as Da Nang, Saigon, and Khe Sanh.

After the film, I found Bob. I'm always preoccupied with who might be an Eagle, and I thought he fit the profile. When I told him about my book, his wife, Rose, gave me my answer before he could respond, "You have to talk with Bob; he's an Eagle Scout too!"

Over dinner that evening and in his Texas home months later, Bob continued to help me understand the men who served in Vietnam, this family of veterans. They served well and returned proudly, but in many cases discovered an ungrateful or indifferent reception. Few yellow ribbons and banners awaited these soldiers. Protestors harassed Bob when he arrived at the Chicago airport, companies often discriminated against vets, and many soldiers hid their service records. Nobody ever welcomed these boys home.

"I don't think anyone is *capable* of welcoming a Vietnam veteran home but another Vietnam veteran," Bob mused. "The way we were greeted when we came back from Vietnam wasn't very pretty. We know what we did there; it was honorable. This film is an opportunity for us to share with our fellow citizens and bring honor to the Vietnam veteran. I think the Vietnam veteran is just like any other kid who was called up whether it was to go storm the beaches of Normandy or Guadalcanal or Iraq. It's a group that went out to do the best they could for their country. They just happened to get caught up in a situation where people turned their back, and once they began to hate the war, they hated the warrior as well.

"I thought the film had the opportunity to bring healing to the veterans who are out there," he said. "*They* could see this, and it would be an opportunity for *them* to tell their story in *their* words as opposed to a historian or a news reporter or a talking head. When I got involved with the *Shadow of the Blade* project, my primary belief was that I'd accomplish something significant if I could help just *one* Vietnam veteran deal with his demons and make an improvement in his life."

Bob reflected back on our conversations about Scouting and concluded, "We talked about the citizenship merit badges: Citizenship in the Home, Citizenship in the Community, and Citizenship in the Nation. Well, this film was an opportunity to give back to the community of veterans. That's citizenship."

The Huey Bob's team flew across the country now sits quietly in the National Museum of American History in Washington, D.C. It reminds visitors of Vietnam and, Bob hopes, of the many duties we each have as citizens.

Veterans like Bob Baird helped me settle my gnawing questions about Vietnam. I wondered if these men might be bitter; they were proud. I wondered if they would serve again; they would. I thought most were drafted to fight; instead, most volunteered, considering their service as their duty. Many of these boys were just a few years removed from their Scout troops and games of capture the flag in nearby woods. Then, suddenly, they found themselves in Vietnam. Wearing green fatigues and carrying loaded rifles, these young men—many still teenagers—walked into foreign jungles to face a deadly enemy. Thousands of their friends would not walk out.

I never expected to find such a willingness to serve in these Eagle Scouts. Not that I suspected Eagles might be hesitant; rather, I just did not anticipate the calm sense of duty they exhibited. "Of course we served our country," they seemed to tell me. "It was our duty. We would never do less."

The number of veterans who fulfilled that duty amazed me; I had not realized how many Americans had been involved in Vietnam or in other conflicts. Nor did I realize how integral to citizenship these former soldiers con-sidered military service. Even if the tide of opinion had swung against their war, these servicemen returned to their lives as simple citizens, satisfied that they had given their best and done their duty. And perhaps that makes their service even more admirable. In time, I came to respect these veterans deeply, and I hope that, by now, they have all been welcomed home.

APOLLO

In July 1969, the month when man would first set foot upon the moon, 35,000 Scouts congregated in Idaho for the Seventh National Scout Jamboree. Scouts and leaders from every state descended upon Farragut State Park, blanketing the 4,000-acre site with tents and exhibitions. The Scouts spent a week together trading patches, earning merit badges, and meeting friends from all parts of the nation, a nation that was still highly regional in flavor. Many young men had never traveled far from their homes, and as it had been doing since 1937, the jamboree broadened the perspectives of thousands of boys and leaders.

Quadrennial national jamborees have marked the time in Scouting, reflecting the ebb and flow of membership and the trends of the day's society. Many constants have remained, however, among them, Tony DiSalvo. Tony, whose parents emmigrated to America from Italy, remembers glimpsing President Franklin D. Roosevelt riding through crowds of Scouts in Washington, D.C., as the nation's capital hosted the first jamboree and its 27,000 attendees in 1937. Tony hasn't missed a Jamboree since. He saw a crowd of 53,000 celebrate Scouting's fiftieth anniversary in Colorado Springs, Colorado, in 1960. He joined 32,000 Scouts and leaders in witnessing Scouting's seventy-fifth anniversary at Fort A.P. Hill in Virginia. At the 2005 Jamboree, he suffered through the oppressive summer heat with 43,000 others, including the president of the United States. There, Tony was already looking forward to celebrating the movement's one-hundredth birthday at the seventeenth National Jamboree in 2010.

In Farragut State Park for the seventh National Jamboree in 1969, Tony stood among 35,000 others and watched a fellow Eagle Scout make history. On July 20, he gathered together with thousands of Boy Scouts and leaders to listen as news anchors reported the final minutes of Neil Armstrong's descent to the lunar surface. The Eagle Scout from Troop 14 in Wapakoneta, Ohio, steadily guided Apollo 11's lunar module over a field of threatening boulders on the moon's Sea of Tranquility. Inside the cabin, Armstrong saw warning lights illuminate. The Scouts on the ground heard reports of the fuel gauge falling. Armstrong still couldn't land; too many obstructions below. He pushed the lunar module, nicknamed *Eagle*, further across the moon's surface, using more gas. Fuel ran lower still. Armstrong, the mission commander, concentrated on landing, not letting the slipping gauges distract him. One minute left. Fifty seconds. The dwindling fuel supply placed the landing and the astronauts themselves in jeopardy. Fear gripped Mission Control in Houston. Scouts in Idaho were rapt. People around the world held their breath. Then, with precious little descent fuel remaining, Armstrong settled his craft on the moon. The nation breathed again.

On the lunar surface, the Ohio Eagle Scout toggled his radio: "Houston, Tranquility Base here; the *Eagle* has landed."

In Mission Control, an Eagle Scout from South Carolina and a future moonwalker grasped the microphone and responded. "Roger, Tranquility," said Charlie Duke. "We copy you on the ground. You got a bunch of guys about to turn blue. We're breathing again."

Hours later, as nearly every Scout at the Jamboree watched via television, Neil Armstrong climbed outside the *Eagle* and made the first footprint in the moon's dusty surface. The Apollo program had succeeded. In a sense, Scouting had succeeded. That day, the boys in Idaho watched two fellow Scouts walk on the moon. Of the 12 Apollo astronauts who eventually became moonwalkers, 11 had Scouting experience. Of the 312 men who have served as NASA astronauts since 1959, more than 180 had Scouting experience; 40 earned Eagle.

Sadly, the pursuit of space exploration claimed two of these Eagle Scouts. Ellison Onizuka of Hawaii died in 1986 aboard the shuttle *Challenger*, and Texan Willie McCool perished in the 2003 *Columbia* disaster. In 1970, space almost claimed the life of another Eagle.

JIM LOVELL

TROOP 60, MILWAUKEE, WISCONSIN

EAGLE SCOUT, 1943

Jim Lovell later described the event as a "bang-whump-shudder," and its re-
verberations pulsed through the spacecraft, knocking the astronauts into the
walls of the cramped ship. Lovell, the mission commander, looked wildly to
his crew. He hoped to meet a calm pair of eyes. He hoped Fred Haise or Jack
Swigert knew what had happened. When their eyes met Lovell's, they reflected the same bewilderment. A warning light illuminated. One claxon
sounded, then others. More warning lamps began lighting the interior of
Apollo 13's command module.

"Houston, we've had a problem," Lovell called to NASA Mission Control
in Houston, 200,000 miles away. His words hung ominously in the air.

Simultaneously, flight directors in Texas and astronauts in space began
to gather the scope of Apollo 13's problem. Instruments showed that two fuel
cells had disappeared, along with a tank that held half the ship's oxygen.
Pressure in the second oxygen tank nose-dived. A main section of the electrical system crashed; communication systems failed; the computer
restarted. Technical glitches, in turn, created thruster problems, and soon
short bursts from the small maneuvering jets began jolting Apollo 13 from
port to starboard, pitching it forward and back. To the astronauts, it seemed
in some ways terrifying, in other ways unreal.

"We could have panicked and bounced off the walls for ten minutes,"
Lovell later explained, "but then we'd be right back where we started. As long
as it wasn't a catastrophic situation like *Columbia* or *Challenger*, but one
where we were still breathing and the spacecraft was not violated by a meteor,
we just had to think. You had to be objective and positive in your thinking,

not looking at your hands wishing for some miracle to happen. If we'd all gotten in a fetal position to wait for a miracle, we'd still be up there."

The crew stayed calm, matter-of-factly reporting the situation to Houston and quietly following the returning instructions. Then Lovell, for a reason he can't recall, looked outside. He realized how serious his problem had become. "It looks to me that we are venting something," he told Houston. "We are venting something into space." These words hung in the air even more heavily than had his original announcement of the ship's situation. Any hopes that Apollo 13 had just experienced a severe instrumentation problem vanished. An explosion, a meteor, something had damaged the ship. Gas, likely precious oxygen, continued seeping into the vacuum outside.

Everyone on the ground and aboard 13 realized they had to stop the venting. The ground crew eliminated each option they considered, then arrived at the last resort: shutting down the valves to the fuel cells. With the sealing of these valves, all chances of a lunar landing evaporated. When the order came through Lovell's headset, he realized their goal was not to salvage the lunar landing on Fra Mauro; their new goal was just surviving.

When oxygen tank two exploded on April 13, 1970, at 9:07 in the evening, the Apollo 13 spaceship was really two craft linked together: the cone-shaped command module *Odyssey*, with its attached cylindrical shaft of engines, fuel, and oxygen, and the spidery lunar module *Aquarius*. The initial explosion had stricken computer and life-support systems aboard *Odyssey*, and less than two hours after the first shudder of trouble, the crew abandoned the dying command module. *Aquarius*, a craft designed to sustain two men for forty-five hours, became a lifeboat that would have to support three men for nearly ninety hours.

They had minutes to transfer precious navigation data from *Odyssey*'s computers to those in *Aquarius*. If they lost or misentered the data, navigating through space would become nearly impossible. In 1970, even NASA's newest ships had no direct data links, so Lovell figured transfer calculations with his pencil and paper, and he did so before time ran out.

Meanwhile, to recover the astronauts, Mission Control decided to alter 13's course and sling-shot the ship around the moon on a trajectory that would let gravity, not engine power, send the ship directly back to earth. A naval aviator and veteran of Gemini 7, Gemini 12, and Apollo 8, Lovell ranked among NASA's finest pilots, but he had never flown a craft as unwieldy as *Aquarius*. Despite *Odyssey*'s 60,000 pounds of deadweight, Lovell positioned his ship perfectly for an engine burn that placed him on the course home. Their odds began to improve, but on earth, they still remained long shots.

On board, Commander Lovell quietly reviewed the odds himself. "As long as we were still breathing," he said, "we were going to go as long as possible. If you want to put it in percentages, there was a ten percent chance we'd make it home again when the tank exploded. As we solved one problem after another, the percentages went up until at splashdown it became a hundred percent again."

From their position 200,000 miles away, they still remained—literally and figuratively—dishearteningly far from splashdown. Once they swung

Jim Lovell, commander of Apollo 13

NASA

around the moon, the crew pointed their ship toward home and burned the engine to build speed and shorten their return time. When the engine stopped, the crew powered down *Aquarius* to conserve the scant battery power that remained on board. Until they approached Earth several days later, Apollo 13 reportedly used as much electricity as a coffeemaker. Cabin temperatures dropped to 34 degrees, and the crew could barely sleep. Two essentially dead ships and three cold, tired astronauts hurtled across empty space toward Earth, covering thousands of meters per second.

Just when they had overcome their first slew of obstacles, another appeared: carbon dioxide. With every breath the astronauts exhaled, they added carbon dioxide to the cabin. The lithium hydroxide devices that removed the toxic gas from the atmosphere in *Aquarius* became saturated, but the similar devices in *Odyssey* would not fit into the environmental systems of the lunar module. Working with a team on the ground, the crew overcame this hurdle as well by hobbling together a contraption of paper, plastic, tape, and cardboard that scrubbed the air. They had solved another problem. But as they had almost come to expect, another issue arose shortly thereafter.

To reenter the earth's atmosphere safely, Apollo 13 had to fall into a narrow wedge two degrees wide. Any shallower, and they would skip off the atmosphere like a flat stone off a lake and enter a permanent solar orbit. Any steeper, and the atmosphere would incinerate them. As it was, they were approaching too shallow. They needed to burn the engine again and correct their course, but the dire power shortage barred them from using computer guidance. Lovell again took the controls and manually flew his ship. With the Earth's terminator (the line between night and day) as his guide, he used his eyes and instincts to deepen 13's approach. The crew cleared one more obstacle, but two more remained.

First, they had to restore power to the command module, their vehicle for reentry. With procedures developed by a team of exhausted NASA technicians, they returned *Odyssey* to life and jettisoned the service module that carried the ruptured tanks of fuel and oxygen. As the module floated gently away into space, it rolled slowly to show the crew the tangle of twisted metal left by the explosion of oxygen tank two. The astronauts could hardly believe the severity of the damage, and they began to worry that the explosion had cracked the adjoining heat shield. If the shield had sustained damage, the craft and crew would melt as they reentered the earth's atmosphere. About that, however, they could do absolutely nothing except wait and see. NASA also knew Apollo 13 had again drifted dangerously near the shallow end of the reentry corridor. Neither the staff in Houston nor the astronauts aboard 13 could fix the situation, so Houston remained silent on the matter. Again, they would wait and see.

At 11:53 a.m. on Friday, April 17, 1970, Apollo 13 crossed into the earth's atmosphere, and for the fourth and final time, Lovell watched flames lap at the windows of a reentering spacecraft. The intense heat and ionization blacked out communications, and the entire world stood before television screens waiting for word. The typical three-minute blackout period passed with no contact. An agonizing minute after they had expected to hear from the crew, millions of people finally heard Jack Swigert's voice announce their safe return. Under a canopy of parachutes, Apollo 13 settled onto the waves of the Pacific Ocean.

From Mission Control: "*Odyssey*, Houston. Welcome home. We're glad to see you."

"That old Scout motto, 'Be Prepared,' was very apropos in my situation," a retired Captain Lovell mused years later. "Being prepared means being knowledgeable about what you're working with and what you're doing, what the odds are, and how you can get out of certain situations. For instance, we never trained for more than single-point failures in the space program because if we trained for every possible failure that could go wrong, we'd still be down there waiting for the first takeoff."

Apollo 13 suffered a *triple*-point failure, something NASA never truly considered since the chances were just too remote. Nobody ever devised ways for astronauts to address simultaneous electrical, fuel, and oxygen problems. If that much were to malfunction in space, the engineers assumed the ship would be lost. But, thankfully, crews in space and in Houston understood ingenuity and teamwork.

"You've got to rely on other people, especially in a space activity," explained Lovell. "You gotta trust each other to do the right thing, push the right buttons. You had to have trust that the control team in Houston knew what they were doing and wouldn't get you in trouble!"

His modesty aside, teamwork by itself could not have brought Apollo 13 home. Ultimately, only three men could ensure the safe return of the ship, and these three men were roughly 250,000 miles away from Earth at their farthest. The decisions they made and the actions they took on board *Aquarius* and *Odyssey* would lead to the mission's success, if only relative, or to tragic failure.

As he recounted his story in his Illinois restaurant, where the magnificent mural *Steeds of Apollo* reminds guests of the owner's accomplishments, I found myself terribly preoccupied with how *I* might have handled the situation had I been inside *Odyssey* alongside a young Jim Lovell. The crew existed in two tiny, fluorescent-lit metal bubbles of light and oxygen. These bubbles were hurtling freely through the vacuum of space, days away from home, with only unreliable systems to return them there. I couldn't imagine the fear and the pressure that must have permeated the atmosphere of the spacecraft. Yet the crew managed one emergency after another and got their ship and themselves back to Earth. Could I have stayed as focused as they did?

Now firmly back on Earth for more than three decades, Jim Lovell traced his ability to handle the situation to his days in Troop 60. He recalled summer camporees at Indian Mound Scout Reservation in Wisconsin, where he served as a counselor for several years. His Scoutmaster placed him in charge of a group of Scouts and tasked him with assembling the boys, pitching tents, cooking, and generally running the group. The Scoutmaster left Lovell to succeed or fail on his own. He quickly learned about self-sufficiency.

"I learned to work on my own," Lovell said, "to develop, hopefully, some leadership qualities: learning to work together to get things done better, using your imagination in getting things done. This is the thing Scouting does for you. It gets you away from your family. It makes you think for yourself."

Now that our conversation had arrived back at Scouting, we mused together about the 180 Scouts who have served in the astronaut corps, including 40 Eagles. "There's a lot of commonality between Scouting, astronauts, and spaceflight," observed the veteran astronaut and past president of the National Eagle Scout Association. "That's why a lot of Scouts gyrate in that direction. I think that Scouting is also the pursuit of exploration. Scouts are people who want to see things, who are curious, who are always wanting to look over the next horizon. That's why they go to camp; to learn things, to go hiking, and to be active. This is [sic] the same criteria, the same elements that make up astronauts. They sort of live on the edge. They are very curious, they want to explore."

"They also want to accomplish things," he said of both breeds. "You work by objective. You're not a nine-to-five kind of guy. You're not a guy who just puts in hours to do a job to get a paycheck. You usually want to do things to see things happen. You want to have a sense of satisfaction, a sense of accomplishment in whatever you do, whether you're going to the moon, going around the earth, going to the space station, or getting your Eagle badge.

"You learned to continue to go, not to give up too early," he added. "Earning a merit badge, you could say, 'Oh, I'll wait until later; but I kept going. When I applied to the Naval Academy, I didn't make it the first time, and

I had to apply a second time. When I got into the space program, I didn't make it the first time with the Mercury program. I applied again and got into the Gemini program. Perseverance also helped me after I got into these programs and was very important to me." Every day, his wife Marilyn is thankful her husband always kept going during those cold, sleepless hours aboard Apollo 13.

As we closed our conversation, Jim Lovell shared one more Scouting memory with me. His cousin, Bill Leedy, had originally inspired Jim to join Scouting, and Lovell's parents had sent their young Tenderfoot Scout into Bill's care at Camp Krietenstein in Indiana. When he arrived at Krietenstein, Jim dragged his duffle bag into the cabin where Bill served as counselor. "On the first day, no sooner had I walked out the cabin's front door than I tripped and broke my arm and was back in town," Lovell remembered. "On the first day of camp life I was back in town getting my arm set with my mother worried and my cousin in deep trouble. But it turned out that it was a lesson that things don't always go right. I've certainly learned that one over the years!"

When Apollo 13 splashed down, Jim Lovell became the world's most famous astronaut. He had already spent more days in space than any other American and as navigator of Apollo 8, became one of the first men to orbit the moon, a feat that earned his crew the honor of *Time* magazines's Men of the Year. Then he ended his career with Apollo 13. Although he never set foot on the moon—still a deep regret of his—his notoriety has probably lived much longer as a result of Apollo 13's shortcoming. In a way, it was sad to see one of NASA's greatest astronauts end his career with an incomplete mission. I soon discovered that with the perspective of time passed, Lovell views Apollo 13 as a failure from a mission standpoint but as a tremendous success from another. "Thirteen was an outstanding success in the way people reacted to a crisis and the leadership that was shown and the initiative that was produced," he said. "It was a triumph in that area. So I have a different feeling about it now. I couldn't think of a better thing to come through to show what we can do if we put our minds to it."

President Richard Nixon flew to Hawaii to welcome the Apollo 13 crew home. With the astronauts behind him, he held up their mission as a reminder that "In this age of technicians and scientific marvels, the individual still counts. That in crisis, the character of a man, or men, will make the difference."

As I read those words three decades after Richard Nixon spoke them, they struck me as ironic. Several short years later, his actions would precipitate a crisis that would severely test the character of the country and its new leader. When Nixon resigned as president in 1974, Vice President Gerald R. Ford became the thirty-eighth president of the United States. The sixty-year-old Eagle Scout from Troop 15 in Grand Rapids, Michigan, inherited an office tarnished by Vietnam and dishonored by Watergate. Ford faced the unwelcome challenges of restoring faith in the presidency and moving the nation beyond the consuming scandal created by the Watergate break-in and cover-up.

For the first challenge, Ford could rely only on his integrity and reputation as a fair legislator. For this he seemed well suited. The second challenge proved more taxing, and to overcome it, Ford sacrificed his career. In an act of true political courage, President Ford pardoned Richard Nixon. Ford knew that in all likelihood he was signing away the most powerful post in the world. He knew the pardon would create widespread uproar. It did. He also knew a pardon would allow Americans to finally move forward and heal. It did that as well. Pardoning Nixon cost Ford reelection to the presidency in 1976, but his act of courage ultimately earned him lasting respect. As I was beginning to discover among other Eagles, Ford showed a willingness to delay—or perhaps surrender altogether—gratification for the sake of a higher ideal or larger group.

Ford's successor, Jimmy Carter, acknowledged the eventual sentiment of the nation by beginning his 1977 inaugural address with these words: "For myself and for our nation, I want to thank my predecessor for all he has done to heal our land." In the case of Gerald Ford, as in the case of Jim Lovell, the character of a man made the difference.

WALL STREET

Because of his training in Boy Scout work, Sammy Walton, 14-year-old son of Mr. and Mrs. Tom Walton of Shelbina, rescued Donald Peterson, little son of Prof. and Mrs. K. R. Peterson, from drowning in Salt River Thursday afternoon. . . . Donald got into water too deep for him and called for help. Loy Jones, who had accompanied the boys, made an effort to get him out, but Donald's struggles pulled Mr. Jones down several times. Young Walton, who was some distance away, got to the pair just as Donald went down a fifth time. He grasped him from behind, as he had been taught to do, pulled him to shore and applied artificial respiration that scouts must become proficient in.

—*SHELBINA DEMOCRAT*, 1932

S am Walton, the youngest Eagle Scout in Missouri history at the time, saved the life of Donald Peterson that day. Those paying attention might have noticed a pattern emerging: Sam Walton always took action. After leaving the Army in 1945, he began managing five-and-dime stores and honing a new philosophy that changed retailing forever. Businessmen called it "volume discounting," and Sam Walton perfected it. He discovered that buying bulk quantities and offering steep discounts ultimately increased sales and profits. With this philosophy, he opened his first Wal-Mart in 1962, built the business with his unrelenting drive, and turned "Made in America" into a household phrase during the 1980s. He developed the idea of profit sharing with employees, refined the concept of supply chain logistics, and moved all his check-out counters to one location in the store—a novel idea at the time, now standard worldwide. He always ensured his stores helped the communities they served, and throughout his life, he favored hunting dogs and pickup trucks over power brokers and fancy cars.

When he breathed his last day on May 5, 1992, he left a legacy nearly unequaled in business. That year, Wal-Mart grossed more than $43 billion. Shortly after the turn of the century, Wal-Mart sales were $220 billion, and the company employed 1.4 million people worldwide. The discounter stood as the largest retailer in the world because of the ambition that burned in one Eagle Scout.

Ambition—that's what earning Eagle teaches a young man, believes Herkey Harris. A veteran of the Carter administration, Herkey served as chief executive officer of INVESCO North America, a well-regarded investment management firm, until his retirement in 2005. Although noticeably smaller than Wal-Mart, INVESCO demanded the same traits in its executives. Herkey rates ambition as the essential element in any career.

"I'm not sure I even knew what the term *goal* meant," he reflected of his days in Troop 31, chartered by the Virginia Avenue Baptist Church in Atlanta, "but earning Eagle was something I set out to accomplish and I did. It sets a pattern. When you're young in life and do something that's hard and you achieve it and not everyone can achieve it, I think that helps you become ambitious and reach goals as you go forward in business or whatever career you choose. The Scouting program helps you create that ambition early in life, and it stays with you. It comes out of this effort to climb up the ladder of advancement where the only person keeping you from succeeding is yourself."

By the early 1980s, a new generation of business leaders was rising to the fore. These leaders personified their companies and burned with ambition for themselves and even more importantly, for the people who worked for them. Chief executives such as Sam Walton, Ross Perot, Bill Marriott, and Michael Bloomberg embodied vision, drive, and an ethical code strikingly similar, considering their disparate backgrounds: one a middle-class boy from Missouri; one a small-town Texan; another the son of a successful Washington businessman, the last an upstart from a blue-collar Boston suburb. But they all shared Scouting.

ROSS PEROT
TROOP 18, TEXARKANA, TEXAS
EAGLE SCOUT, 1943

The U.S. government had evacuated thousands of American citizens from Iran as the Shah's reign came to an end in 1979. Likewise, the chief executive of Electronic Data Systems (EDS), Ross Perot, had ordered the evacuation of all nonessential EDS employees and families. The streets of Tehran filled with revolutionaries, and as the return of Ayatollah Khomeini became imminent, the situation for the remaining Americans grew bleak. Shortly before the revolution, the Iranian government suddenly arrested two EDS executives. Bill Gaylord and Paul Chipparone found themselves in a Tehran prison, facing charges they believed were intended to keep EDS working in Iran despite the government's failure to pay its bills.

Once Ross Perot received news of the arrests, nobody ever doubted these men would come home. Perot launched a persistent diplomatic campaign, hounding the U.S. government to win the release of his men. Henry Precht, the director of Iranian affairs in the U.S. State Department at the time recalled, "Every day I began by calling Tehran, and the first question I asked the embassy was 'What have you done for EDS today?' That was because I knew that at some point later during that day, the pressure to find out what we had done would start, and I had to have an answer . . . Perot was certainly the most effective and persistent person I have ever encountered."

When diplomatic channels faltered, Perot flew to Iran to visit his jailed employees, reassuring them that he would bring them home safely. He tried his best to win their release, but found that the Iranian government was rapidly dissolving as mobs began taking over Tehran in anticipation of the Ayatollah's return. Paul and Bill remained imprisoned, but Perot's loyalty drove him to contemplate another option.

Back in Texas, he talked over the problem with his mother before making a final decision. "I went to talk to my mother and explained it to her and she looked me right square in the eye and said, 'Those are your men. You sent them over there. They haven't done anything wrong, and it's your responsibility to get them out.'"

Perot would not leave his men behind, so he organized a crack team of Vietnam veterans from EDS, led by Colonel Bull Simons, and flew with them to the Middle East to help Bill Gaylord and Paul Chipparone escape. By the time the EDS team arrived in Iran, revolutionary mobs had inadvertently freed the two American executives from prison as they liberated thousands of inmates. Remnants of the Iranian police were still after Bill and Paul, so the EDS team decided to smuggle them across the Turkish border. Narrowly avoiding confrontations with anti-American militias en route, they finally crossed the border to safety in February 1979, ending the six-week nightmare. *A New York Times* headline said it well: "Perot 2, Iran 0."

Ross Perot viewed the feat as a simple act of loyalty, an extension of his two guiding principles: treat others as you want to be treated and never leave a man behind. Understand those two things, and this intriguing figure becomes much less complex. From his early years, those two principles have influenced every step along his long and unabashedly eccentric path.

Ross Perot was born June 27, 1930, in the small town of Texarkana. He and his sister, Bette, were heavily influenced by their modest, working-class parents and by the realities of the Great Depression that gripped the nation during much of their childhood. Throughout his life, Perot would trace any success he had back to his parents and the lessons he learned during those early years in East Texas.

"During the Depression, we lived five blocks from the railroad tracks," Mr. Perot recalled as we sat together in his Dallas office, which resembled a personalized museum more than a place of commerce. "Hobos would get off the train, come by our house, and knock on our door . . . and my mother would never turn down a hobo who wanted food. She'd always give them food even though we didn't have much to give."

One day, a guest from the tracks asked if the Perots ever wondered why so many homeless men came to their door. To explain, he showed them a curbside mark by their house, hinting to other wanderers that a badly needed meal might await them inside. After the Perots served this guest and watched him leave, young Ross asked, "Mom, do you want me to wash that off?"

Mr. Perot never forgot her response. "She looked me right in the eye and said, 'No, son. Those are people just like us who are down on their luck. We need to help them.'"

"This goes back to the values of Scouting, you see," he explained to me from a chair beside his desk. His face glowed. "I got it at home, I got it in the Boy Scouts, I got it at school, I got it at Sunday school and church. I got doses of those values everywhere I turned, and finally some of the vaccination took!"

In all these places, he was learning to treat others with respect. In Troop 18, sponsored by the Offenhauser Insurance Agency, he was also learning the skills he needed to be successful in business. "I became a Boy Scout and realized as I read through my handbook, you could become an Eagle Scout at thirteen months," he said. Then he continued in a matter-of-fact manner, "And I decided I'd be an Eagle Scout in thirteen months. For the first time in my life, I set goals and objectives and achieved them. And that's very important in a person's life, to set goals and achieve them. To have those experiences at twelve years of age is a pretty unique thing."

In Scouting, Perot found a number of people who would influence his life in important ways. Chief among them was Eagle Scout Josh Morriss, who inspired Ross to reach Eagle. Ross was so impressed with this older Scout that he decided to follow him into the U.S. Navy. "He was a role model for me," Perot said. "I was going to try and be the kind of man he was. Then, he went to the Naval Academy, and I'd never seen a ship, never seen the ocean, and I wanted to go to the Naval Academy." After he achieved Eagle, Perot set his next goal. He applied to the U.S. Naval Academy. He was neither accepted nor discouraged. He applied the next year and was again rejected. He applied for the third consecutive year, and only then did he receive his appointment. In the Naval Academy, he found another place where virtues formed the bedrock of daily life.

Along with future admirals William Lawrence and James Sagerholm, Ross Perot made the principles of Scouting a central part of the Academy's culture. These three midshipmen, as students at the Naval Academy are called, led the effort to establish an honor system for the student body: the Brigade of Midshipmen. They saw ethical problems within the Brigade and decided the students should no longer tolerate lying, cheating, and stealing. They didn't look to the faculty or staff to run the system; however, they turned to their fellow midshipmen to design and manage this new concept.

"I felt very strongly that the honor code should come from the midshipmen, not the senior officers," Perot explained. "It should be *their* honor code. I went to every company, every platoon, and talked with everybody, and it was theirs." He was learning to lead; if he were a midshipman, he would want his opinion heard. He understood the value of extending that same courtesy to others.

Having established the honor system that still guides midshipmen today, Lieutenant Perot left Annapolis in 1953 with an officer's commission and the love of Margot Birmingham. After marrying Margot and serving in the navy for four years, Perot became a computer salesman with IBM in Dallas, Texas. But in the early 1960s, this ambitious young man grew frustrated in IBM's corporate structure. He had aspirations that he feared would never be realized. He felt smothered. He wondered if he would ever live his dreams. Then, as he waited for one of the haircuts that always keep his hair closely clipped, he read a passage penned by Henry David Thoreau: "The mass of men lead lives of quiet desperation.

"I said, 'That's me,'" he remembered. He realized the time for waiting passively was over. He followed his passion and set out to create a new business and realize his dreams. "The rest is history," he said confidently. "And now it's a giant industry: When I started EDS, they didn't know whether it was a company or a disease!" Electronic Data Systems (EDS) started as a dream, and it might have remained such without a loan from a key supporter. He still has the original $1,000 check his wife Margot wrote to launch the company in 1962.

In 1962, EDS was far from the 124,000-person, $5.2-billion behemoth we know today. The company did not have a single client. Perot's first goal at the firm was to sell unused processing time on a mammoth transistor computer in Dallas. With 110 prospects in mind, he set out to sign his first client.

"I called on 77 prospects face to face and didn't sell a minute of time," he explained. "I was well past half the market: There were 110; I'd gotten to 77. Seventy-eight I made the big sale. My experience is that the difference between winning and losing is not giving up."

By the end of that first project, he had enough cash on hand to begin building his business into one of the world's top technology firms. "It was just a dream, and I think the dream materialized because we put the emphasis on hiring the highest-quality people. Teaching someone technology is a piece of cake when compared to trying to straighten a person out who's just a mess." He carried the lessons of his youth with him to EDS and took the company public in 1967. He set his salary at $68,000, and there it remained as he cast his fate with his shareholders. All his additional benefits would be tied to the performance of the stock. "Sixty-eight thousand is all I ever got," he said. Then he chuckled and added, "But the stock worked out well. I was totally focused on making the company successful."

In 1984, he sold EDS to General Motors for $2.5 billion. Four years later, he founded Perot Systems. Anyone who had not heard of Ross Perot up to this point found out about him in 1992, when he entered the race for the presidency of the United States. Perot captured the attention of the nation and reinvigorated millions of disenchanted voters as he waged one of the most successful third-party candidacies in history. His charts, infomercials, and straight talk became hallmarks of his unconventional campaign; he never shied from speaking his mind. He saw a problem in our government, and he wanted to fix it. He and running mate Admiral James Stockdale, a former POW, received 19 percent of the popular vote, but his United We Stand America ticket lost to Bill Clinton and Al Gore. After the election, he returned to the business world and took Perot Systems public in 1999. The young information technology firm's revenues exceeded $900 million that year and have since doubled.

When we met in his office on the Perot Systems campus outside Dallas, Texas, Perot had just been elected chairman emeritus. He met me at the elevator bank and walked me across a short bridge, lined with statues of his grandchildren, that led to his office suite. The suite itself was a museum. He had collected pieces of history and American artwork to accompany the artifacts he has kept from his past. Stepping into his spacious office, I found the walls and shelves filled with Americana and seventy years of memories. Above the low shelves that circle the room hang paintings that serve as his daily reminders. *The Spirit of '76* and *Washington Crossing the Delaware* remind him of what our ancestors sacrificed for the nation. Norman Rockwell's *A Scout Is Reverent*, a print of which hung on his wall as a boy, reminds him of a higher duty. In Rockwell's *Breaking Home Ties*, he sees his own life and a

Three generations of Eagle Scouts: Ross Perot, Sr., Ross Perot III, Hunter Perot, and Ross Perot, Jr.
COURTESY OF CIRCLE TEN COUNCIL, BSA (DICK PATRICK, PHOTOGRAPHER)

representation of one generation's obligation to the next. "See," he said, motioning to Rockwell's picture of a poor working father sending his son off to college. "This man sacrificed everything so his son—that next generation— could have a better life. Today's generation is *spending* the next generation's future. And that's sad."

His son Ross Perot, Jr., was now CEO of Perot Systems, and mementos of his namesake's accomplishments occupied one corner of the elder Perot's office. When we came to these pictures, I found a framed photograph showing Ross Jr. standing alongside his beaming father and his two sons. The picture paid tribute to the Perot family's Scouting tradition. Reflecting on his son, the senior Perot noted, "The leadership training, the decisiveness, all the things that made him successful in business started in Scouting."

The training continued at home: no special favors for this son of privilege. "Ross had to work for whatever he wanted, like I did as a boy," Ross Sr. recalled, lighting up the office with his smile. He recalled an incident when Ross Jr. had walked into a room while his father was being interviewed. The reporter turned to the younger Perot and asked, "What does it feel like to be the son of one of the richest men in America?" Perot's eyes gleamed. He delivered the punchline: "Ross just looked at him and laughed and said, 'Mister, all I know is I get twenty-five cents a week!' "

Mr. Perot has also tried his best to give those same lessons in humility to his grandsons and remembered talking with them about the meaning of their Eagle rank. "I told them how much I admired them and how much I respected them for having done it," he recounted. "Earning the Eagle Scout rank certainly has a positive impact on young men, and it's very clear that when you earn that badge, you need to be honest, trustworthy; you need to conduct your life in a way that is proper and that you can be proud of. You need to reach out and help. These guys at Christmas are out there helping the Salvation Army raise money every year. They're out there helping gather food for people, and on and on and on. And that comes back to Scouting: Help other people at all times."

Treat others as you would like to be treated. Never leave a man behind.

Less than a decade after he founded EDS, Perot landed on the international scene when he learned about the many Americans who had been left behind in Vietnam. He heard the story of U.S. servicemen held as prisoners of war and discovered their families were living in an agonizing world of uncertainty. The North Vietnamese now had a new enemy.

Working with the federal government, Perot brought worldwide attention to the plight of American POWs being held by the North Vietnamese. The Communist government in the North treated U.S. prisoners brutally, torturing them and offering no information about the status of U.S. servicemen missing in action. American families were left to wonder if they would ever see their loved ones again. Perot decided to try the Vietnamese in the court of world opinion, and in December 1969, he personally flew thirty tons of supplies, including medicine, Christmas presents, and letters from home, to Southeast Asia for the POWs. North Vietnam predictably rebuffed the planes, but Perot had won a victory.

"They had worldwide publicity for ten days," remembered Perot, smiling. "The whole world was upset about these POWs, and they suddenly stopped the treatment. Then we had wives and children going into the Vietnamese embassies everywhere they had an embassy in Europe. We'd take wives and children of POWs over and visit with the Vietnamese. It's not those visits that counted, it was the huge amount of press coverage in various countries." Perot worked tirelessly to bring POWs home and was often instrumental in supporting them and their families once they returned. He still has moving and heartfelt handwritten letters of thanks from POW families posted throughout his office, and since the 1970s, he has remained a leading figure in POW issues, making sure we never leave a man behind.

"The military families are in Ross's heart and in his soul and in his actions every day of his life," said Carol McCain, the ex-wife of one POW. "There are millions of us who are extremely grateful to Ross Perot."

Holding back tears, Brigadier General Robbie Risner, a prisoner in North Vietnam for nearly eight years and a prison mate of George Coker, said, "I can't help become emotional when I think of what he has done; he has forfeited, he has paid, he has given for the military, especially for the POWs." This comment comes from a man whose bravery inspired his fellow POWs to support him by singing patriotic songs for three hours while he was being tortured nearby. Their voices gave him the strength to survive; he recalls feeling "nine feet tall." Following that description, the statue of Risner at the U.S. Air Force Academy stands exactly nine feet tall; Ross Perot made sure of it.

The more time we spent together, the more I began to discover the deep passions that drive this Texan: his love of country and belief in helping others. These sentiments are evident in his words and in his flawlessly quoted passages from American history; and they are also captured in the pictures, handwritten letters, and mementos from grateful individuals that fill his office: notes from a crippled child, a veteran struggling with a debilitating disease or injury, a soldier's widow. They all found help in Ross Perot, and in them, I think, Ross Perot found his passion.

One example came during the Gulf War when an Iraqi Scud missile slammed into a military barracks in Bahrain, nearly taking the life of Army Sergeant David Campbell. "I was looking toward the door, and I remember watching the wall separate and the roof blow in," Campbell said. That was the last thing he remembered.

"They said he had less than a ten percent chance of surviving and that we should get over there as soon as possible," recalled Gail Campbell, who received the dreaded call from the army while she was at home with their two young daughters. "And the next thing I knew, I got a phone call from Ross Perot, and he wanted to help: 'What can we do for your husband?'"

"Suddenly, I'm talking to Gail Campbell," remembered Mr. Perot, "and she was wondering if there was any way that she and the two girls could see him before he died. I said, 'Certainly we can do that, but my question is: 'Is there any way to save his life?'"

Perot called Texas trauma specialist Dr. John Weigelt, and together they identified three experts who were currently serving in the Middle East. They didn't know their location or service branch, but Perot made a personal phone call to the Pentagon and things began to happen. Within hours, the military had located the three doctors, and Perot had vital medical equipment on the way to the Middle East. "They sent a Marine general out on the street to find the three doctors," Mr. Perot recalled. "He found all three of them . . . for a sergeant."

Ross Perot arranged a satellite hookup, and Dr. Weigelt coached the doctors in Bahrain through the procedure. Twenty-four hours later, the team of doctors had stabilized Sergeant Campbell. Soon he came home to his family.

"You never ever leave the wounded behind," Perot concluded.

Many cases exist where Ross Perot has funded research to help heal a patient, arranged for a sick or wounded soldier to have medical care, or supported a family through the hardship of losing a loved one who has died in the line of duty. In cases where government programs have fallen short, Ross Perot has stepped in.

At a dinner honoring Perot's service that was attended by all the Joint Chiefs of Staff, Richard B. Meyers, the chairman of the Joint Chiefs, reflected, "Just knowing that he's there for those circumstances, which unfortunately turn out to be all too many, where for some reason or other we can't properly take care of our men and women in the armed forces, we all know that Ross Perot is just a phone call away and he is a man of action. And that added dimension of support means so much to all our military family and it's exactly what our servicemen and women deserve."

One solider Perot helped observed, "It's not that he has the *capability* to do the things that he does. It's that he *wants* to do the things that he does."

His desire to do these things for others stems from a profound loyalty to his country. This loyalty shows in the paintings on his office walls, in his knowledge of history, and in his actions as well as his words. During our conversation, his typically colorful anecdotes always returned to his duty as a citizen. That loyalty stems from the opportunity this country gave a middle-class boy from rural Texas. By starting new companies and helping those in need, Ross Perot hopes to pass that opportunity along to others.

We visited in his office late into the afternoon, and when our conversation ended, Mr. Perot and I walked together toward the parking lot by way of Perot Systems' lofty atrium. There, we passed beneath the likeness of another tenacious man, one who lost one election after another before winning the presidency of the United States. It was Norman Rockwell's *Young Lincoln*. The towering portrait depicted Abraham Lincoln in his twenties, a rail-splitting axe held lightly his right hand and his head bowed gently toward a book he held open in his left. Our sixteenth president owns a special place in the heart of Ross Perot, whose humble roots reflect those of Lincoln.

"Lincoln started with nothing," Mr. Perot said, explaining his attachment to the eight-foot piece. "Self-educated, came up the hard way, had such courage. Now you think nobody has the courage to deal with the deficit now and all of the other things? Think what it took to get rid of slavery."

Then the favorite son of Texarkana continued, "In this country, you don't have to come with a pedigree. You just have to have the principles and the moral and ethical standards, and then you need to have the drive to get things done. All those things you get taught in Scouting."

We pushed through the building's doors and ambled toward the parking lot, which was still warm with late-afternoon sunlight. I looked for his waiting limo and chauffer but saw neither. Walking toward the few remaining cars, we said our good-byes, and then Ross Perot, self-made billionaire, unlocked his Ford Crown Victoria, slid behind the wheel, and drove home.

I found an echo of Mr. Perot's story several months later in Ed Crutchfield, another executive who rose from humble roots to build and lead a respected national firm. Shortly after turning thirty-two, Ed became president of First Union, a bank that in 1973 had $5 billion in assets. When he retired a quarter century later and handed the reigns to another Eagle Scout, First Union—now Wachovia—had $250 billion in assets. Yet, when we met in his office overlooking the fast-growing city of Charlotte, North Carolina, something struck me. This Eagle Scout talked very little about the decisions and strategies that marked his exceptional banking career. All that was in his past, a closed chapter. Instead, he dwelled on his passion for conservation, the joy he receives from helping young people receive a better education, and his involvement at Davidson College. He reminded me of Ross Perot. Like Ed Crutchfield, Perot finds his current passions in areas that have little to do with making money. He genuinely values helping others who need and deserve special attention. Granted, for many years the traditional pursuit of success consumed Perot and many other business titans, but I observed that as they aged, these corporate Eagles fully grasped an idea that was slowly taking root in my own mind: Success was not about them.

"I think we have a worldview that is often tied to success but not to significance," reflected Mark Sanford as we sat together in his office in the South Carolina State House. "What's unique about Scouting is that the Scouting program is a *value*-based leadership program. There are plenty of people out there chasing success, but they're missing how you get to significance and that is by living a life tied to those core values and principles. To me, that's the biggest thing I got out of Scouting: the idea of service to others."

"I tell my boys this all the time," the young governor continued. "Each one of you has been given a mission here in life, and the tricky part, and the difficult part, is finding your mission and recognizing that *your* mission is not another's mission. But we all have a mission and to get real passion in life means living an adventure tied to some mission, that again," he emphasized, "is bigger than ourselves."

When Mark Sanford and I met, I'd traveled almost every week for the preceding seven months, spent most of my savings, and passed the 30,000-mile mark somewhere between Atlanta and Columbia the previous afternoon. Different weeks found me in different states, always hearing new perspectives. The unfortunate but perhaps understandable result was this: I hadn't digested what I was hearing. I'd become worn out, frazzled, and so focused on recording and preserving these stories that I failed to *hear* them. I missed the familiar imperative these Eagles were collectively drilling into me: Help other people at all times.

To the extent I did realize their message, I wove it into my manuscript and my understanding of this legacy. I never bothered to apply their advice to my own life. After I met with Governor Sanford however, I took a long run along the Congaree River, which runs just below the capitol in Columbia. Beside the waters, still high from spring rains, and under a hot Carolina sun that somehow managed to penetrate the trees overhanging the dirt trail, I ran deep in thought, not really noticing the path before me.

Recently, people had begun asking about the effects this trip was having on me. What was I learning? How was I changing? Well, I didn't understand; the trip wasn't supposed to *change* me, just settle a few questions. So I had answered their queries lightly, almost flippantly.

Running never fails to clear my mind, and as I clicked off miles that Monday afternoon, I finally started to understand that the questions others asked me were more valid than I'd originally thought; this trip was, in fact, affecting me at a deeper level. I began to comprehend what Governor Sanford and so many others were telling me: A life lived for yourself has little value or significance in the end. Suddenly, this fundamental part of the Eagle legacy became glaringly apparent.

I now faced the uncomfortable task of comparing myself to their example, and I quickly realized that comparing my position in life to that of many of these Eagles would lead me nowhere. The obvious fact was, nobody had elected me governor or senator, or installed me as a chief executive or general, but then most people don't rise to those levels of rank. That does *not* mean their actions are less important or their obligations any fewer. So I couldn't escape this reality: No matter my experience or position, I could be doing something significant for others. I couldn't share an equivalency of rank with many of these men, but I *could* share a level of service and devotion. No longer did I have an excuse; I had a challenge.

I reached the trail's northern end, briefly caught my breath, and then turned to retrace my steps. As I ran south, at a slightly slower clip than I'd run north, I continued digesting the thoughts that were at long last beginning to arrange themselves coherently in my mind.

You cannot meet these Eagles, hear their words, and see what they have accomplished without feeling slightly inadequate, at least at first. I eventually realized that these examples and perspectives were reminders, not benchmarks. They are thousands—millions—of instances that show us that the principles of our younger days never expire. They reminded me of an oath I took in Troop 103.

When a Scout stands up with his troop and recites those words each week, the concepts underlying them are easy to remember and simple to live by. Unfortunately, busy lives and new priorities inevitably distract us as we grow older, and those ideals sometimes become faint and harder to practice. Along my journey, however, I found that once most Eagles adopt this code in their boyhood, its values remain part of them forever. Sometimes, it just takes another's example to remind us about the promise we made decades ago.

J. W. MARRIOTT, JR.
TROOP 241, CHEVY CHASE, MARYLAND
EAGLE SCOUT, 1947

The letter J. Willard Marriott wrote to his son on January 20, 1964, sits in a glass case several floors below the office from which that son, J. W. Marriott, Jr., now runs the family business. The elder Marriott wrote the note as a father to his son and as a seasoned CEO to a new president. In four simple typewritten paragraphs, the company's patriarch set forth the principles he always held close. The letter reminds visitors and employees, as well as the current CEO, about the values at the foundation of Marriott International. Above all, J. Willard Marriott, Sr., treasured his employees.

"Being the operating manager of a business on which probably 30,000 people depend for a livelihood is a frightening responsibility," the letter observed. "But I have the greatest confidence you will build a team that will insure the continued success of a business that has been born through the years of toil and devotion by many wonderful people." The letter, written on Marriott predecessor Hot Shoppes, Inc., stationery is signed "Love and best wishes, Dad."

Reflecting on the letter years later, J. W. "Bill" Marriott, Jr., recalled his father's lesson. "You need to treat people as you would like to be treated," he said. "You need to live the Golden Rule and recognize the great importance in your life and your business of *people*—and reach out to people and be there to help them, to teach them, to counsel and guide them. Basically, let them know you're there to clear the highway so they can get their job done and that you'll be supportive of them, listen to their concerns, help them solve problems, and get their advice on certain things. You need to be a servant-leader."

Turning to the Hurricane Katrina disaster that had ravaged the Gulf Coast, he explained that once the storm left the city, Marriott set out to locate their 2,800 New Orleans employees. They accounted for each and ensured that these associates and their families had cash for necessities. They also committed to finding jobs for these displaced employees in locations outside New Orleans. Bill always viewed Marriott as a family, perhaps because he remembers the company when it had several hundred employees instead of over 100,000. As he expressed it, when Katrina hit, *his* duty became caring for these people.

"When you saw the situation with Katrina, you saw the volunteerism in this country come forward," he said, moving toward a larger point. "People reached out to help these people that were so devastated in the hurricane. Those are the values of Scouting. As a nation, we really 'helped other people at all times' in what was a very difficult situation."

Those are also the values underpinning Marriott International, and the current CEO heeded his father's words. "The biggest obligation I have is to make sure our people have stability in their jobs, a full work week, and job security," he said. "Beyond that, I'm committed to providing them an opportunity to grow. We make sure they have training opportunities so they can move ahead with their careers to take care of their families.

"That's the right thing to do, but you also have to realize that the role of people in our business is huge. We don't manufacture anything. Ours is a service business and ninety-five percent of our people interact with customers all day long. They are the key to our success."

When young Bill Marriott joined Boy Scout Troop 241 in Chevy Chase, Maryland, he learned about the values that would help him lead the people of Marriott International. He explained, "When other kids were off doing things they wanted to do, playing baseball or soccer or whatever, you're out trying to earn merit badges, and you're out camping or learning skills which are totally different from what you learn in a normal urban society. I think the thing I learned was the importance of setting goals and the importance of having the determination to meet those goals and to work hard at it until you *do* get it done. That has been the hallmark of my parents' lives and my life. That's really what Scouting taught me more than anything else.

"Earning Eagle means you've achieved the highest rank in Scouting. You've done it through hard work and determination and a lot of help from your parents! I don't care who you are, there's not an Eagle Scout in the world that didn't get a lot of help from either his mother or father, and usually his mother."

Bill's father spent many nights away from home building Hot Shoppes, Inc., which he started as a single A&W restaurant franchise in 1927. In 1937,

the growing company ventured into airline catering and in-flight meals. When Bill reached his teenage years, Hot Shoppes welcomed him as an accounting assistant, cook, and dishwasher. When he graduated from the University of Utah in 1954, his father's company posted yearly sales of $21.5 million. J. Willard Marriott made Hot Shoppes successful with his relentless work ethic and penchant for perfection. The accompanying success, however, left Alice Marriott with much of the child-rearing responsibilities. By Bill's account, her work ethic equaled her husband's. She faithfully

J. W. Marriott, Jr., Eagle Scout
COURTESY OF J. W. MARRIOTT, JR.

encouraged Bill in his Scout work, reminded him to schedule appointments with merit badge counselors, and usually drove him to each meeting. She always attended his courts of honor.

"She didn't preach to me," he said. "She was trying to be helpful: 'How can I help you get this done? When's your next appointment? When can we get together to sort things out and put things together?' She was terrific.

"Dad was always busy, and she was there and she thought it was important for me to become an Eagle—and I did too," he explained. "It was a great collaborative effort between my mom and me that got me to Eagle. In your life, you need support in everything you do, and in this particular case, my mother really came through for me. They used to give mothers an Eagle pin. I don't know if they still do or not, but they should." They still do and the Marriott women have received many: Three of Bill's sons and four grandsons earned Eagle, and when we spoke, a fifth Marriott grandson was nearing the same rank as his grandfather.

"At home and at our church, we try to teach our kids the importance of work and achievement," he explained, answering my question about his family's well-established Scouting tradition. "Whenever you have the opportunity to improve yourself and achieve, go out and do it! That's what we encourage in our family, and that's right in line with the teachings of our church and Scouting." I began to gather how important Mr. Marriott considers his Mormon faith. After probing, I learned that even as CEO of Marriott, he still found time to serve as bishop for the local ward of his church. He recalled the experience warmly. "We had about eight hundred people," he said. "I was there to help them find jobs, help them find housing, help them get food on their plates when they didn't have any. I think that's where the rubber meets the road. All of us in corporate America contribute to charitable causes, but . . . what was most satisfying to me was when I was able to get in with people and help them personally."

He observed that Scouting taught him to be engaged on that level. To earn the next rank, he couldn't rely on others; he had to do the work himself. His merit badges demanded Herculean amounts of dedication, he recalled, then added his opinion that the extra difficulty of the merit badges from his era made up for the lack of a capstone service project, which was not introduced until 1965, the year after he became president of Marriott. He talked about spending hours on end trying to identify fifty different bird species for Bird Study merit badge and spending fifty nights camping, some in the woods of Virginia, some in his suburban backyard.

"You're learning a lot of different things from the different merit badges," he said. "They give you a whole new perspective on your personal education in life that you don't get in school. You take the same values, and you can use them in your life. I think I've always been a person who's tried to learn and I learned a lot in Scouting, and that continued as I've gone into business and other activities. I've been a student of history and of the world and of events, and that was promoted by what I learned in Scouting. I learned about civics; I learned about personal health; I learned about safety and also all kinds of things you wouldn't normally learn in school. It was a great experience, and it sparked my interest to continue to learn."

He admitted that his most memorable challenge came in starting a fire for Camping merit badge. He explained, "You had to keep working those sticks until you could get a spark; then you had to get the spark into the tinder and get it started and that took me a long time. I almost didn't make it. I finally just eked through and got it done."

I asked him about the chances of him starting a fire today. "I *start* a lot of them," he said, issuing a tremendous laugh. "It's putting them out that's hard!"

His laughter slowly subsiding, he explained how he extinguished the figurative fires that continually erupt in the $11-billion company, with its 500,000 guest rooms spread across 68 countries. "Taking action is the key," said the veteran executive. "You have to get your facts, then you have to do something. You just can't stand there and watch the train leave the station. You better be on the train, you better be at the head of the train leading it up, making things happen, and working with your people."

Leadership with a bias for action. I remembered South Carolina Governor Mark Sanford telling me the same. "If there's a bear outside your tent at Philmont," he'd said, "you've got to do something about it *now!*"

I shared Governor Sanford's comment with Mr. Marriott, who, in very typical fashion, responded with a joke punctuated by a hearty laugh. "In that case, you'd better have a good pair of shoes, right?"

The seasoned CEO has faced bears before. He remembered one particular challenge that arose in 1990, when the real estate market suddenly crashed, war loomed in the Middle East, and the country slid into a recession. Marriott had been building hotels across the country and found itself holding nearly $3 billion in real estate assets when buyers suddenly disappeared because of the economy. "Our stock plunged from $42 to $8 per share," Mr. Marriott remembered, the always-jovial tone of his voice not indicating the stress he must have felt at the time. "But we pulled ourselves out of it. We got our team together quickly, got them focused, and found capital in lots of places we'd never looked before. We were able to keep the company afloat by being creative. We engaged the whole team—one hundred and fifty to two hundred senior executives—in a crisis-management effort." He acted quickly and led the effort.

"But as part of this, we had to shut down our architecture and construction departments," he continued. "We had to let one thousand good people go, but we set up an out-placement service for them and placed ninety percent, at a time when the real estate industry was at a halt."

"When you've got a problem, you've got to solve it," he concluded. "So we did our best to keep Marriott afloat and also exercise compassion for our people and help them survive, care for their families, and move forward."

When he began leading Marriott as its president in 1964, Bill Marriott oversaw a company with four hotels and 9,600 employees. By the time he found himself talking with me, his company had 2,800 properties and 143,000 associates worldwide. Those statistics led to a question that had burned in me throughout our conversation, but I wasn't sure how to ask it. I had learned that many business titans have humble roots, Sam Walton, Ross Perot, and Ed Crutchfield among them. Ambition and hunger drove these Eagles to succeed. As Eagle Scout Richard Schmalensee, dean of MIT's Sloan School of Management, observed, many CEOs and business leaders come from modest backgrounds as do many Eagle Scouts. Bill Marriott's circumstances were not those to make a young man hungry. In many ways, he was born a son of privilege, the son of a successful businessman. As disarmingly as I could, I asked him where he found the ambition that spurs him to spend weeks on the road inspecting hotels and long hours at the office.

"I think a lot of any drive I have comes from our church's teachings," he reflected. "We believe in the value of work, we believe in the value of service, we believe in the value of helping other people. We believe we were put on this earth to accomplish something and achieve something and develop our talents. That's why I think Scouting connects so well with the values of our church. If you're going to achieve in Scouting, it requires you to give an extra amount of effort."

As we ended our conversation, Mr. Marriott added one last story that he felt was important. He told me about a phrase coined by the president of his church, a phrase he proceeded to relate to the purpose of Scouting. "The idea of 'deciding to decide' gets to the importance of deciding early on that you'll do the right thing whenever you face a choice later in life," he explained. "If you stay with that until the end, you'll be fine. If you *don't* decide ahead of time, you'll let the world pull you astray. Once you make that decision to always do what's right, you've already made thousands of choices that'll come up later. It makes life a lot easier to live!"

J. W. Marriott, Jr., decided decades ago how he hoped to lead his company and address the challenges that would arise: decisively and compassionately. With an obligation to his employees and shareholders always first in his heart, his vision is clear, and so are the results.

Section Three of the Boy Scouts of America's Federal Charter reads: ". . . the purpose of this corporation shall be to promote, through organization and cooperation with other agencies, the ability of boys to do things for themselves and others . . ." Accordingly, Scout troops do not exist independently. Each troop relies on another agency or organization for sponsorship. These outside groups provide 125,000 Scout units with support, leadership, a place to meet, and a place to store tents, trailers, and other gear. These institutions invest in the boys of their community.

During our conversations, Bill Marriott continually returned to his church. To him, Scouting was forever linked to the congregation of the Church of Jesus Christ of Latter-Day Saints that sponsored Troop 241. The values of his church and the values of Scouting became inseparable and forever shaped his character. Sometimes troops heavily reflect the character of their sponsoring organizations, as in Mr. Marriott's case; other times they do not. As I heard stories from troops of all stripes and sponsorships, I realized the vast diversity of "the Scouting experience." No two units are exactly alike. For all the standard uniforms, policies, and handbooks, individual sponsors, troops, and their leaders truly define Scouting.

When I considered the thousands of institutions that charter Scout troops, I began to understand another unique aspect of Scouting: The program's reach into America is unsurpassed. Its ability to join organizations of every type to one common cause astounded me. Synagogues and Islamic centers, labor unions and large corporations, schools and Rotarians, Catholics and Buddhists all sponsor Scouting. They believe that the troops they charter can accomplish something vitally important for young men.

The organizations that support Scouting often have beliefs and opinions that conflict with one another, but they all agree on the fundamental values contained in the Scout Oath and Scout Law. In Scouting, they tacitly focus on those things that unite all Americans. They find the common ground so important to our nation's fabric and future. I think Scouting reminds people—often members of these sponsoring groups—who have never even considered wearing the khaki uniform that there are some things upon which we all agree.

MICHAEL BLOOMBERG

TROOP 11, MEDFORD, MASSACHUSETTS

EAGLE SCOUT, 1955

Unlike Bill Marriott, Michael Bloomberg's family could not afford summers at camp. So at an early age, the future entrepreneur learned to make his own way. "I went to Boy Scout camp for each summer up in New Hampshire—five summers—paid for it by selling Christmas wreaths," he explained. "If you sold the most Christmas wreaths in your troop, you got a free week or two weeks at camp." This Jewish Scout sold more Christmas wreaths than anyone else and earned his free trips to camp. In selling wreaths each year, he learned about tenacity, which, time and again, would prove the key to his success.

Decades later, that success landed him in New York's City Hall, where I found him on a blustery December day. The centuries-old building stands on an island of trees and grass in the midst of downtown Manhattan, and the campus muffled the sounds of traffic as I passed through the gates and walked toward the main building. I wove through the press corps that had assembled on the front steps and then entered a building that seemed too small for the city it administered. A member of the mayor's staff guided me through the interior corridors, where I enjoyed the trappings of a bygone era: elaborate moldings, classical paintings, ornate columns. She soon ushered me through two French doors and into a cavernous room whose ceiling, high columns, and paintings matched the rest of the 200-year-old building. As I lowered my gaze, however, I saw something that seemed very out of place until I considered the leader of the current administration.

When Michael Bloomberg stepped from his office as CEO of Bloomberg LP, a $3-billion international information firm, into the mayor's office in 2002, he brought a new perspective. He transformed the ceremonial mayor's suite into a space reminiscent of the trading floors he worked on as a rising star on Wall Street. Several rows of low, modern office cubicles sat beneath the now mismatched regal ceilings. A black swivel chair and computer screen sat at each desk, and on many sat Bloomberg LP's trademarked dual monitors, which brought the staff near-instant information from the city, nation, and world. Squarely amidst the sea of low partitions sat Mayor Bloomberg's office, a low cube no different from any other in the "bullpen." No doors, no walls, just a low partition that rose only one foot above his desk. Everyone can see and hear everyone else in the room, and one staffer noted that when people several cubes away called the mayor via phone, he'd hang up, look at the staff member, and say, "I'm right here, just yell!"

At City Hall, Michael Bloomberg re-created the environment that made him successful. Together, we surveyed the never-quiet bullpen from the slightly disarrayed staff conference area, not quite the posh surroundings in which I pictured meeting an executive as accomplished as Bloomberg. The mayor wore a dark, well-fitting suit, and his sharp eyes and quick comments hinted at his commanding position and his successful past. He gestured to a simple folding table where we sat down in equally simple chairs. Then I began learning about his legendary career.

From his humble background, Bloomberg entered Johns Hopkins University and later Harvard Business School. He encountered little failure at either institution. He also met success as he forged his work ethic at a Cambridge real estate firm where he routinely opened the office. He knew customers looking for housing would call early to set up appointments for the afternoon. Being the first one in the office, he answered the calls and scheduled engagements for later in the day. It took others in the firm a long time to figure out why so many customers walked into the office each afternoon asking for Michael Bloomberg.

He likewise confronted little failure at Salomon Brothers, the Wall Street firm where he built his career. He remembers that only Billy Salomon, the firm's founder, beat him to work in the mornings and few stayed later in the evenings. Even with his highly regarded diplomas, this Russian-American from working-class New England seemed to have something to prove. His work ethic paid dividends, and until 1981 he rocketed upward. Then, suddenly, Salomon Brothers was acquired, and he lost his job. For the first time, he confronted failure.

When most people lose their jobs, they don't have $10 million in the bank. Bloomberg did, all of it self-made. By focusing on his bank account, however, one misses the real lesson. The important lesson comes from being knocked down, having a dream, taking a risk, and *making* it happen.

Jobless, with a family to support, and still burning with sizable ambition, Bloomberg considered his future. Like many entrepreneurs, he needed to escape the reigns of corporate structures and chart his own path. He left Salomon as an information systems executive, and he knew finance as well as anybody. Realizing that Wall Street still ran largely off complex computers and hand-entered information, Bloomberg saw an opportunity. He conceived a computer system that would deliver electronic information about stocks, bonds, and the market to the masses in real time, in a simple format. No longer would companies need experts to analyze raw financial data. No longer would each large firm have to collect these voluminous data independently. Bloomberg would provide it all faster and at a lower cost. In a sense, he built some of the first roads of what would become the information superhighway. People laughed. They thought he was crazy.

His first sale came in December 1982. Alone, he walked into a Merrill Lynch board room to pitch his yet-to-be-fully-developed product. Merrill Lynch thought they could build their *own* system, but they couldn't start for six months. Bloomberg shot through the opening: "I'll get it done in six months, and if you don't like it, you don't have to pay for it!"

Six months to the day later, the Bloomberg team delivered. They earned a handsome fee for installing the system and leased twenty-two special Bloomberg terminals to Merrill Lynch for $1,000 a month. Bloomberg had its first customer, and they made sure the Wall Street giant remained happy; they knew one satisfied customer would draw many more.

Twenty years after Bloomberg LP closed that first deal; the firm leased more than 170,000 terminals to clients in 110 countries and posted revenues of $3 billion. Bloomberg LP lists most of the world's major financial firms and central banks as clients. As its founder gambled in 1981, people would pay for good information. It became his job to make sure nobody provided better information than Bloomberg LP.

To cement the place of his terminals on desks worldwide, Bloomberg ventured into all types of media, creating Bloomberg News, Bloomberg Information Television, and Bloomberg Magazine. He started by providing news stories based on stock and bond data, then ventured into financial and traditional reporting, knowing that his credibility as a dependable news source was increasing steadily. He worked relentlessly. By 1995, only Associated Press stories were published in more U.S. newspapers than Bloomberg News, and today Bloomberg Information Television broadcasts news stories twenty-four hours a day from desks located in cities around the globe. But Michael Bloomberg has to be careful; he *is* Bloomberg LP. He realizes that he must always conduct himself accordingly, keeping in mind those Scouting principles he learned in Medford.

In 2001, he became a personal representative of another institution, New York City. On the winter day we met, Michael Bloomberg was leading America's largest city, home to more than 8 million people of all races and nationalities. He had just come from a ceremony honoring New York firefighters, and he gently deflected a question about his role in public service, commenting instead on the risks members of the New York Fire Department take in the name of duty. His risks are of one nature; the ones those men and women take are entirely different. Later on the day we met, he planned to visit a nearby hospital to see a firefighter who was badly burned in a fire that morning.

He sees the life of every New Yorker as important to every other, regardless of his or her position. That philosophy grew from his experiences in Troop 7, and he mused that his summers at Scout camp in New Hampshire taught him that even a self-confident entrepreneur like himself isn't entirely independent. Whether the boys of Troop 11 were pitching tents, cleaning campsites, or working on projects, they'd do it together. To him, that provided a larger lesson, and he sees that even as a chief executive surrounded by busy assistants and the trappings of success, the lives of every New Yorker can affect him and millions of others in some way. "We're in the world together," he said simply. "You can't find one person or job that isn't dependent on others."

Those in public service, like the firefighters Michael Bloomberg met that morning, touch the lives of New Yorkers in a uniquely meaningful way. But the closest-held goals of these public servants are likely similar to their mayor's: to make the world better for the people dearest to them. For the mayor, this means his two daughters. Irrespective of his wealth and office, he is a father like millions of other men in America, and I wondered what he did for Georgina and Emma at home, away from the press and their cameras. I asked him one of the haunting questions that I expect often causes millions of fathers to lose sleep at night: "What do you want your children to learn from you?"

He contemplated the question. Then, perhaps remembering his own path, he said, "I hope they learn not to worry about what people think. I've told them a million times that if at the beginning everybody laughs at you when you do something, don't worry about it because you're learning and they're not. And eventually they forget that they used to laugh, but they respect you because you have a skill now." Or, in his case, a $3-billion company. "If you wait and only do things once you know how, you're never going to make a lot of progress. So just go out and do it."

For that lesson, the Bloomberg girls have a fine example in their father. Michael went out and earned Eagle. He rocketed through the corporate world of Wall Street. Then he stepped out independently and heard the laughter as he started selling stock and bond information via bulky monitors labeled with the meaningless brand of "Bloomberg." Then the laughs stopped as the company flourished; others took note and started learning from *him*. He heard snickers once more as he entered the race for mayor of New York City, and they grew louder when this political novice actually won. With some sarcasm, he said, "There's an article in the *New York Times* today—front page in the *New York Times*—that says I've learned something in three years. I don't know if that's true or not," he added with a small laugh. "Eventually they stop laughing. I put a smoking ban in, and everybody hated it. Today, you'd never get rid of it. Never."

Returning the conversation to Scouting, I asked, "Think back on the Scout Oath and Law," and then qualified, "which you probably haven't thought of in some time."

He responded by repeating the Scout Law flawlessly: "A Scout is Trustworthy, Loyal, Helpful, Friendly, Courteous, Kind, Obedient, Cheerful, Thrifty, Brave, Clean, and Reverent."

"Well, maybe you have," I allowed, laughing at his quick response and the contented grin it left on his face. I asked him about the values of those creeds and, as an Eagle Scout, how they shaped his life.

Michael Bloomberg receiving his Eagle Scout award as his mother looks on
COURTESY OF MICHAEL BLOOMBERG

"I think they're all the American values, hopefully the world's values, but certainly America's. Americans have quaintly simplistic ways and direct ways of phrasing things that is [*sic*] unique to this country. I think it's one of the great strengths of this country: There's a lack of ambiguity. Nobody suggests that as an adult that everyone's going to be perfect and follow every one of those things. But hopefully you [as an Eagle] do more than you would otherwise.

"Being an Eagle Scout means that you took control of your own life," he elaborated. "You set an objective, a reasonably complex one for a young man, and that you pursued it through difficult times. Not every merit badge is easy. Sometimes things don't work out, and you fail. But the person you see in the mirror is the person who should be most proud that you became an Eagle.

When you go on in life, generally nobody walks up to you in the street and says, 'Were you an Eagle Scout?' And you don't walk up to somebody and say, 'Were you an Eagle Scout?' " *Unless you happen to be me,* I thought.

"But you know you accomplished something," he continued. "You set a goal and accomplished it. When you're an adult, there are a lot more serious goals. Fighting for the country or raising your own family or helping people who just weren't as lucky as the rest of us. The decisions when you're an adult get to be much more complex. There's oftentimes no right or wrong answer, and ascertaining the facts is probably as big a problem if not more so in decision making. When you are at the age of Boy Scouts, the facts are clear. Later on they're not. Learning to deal in the simple cases helps prepare you in terms of analytical abilities and confidence in yourself to take on the more complex tasks. And I think the confidence Boy Scouting builds in young men is what it's all about. It's not the individual skill you learn in merit badge A, B, or C.

"There are plenty of times when you want to throw up your hands when things don't go well," he observed from experience. "You get fired in your career or your kids aren't behaving the way you'd like them to behave or you lose something that you wanted. It's being able to deal with those situations. And I don't think you go back to thinking 'I dealt with this as a Boy Scout,' but life is a series of additional steps, and each builds on what comes before and is a prelude to what comes after. For me, the Boy Scouts were a big part of that."

Like I was finding in the lives of so many other Eagle Scouts, Michael Bloomberg's path eventually led him toward public service. Scouting's emphasis on citizenship seems to have an almost inevitable effect on the young men who reach Eagle. At some point later in life, they remember their training and invest deeply in something larger than themselves.

Michael Bloomberg had little to lose when he invested in New York City. He had already amassed his fortune. He could pay for private cars and helicopters. His name was known worldwide, and he could always return to his namesake company. That makes him no less or more admirable than any other public servant, however, but it did make me think.

I remember studying politics at Washington and Lee University and spending two summers working in Congress. During all that time, however, something never occurred to me: truly *why* people enter politics in the first place. We studied *how* people won—or lost—elections and *how* they governed. I never really learned *why* they ran. The cynical and superficial answer might have been fame or glory or perhaps, at worst, power. Before I began this trip across the country, I thought those reasons might be fairly common. Particularly after I met with Michael Bloomberg in City Hall, the trappings of elected life seemed mighty enchanting. But as I met more and more elected officials—many poorly paid unsung local representatives—I learned that difficulty, not glamour and excitement, marks life in politics.

"Public office," sighed Georgia legislator Edward Lindsey. "Let me tell you about the glamour. During the session, I'd generally be up around 4:30 in the morning. I'd answer my constituents' e-mail between 4:30 and 6:15 and help Elizabeth get the boys off to school. Then go back to it around 7:45 and then try to prepare for what was going to take place that day in committee and in session. Session would begin at 10:00; that'd usually be about three to four hours. Then we'd do committees all afternoon, and I'd sit down around five o'clock and I'd start reading the bills that were coming up the next day or working on a particular bill my committee was interested in. I'd stay with that until about 7:30 or 8:00. I'd then go to dinner with somebody if I was asked to go to dinner. Get home, go back over what I had to do the next day, then go to bed around midnight and start again four and a half hours later. And even now, out of session, I've got something going on three nights a week." All this amidst sustaining a young family and a law practice.

"Don't get me wrong; I absolutely love having this opportunity," he stressed, "but I think the reality is different than the broad perception." That settled the issue of glamour, but the question remained: "Why?" I found one poignant answer in one of Lindsey's Minnesota counterparts.

Cy Thao still remembers Laotian Communists interrogating his father shortly after U.S. forces left Southeast Asia. The Thaos, along with many other Hmong, had aided the United States during the Vietnam War and become targets for the victorious Communists. When suspicious government agents began investigating Cy's father, the family fled across the Mekong River and into Thailand. In 1980, after five years in a refugee camp, they emmigrated to Minnesota. Shortly thereafter, Cy discovered Scouting as he tagged along with his older brother on Troop 100's first camping trip. Although its boys were the poorest in the area, Troop 100 provided an entrée to American life for Cy Thao. It also fostered the values that would lead him to the Minnesota House of Representatives.

"The whole Scouting process was a rite of passage," the artist-turned-legislator explained. "It turns a young boy into a man and teaches him his obligations to help his community. I felt like Scouting taught me to slowly transition to American culture and to learn responsibility and practice leadership. Then, you grow up and become an adult. You take what you learned and use it to help other people."

He explained how he started helping others through local politics. During that discussion he never used the word *I*. He simply viewed himself as the representative for a group of activists who cared. "We were in a position where we could help change society around us and help people who needed some support," he said. "We looked at our community and saw that people weren't being involved politically. Lots of poverty, lots of people who didn't know how to vote, people who weren't getting health care. People were just reacting to situations. Instead of letting things happen to us, particularly within the immigrant community, we needed to get the community's voice heard. We had a great desire to change what's around us. Through public service, we've been able to help people here in St. Paul and around the state."

Then he laughed and made a more personal admission. "Now that we got elected, I worry most about messing up and letting everyone down! So there's also an obligation—a duty—that you can't let yourself fail. Everyone is watching you and expecting you to have the highest standards. It's just like being an Eagle Scout!"

Legislators like Cy Thao and Edward Lindsey, and a mayor such as Michael Bloomberg, reached positions of great responsibility and, concurrently, of great expectation. Their constituents expect their hard work and honesty. In response, these men hold themselves to the same standards they did as Scouts. They seem to remember their oath to help other people at all times. They do their best. They follow the Scout Law. And I think they always bear in mind that their actions will reflect upon all others who share their rank of Eagle Scout.

BEYOND THE COLD WAR

Throughout the latter half of the twentieth century, the Scouting program underwent many alterations as it adapted to a changing nation. The Explorer program, which helps older Scouts investigate particular career paths, began in 1959 and opened itself to young women in 1971. In 1972, Scouting began its first public antidrug campaign. Soon thereafter, women were allowed to become leaders, and Scouting registered 6,524,640 members, the largest number in its history. New merit badges emerged, and old merit badges disappeared as technology and interests shifted. No longer were old badges such as Signaling and Blacksmithing of interest to Scouts; new badges like Atomic Energy, Climbing, and Fly Fishing certainly were.

Scouting attempted to engage more youth from different backgrounds during the 1990s by introducing several new initiatives, including Operation First Class, which promoted Scouting in urban areas, and Learning for Life, a separate program that teaches character in public schools. Shortly before the turn of the century, Scouting launched the Venturing outdoor high adventure program for young men and women aged fourteen through twenty.

In 1981, the Scouts faced the first of many lawsuits concerning the organization's membership policies. Although the BSA offers options for girls and young women, the Boy Scouting program itself remains single-gender, and openly gay and atheist adults are not allowed as leaders in Scout troops. These regulations resulted in lawsuits that continued for two decades until the U.S. Supreme Court ruled that the organization could establish its own guidelines. While individual troops continued to thrive, the Court's decision in 2000 presented new challenges for the Boy Scouts of America. In the latter decades of the twentieth century, Scouting also faced competition for boys' time and interest as other activities for teenagers, sports in particular, proliferated. Yet despite the changes time has naturally brought to its programs, Scouting has remained remarkably constant.

"In my day, you didn't have to do a service project," recalled Eagle Scout Dick Leet, a former president of the Boy Scouts of America. "I also earned some different merit badges than Scouts do today. The Scouting program and requirements changed in a lot of ways over the last decades to keep up with the times. So 'was an Eagle' and 'is an Eagle' could be argued to be different, but they're not because the heart of the program—the Scout Oath and Law—has stayed the same. We're still teaching young people the same basic truths."

During those decades in which Scouting was evolving, the United States and the Soviet Union were locked in a conflict that cast a shadow over America's communities. Sam Nunn still remembers growing up under the threat of the Cold War. Warner Robins Air Force Base lay just sixteen miles away from the small house where Troop 96 met in Perry, Georgia, and Sam knew that somewhere behind the Soviet Union's "Iron Curtain," a nuclear missile waited for the order that would send it to destroy his hometown and its air base. "We were certainly aware of the threat, but we didn't have anywhere to run," Sam explained. "We couldn't afford schools, let alone fallout shelters!"

Like Sam Nunn, millions of Americans still remember the forty-year standoff between the United States and the Soviet Union, during which nuclear tension remained constant. Strategists appropriately called the principal component of the fragile peace MAD (Mutually Assured Destruction). If one side attacked, a global nuclear holocaust was certain. Millions remember fallout drills in schools and churches. Millions remember the specter of a mushroom cloud ballooning upward from an atomic explosion. Few, however, had a chance to help.

Years later as a U.S. senator, Sam traveled throughout Eastern Europe and the Soviet Union, meeting adversaries who would eventually become allies. In 1989, when the Soviet Union and its military began collapsing along with the Berlin Wall, the Georgia senator and leaders of the former Soviet bloc discovered a terrible emerging threat: the spread of weapons of mass destruction. He understood the stakes and fortunately was in a place to act.

"Trace it back to the Scout Law," he observed. "Trustworthy. Really, all those other points are just ingredients you need to be trusted. You can't lead unless you enjoy the trust of your colleagues and constituents." And former adversaries. Eastern Europe's leaders knew Senator Nunn and his reputation. They trusted him to help. All he needed was the right partner.

RICHARD LUGAR

TROOP 80, INDIANAPOLIS, INDIANA

EAGLE SCOUT, 1946

"I can still see that cartoon on the front page of the *Indianapolis Star*," reflected Richard Lugar, carrying us back to 1968 Indianapolis, Indiana, where he had just been elected mayor. He had scarcely moved into his new office in city hall when his reputation landed his caricature on the front page of the city's leading newspaper. With that cartoon, the *Star* echoed the questions many people were already raising about the ethics of their new thirty-five-year-old mayor. The questions weren't surfacing for the usual reasons, however. Ironically, people wondered if the young, idealistic mayor was *too* ethical to get the job done.

Warming up, Lugar continued describing the cartoon. "The *Star* had a picture of little Dick Lugar in his Boy Scout uniform, and it was meant to show me still wet behind the ears. And then there were the great vultures of urban life, the people who are going to eat your lunch twice a day, all surrounding him," he said, motioning to describe the swarming birds and edging forward in his seat. "All with the idea that this poor guy has no clue what's about to hit him. It's all well and good to be the Eagle Scout, but, nevertheless, life in the big city is pretty tough, unyielding, and unforgiving.

"And a lot of people felt that way about it," he observed as he settled back into his chair. "On the one hand, they admired me, because they liked the Eagle Scout image and felt, all things considered, this is the kind of role model, the kind of person you want to deal with. On the other hand, there always is a certain amount of skepticism with people. Do people like this really ever get the job done in circumstances that are less than perfect or, worse still, just a mess?"

Leave it to a political cartoonist to capture in a simple picture one of the fundamental questions with which I'd been struggling and trying to articulate in, as the saying goes, a thousand words: Can honest people succeed in a harsh and complicated world? While the cartoonist had posed the question, he didn't provide the answer. That chore fell to Richard Lugar.

In 1976, after serving two successful terms as mayor of Indianapolis, the people of Indiana sent Richard Lugar to represent them in the U.S. Senate, where I found him twenty-five years later. One bright morning, I emerged

Richard Lugar, U.S. Senator, Indiana
COURTESY OF SENATOR LUGAR

from the Union Station Metro stop and walked south down a park-lined street toward the stately dome of the U.S. Capitol. I turned onto Constitution Avenue and walked toward the entrance to the Hart Senate Office Building. Inside, I wandered down flag-lined hallways and began to wonder how a quarter of a century in Washington, D.C.'s heady, powerful atmosphere had affected this Indiana Boy Scout.

I learned the answer soon enough. Shortly before eleven a.m., I walked between the U.S. and Indiana flags that guarded the glass doors of Lugar's suite. A young staffer ushered me down

a long corridor and into a cavernous but cluttered office. The office's deep blue carpet was set off by dark wooden bookshelves and lit in part by a pair of towering windows. On the rich carpet sat a round, paper-covered conference table and a graceful desk. Amidst all of this, almost dwarfed by the office's regal trappings, waited a warmly smiling Richard Lugar.

I stepped forward and shook hands with a gracious, silver-haired Hoosier who carried not a trace of the arrogance that part of me had suspected might be endemic in the U.S. Senate. His constant grin and sparkling eyes chased away any remaining hints of my earlier apprehension, and we were soon discussing our common Scouting memories. The subject of the

Star's cartoon quickly surfaced, and with that image, the Rhodes Scholar instantly crystallized the question of the day. Can an Eagle Scout succeed in today's world, particularly in the tough realm of politics? More precisely, can he succeed and remain true to his principles?

For Lugar, the answer came easily. He has never personally felt a conflict between virtue and success. To him, political success and success in life in general never entails compromise; well, perhaps it does when it comes to legislation but certainly not when it comes to principles and beliefs.

"This question means coming to grips with the whole problem of truth and integrity and having somebody you can rely upon, who you can believe in," he said. "Success comes back to the whole issue of credibility, which I think crucially important in public life, observed almost as much in the breach as in the observance! I sort of believe that you are not obligated to blurt out everything that you know, but particularly as president or as somebody who has responsibility, the things you do say have to be truthful insofar as you know, because almost everybody relies upon it. If you're an American president and you constantly need to be reinterpreted or be read between the lines or if you always put a spin on things, well you're going to

Richard Lugar, Eagle Scout, Troop 80

have enormous problems because people who rely upon you as allies will begin to have their qualms, and those who are adversaries will be reading between the lines and will not take you seriously. So I sort of get back to this bedrock aspect that integrity is very much the thing that is required. This is derivative from Scouting: the discipline of the program, the repetition and observance of the Scout Oath and the Scout Law, and the various ways that's manifested."

I pressed Lugar about how Scouting's program and creeds made a difference in his life. He paused momentarily before replying. "Well, I was eternally indebted to the Civics merit badge, which required me to first of all just get a map of the city and find all the cemeteries, all the parks, to get some idea of how broad and wide this place of Indianapolis was. I was only acquainted with people on the north side, and my life as I found it was very circumscribed, maybe two or three miles as the crow flies. . . . The Scouting situation is the first one that really led me to an idea of my whole community and what was involved there. It clearly was a tremendously formative influence."

As the future senator began to develop the sense of citizenship that would guide him through life, he abruptly learned that his community and his duties as a citizen thereof stretched well beyond the city limits of Indianapolis. The additional lesson came in 1944, when he was twelve.

Each Friday night, Troop 80 met at the Church of the Advent in Indianapolis. During every meeting, the troop assembled by patrol for review, forming neatly spaced lines facing the front of the room. Lugar's patrol, the Lone Pine Patrol, always stood directly before a particular framed picture that hung from the wall of the Scout room. The simple frame held one black-and-white photograph of each of the troop's Eagle Scouts. Every meeting, those Eagles, their faces forever frozen as young men, gazed down on new generations of Scouts, challenging them to reach Eagle and join them on that wall.

Among the young faces in the collage of Eagles was that of Reiman Steeg, the older brother of Lugar's patrol leader. After earning his Eagle several years earlier, Reiman had left Indiana to join so many other Eagle Scouts and young Americans on the battlefields of World War II, which was still raging at the time.

Reflecting on that picture frame, Lugar recalled, "The Lone Pine Patrol looked right at this; we were at attention while being inspected. I could see all of the faces, the Eagles, and the symbolism of wanting to be in that picture was enormous. But, see, Reiman Steeg was there in the picture. Well, tragically, he was killed in the war. Later, word of his death reached us, and they had a funeral service right there at the church where we met. And so this was terribly sobering for each of us." The young Scouts suddenly realized that events halfway around the globe could have very real effects on the people, farms, and towns of the nation's heartland.

Lugar and I shifted gears and turned to the subject of international relations. Judging by his energy and the light in his eyes, if there is something

Lugar enjoys discussing as much as Scouting, it's weapons control. He began an allegory that started when America's old adversary, the Soviet Union, crumbled after the Cold War.

Many leaders used the Soviet collapse as an excuse to shift their attention to other areas; Lugar did not. He saw a real threat emerging in the former Soviet Union, a threat that could devastate not only Russia but also the towns of Indiana and of every other state and, for that matter, of every other country. The trouble was this: When the Soviet Union disintegrated, so did the security surrounding the Red Army's nuclear, chemical, and biological weapons. The old Soviet empire could become a nuclear shopping mall for terrorists and rogue states. Realizing their situation, budget-strapped Soviet generals brought their problems to their longtime counterparts, Senator Lugar and the Eagle Scout from Perry, Georgia, Sam Nunn.

"When the Russians came to Sam Nunn and me eight years ago, these were officers that we had met in various other ways," said Lugar. "They knew us, trusted us, and they said, 'You know, this is very dangerous. Russia is breaking up, and these weapons are not going to be well guarded. In some cases, you can take a tactical nuclear weapon on a flatbed truck off to Iraq or Iran.'

"It was the urgency of that situation that got us going," he explained. "We needed to use the United States to try to bring some discipline to the Russian cleanup. In other words, to get all this stuff bottled up so it did not get elsewhere."

These two senators worked diligently to develop the Nunn-Lugar program, a set of Department of Defense initiatives that assist the former Soviet bloc as they work to secure and destroy their arsenals of mass destruction: their nuclear weapons, biological stockpiles, and chemical agents. These relatively unsung programs have helped ensure that, despite a frightening number of attempts, terrorists and rogue states will never lay their hands on the world's deadliest weapons.

But the heavy-handed diplomacy often typical of international politics has not underwritten the success of these programs over the past decade; personal relationships have. Looking back on dealings with his foreign counterparts, Lugar explained, "Again and again, the layers were taken off because they do trust us. They have a sense that the ups and downs of Soviet-American and Russian-American relations have come and gone, but we have been there steadily working with them to clean up a horrible mess of nuclear, biological, and chemical weapons. So the trust is an important aspect of this relationship."

Sometimes, however, the Russians are not Lugar's toughest sell. He also has to win the trust of his fellow senators and—often even more challenging—that of the public. One of his chief difficulties has been convincing people to pay attention to issues as dry-sounding as "nonproliferation" that involve far-removed places whose names most can't even pronounce.

"Lugar and I worked on senators and congressman one-by-one," recalled Sam Nunn. "Eventually, we were able to convince them how important this legislation was to everyone, not just the Russians and their old satellites."

Trying to convey the importance of his work to me, Senator Lugar uncorked an anecdote that placed him inside a missile installation hidden beneath the rolling hills of the Ukraine. There, he said, former Red Army officers walked his American delegation through an entire ballistic-missile launch sequence, stopping just short of turning the keys that would have sent the silo's missile and its ten nuclear warheads arching toward its target in the United States.

But even if they had turned the keys, no thunderous liftoff would have ensued; that silo no longer had a missile standing ready. All that remained in the empty, thirteen-story launch tube were loose hoses and twisted wiring. The missile and its warheads had been dismantled thanks to the Nunn-Lugar program.

Even though the missile was gone, Lugar still found bone-chilling reminders of the precarious situation that existed throughout the Cold War lingering in the small command room. He remembered: "They had *pictures* of American cities, the targets of this. And so they knew what they were going to hit. And we may not have been the wiser, but literally we were under the gun during this whole period of time." Like a pitcher in a windup, he paused for effect. "Any one of those ninety missiles in that field could have destroyed Indianapolis, Indiana, or Atlanta, Georgia. Totally taken them out. Gone."

He quickly leapt to another fact: Nunn-Lugar concerns much more than just nuclear weapons. He recalled that after touring the Ukrainian missile site, his delegation headed into the remote forests outside Moscow to a place that never existed on any maps. He visited Obolensk, Russia's secret biological weapons institute and the world's "leading" anthrax center. In the labs there, the Soviets had produced terrifying quantities of deadly agents. These agents were not always stored in high-tech facilities but often in dated refrigerators, many times in unlabeled, uncatalogued, and unlocked cardboard boxes, almost inviting an accident or theft.

"Due to the trust between our teams, we had been admitted to biological facilities where the Russians were making all sorts of agents, which they don't admit that they've been doing at all officially," began Lugar. "We were taken to a biological laboratory where it was obvious to me they'd been producing anthrax for many years. I asked one of the scientists there, in a moment of candor, 'How many strains did you produce?'

"He said, 'Six. But now we want to produce antidotes, and we want to have ties with American pharmaceutical and chemical firms to do this.'" Through Nunn-Lugar programs, that scientist now has access to the Western partnerships he needs to make a living by using his skills for peaceful ends, not destructive ones.

Unfortunately someone did manage to find strains of anthrax, and shortly after September 11, 2001, anthrax-tainted letters shut down the U.S. Senate. Lugar and his staff suddenly found themselves huddled together in borrowed conference rooms, afraid to open their mail, as the government quarantined the entire Hart Office Building because of tiny amounts of the same toxins Lugar saw stockpiled in Russia. In the events of September 11 itself, Lugar glimpsed his worst fears: What if those terrorists hijacked nuclear weapons instead of airplanes?

After the attacks, Lugar stormed the speaking circuit to send out the warning: "The ability of a terrorist cell to get their hands on these types of weapons could create enormous devastation that could dwarf all that occurred at the World Trade Center. The bottom line of the war on terror has to be to separate the terrorist groups from any possibility of having weapons of mass destruction, given, obviously, their intent and ability to use these weapons with devastating results."

Suddenly, a buzzer sounded outside the office and I expected someone to sweep in and end our meeting. Well over an hour had passed, and I worried that the chief of staff was growing anxious to shuttle the senator along to his next engagement. And honestly, I thought that would have been fine; I had the answers for which I'd been looking: His integrity and broad sense of citizenship had brought him success in the international realm. But in Lugar's case, there was much more to being an Eagle Scout than that.

Luckily, the office door remained closed, but the interruption gave him a chance to glance at his watch and casually ask, "Do you have lunch plans?"

En route to lunch, we walked down the hallway outside his office, a corridor covered from floor to ceiling with thirty years of political memorabilia. I slowed my pace to look at pictures showing him with various queens, presidents, and foreign dignitaries. But he tugged me along and took me straight to the charts that showed the thousands of missiles, chemical and biological arsenals, and nuclear warheads that his projects have helped destroy. He also quoted one of his favorite facts: "These programs have dismantled more nuclear weaponry than China, Great Britain, and France combined possess today." And each weapon Nunn-Lugar initiatives destroy makes one less that terrorists or fanatical dictators can ever turn against the United States or any other nation.

A short time later, we entered the elegant senate dining room in the U.S. Capitol. Interestingly, the room's overly formal appearance would stand in stark contrast to the conversation we would soon have over our club sandwiches. In this staid room, I began to discover precisely why Lugar makes such a good public servant.

Our conversation in his office had been largely about him: his thoughts, his experiences in Scouting, and his accomplishments in weapons control. But as an affable steward seated us at a secluded corner table, Lugar started asking the questions. At first, I thought it might be obligatory. Before long, however, I realized he'd taken a genuine interest in me.

I watched him unwind as he escaped his own business and genuinely immersed himself in my world, a world we both share but one I sensed he rarely had the opportunity to visit. We discussed hikes gone awry and camping trips spent in rain-soaked tents. We talked about our Scoutmasters and reminisced about the pecan groves on our family farms. He helped me talk through ideas about my future. Then we talked of our time in student government, where Lugar honed his diplomatic skills working with his copresident at Dickinson, Charlene Smeltzer. Even in college, Lugar was a born diplomat and could win the trust of his toughest adversaries: He convinced Charlene to marry him.

The conversation continued, with the senator plainly enjoying his new role as interviewer. By the time the waiter arrived to offer dessert, I felt as if I were seated across the table from my grandfather, not one of the most influential people on Capitol Hill. Once we finished the Georgia pecan ice cream Lugar had insisted on ordering to honor my home state, we left the dining room and shortly after emerged onto the sunlit East Plaza of the Capitol. We ambled back toward his office beneath the ancient trees shielding Congress from the Supreme Court and soon returned to the corridor of mementoes in his office.

Lugar remains proud of his accomplishments, but he gets an equal sense of happiness from the way he has lived his life. As we stood in his office preparing to part ways, he fielded one last question about success in politics. How could an Eagle Scout wrangle with the predatory vultures of national and international politics without tarnishing his badge?

With a mix of contentment and gratitude, he said, "I think all of us have enormous temptations. If you have sizable ambitions, not just personal ones, but for your state, for your country, for the people you're advocating, there are always courses of action that are going to be presented that are somewhat less than the Eagle Scout ethic. And yet, my own feeling has been one of being grateful that I could be the person I wanted to be and at the same time have these opportunities.

Then he warmly encouraged me to pursue the journey I'd begun and couldn't resist adding his perspective. "This trip is really about trying to catch the essence of why the Eagle Scout ideal is important," he observed. "Not only to individual people but to Americans in general for all the life changes this makes in our nation. That there are a number of these people who have made a tremendous difference."

I thanked him again for his time. "Not at all. Scouting is a subject I certainly enjoy talking about, he responded, adding with his grin, as you can probably tell."

Walking back toward Union Station under the still-brilliant fall sky, I began to realize how Senator Lugar answered the question posed by the *Indi-*

anapolis Star's 1968 cartoon. He answered it the way an Eagle should: He lived by his vision of citizenship, earned the trust of his adversaries, and succeeded in a world that too often views the good guy as an underdog.

Beyond that, I recognized Lugar's most defining quality: his genuine interest in others, be they young writers or Indiana farmers. His efforts to bottle up weapons of mass destruction never won him many votes; those issues were never of the flashpoint variety. He spent his time on them not because he wanted votes or recognition but because they mattered to folks at home, whether they knew it or not. He genuinely cares about each of them, and *that* is why he may be an uncommon politician yet a typical Eagle Scout.

In the ensuing months, I met scores of uncommon politicians. Many were Richard Lugar's colleagues. A background in Scouting led a number of Eagle Scouts to the Senate of the 109th U.S. Congress: Lamar Alexander of Tennessee, Jeff Bingaman of New Mexico, Thad Cochran of Mississippi, Mike Crapo of Idaho, Mike Enzi of Wyoming, Ben Nelson of Nebraska, Jeff Sessions of Alabama, and Gordon Smith of Oregon. Among the U.S. population, roughly 1 person in 300 is an Eagle Scout: 0.4 percent. In the U.S. Senate, 9 of 100 are Eagle Scouts: 10 percent of the male membership. That statistic speaks volumes.

‸

SEPTEMBER 11, 2001

Eight months after September 11, 2001, Zayed Yasin's words rolled over the quiet crowd seated beneath the stately trees of Harvard Yard: "I am one of you, but I am also one of 'them.'"

The clean-cut, dark-haired 2002 commencement speaker began explaining his dilemma to the audience of thirty thousand graduating students, friends, and family members. "When I am told that this is a world at war, a war between the great civilizations and religions of the earth, I don't know whether to laugh or cry," he continued earnestly. "'What about me?' I ask. As a practicing Muslim and a registered voter in the Commonwealth of Massachusetts, am I, through the combination of my faith and my citizenship, an inherent contradiction?" For the next five minutes, the graduating senior argued that he was not.

Three years later, Zayed had returned to Cambridge as a student at Harvard Medical School, where I found him, not surprisingly, studying. I convinced him to step away from his neuroanatomy notes, and we walked through fresh February snow to a local Thai restaurant. There I watched this second-year medical student momentarily forget about the mountains of work that consumed his days as he patiently fielded my battery of questions.

I had been particularly interested in talking with Zayed because honestly and regrettably I had little understanding of Islam. Likewise, I had little comprehension of how it must feel to be a Muslim in today's climate, where the events of September 11 and news reports from the Middle East often paint negative portraits of his religion. Over dinner, this Eagle Scout began to help me understand what it was like to be one of "them," as he said in his speech.

He started from our common ground: Scouting. "The sense of honor, the sense of duty to your god and to your country and to your self that's in the Scout Law fits in very well with what I believe as a practicing Muslim," he observed. "Those beliefs—those identities—are not in opposition."

"The Scout Oath and the Scout Law treat religion in a very ecumenical manner," Zayed observed of Scouting's incorporation of faith. "Any of the values that are mentioned formally in Scouting are, at least from my point of view, very universal, and there was never any specific doctrinal focus to it. That belief, that focus on God and religion, in whatever form it may take in your life, was something I felt very positive about."

Zayed Yasin addresses those gathered for Harvard's 2002 graduation ceremony.
STEPHANIE MITCHELL/HARVARD UNIVERSITY NEWS OFFICE

In the coastal town of Scituate, Massachusetts, Zayed Yasin grew up with young men from Irish and Italian families who were devout Catholics. His was the town's only Muslim family. Despite their different faiths and practices, however, these young men all shared the ideals of Scouting, comfortably took the same Oath, and abided by the same Law. They all agreed to fulfill their duty to God and country and recited together the last point of the Scout Law: A Scout is Reverent. "A Scout is Reverent toward God," the Scout *Handbook* elaborates. "He is faithful in his religious duties. He respects the beliefs of others." The Yasin family felt comfortable in this climate, and Zayed's younger brothers, Tariq and Khalid, also reached Eagle in Scituate's Troop 7. Only a service project remains for Rashid, the youngest.

Having learned first-aid skills in Scouting, Zayed became an emergency response team leader for the American Red Cross when he came to Harvard. His teams responded to fires and other accidents that occurred in the Boston area. In part, he served with the Red Cross to help others; he also served to help others understand his faith.

He pushed himself back from his now-empty dinner plate and observed, "Whether you like it or not, whether you accept the responsibility or not, your actions are seen as representing your faith and community. I'd like to think the way I treat people is reflective of the way I'd like my religion portrayed. When you're burned out of your house, and someone helps get you a place to stay, food to eat, makes sure you're safe, makes sure you have the medications you need, and that person is named Zayed Yasin—I'd like to think that makes an impact."

Returning us to the present, he added, "I'm hoping that being a physician, once I eventually get there, that if someone named Zayed Muhammad Yasin takes care of you when you're sick, there's a connection there."

The same connection between service and understanding lies at the heart of Scouting. From the very beginning, Lord Baden-Powell ranked it among his chief aims. As he stood before Scouts of all nations and religions at the 1937 World Jamboree, the aging hero held aloft a Jacob's staff, a long staff crossed near the top by several wooden arms. "This was the instrument by which the navigators in old days found their way across the seas," explained Scouting's patriarch. "Let it also for us today be an instrument of guidance in our life. It is the cross which for all who are Christians points the way, but it is also a cross with many arms; these are held out to embrace all creeds."

All creeds have in turn embraced Scouting. Today, the largely Muslim nation of Indonesia boasts the largest number of registered Scouts in the world: 8.9 million. The Boy Scouts of America registers more than 3 million Scouts of all religions. More than 2 million primarily Hindu youth belong to Scouting in India. Pakistan has 500,000 Scouts, Thailand 1.3 million, and the Philippines 2 million. Hundreds of thousands of Scouts are active in countries as ethnically and religiously different as South Korea and Jordan, Kenya and Brazil. In total, 153 countries host Scouting programs that serve 25 million young men and women of every conceivable creed. Reverence, not religion, defines the Scouting movement.

On September 11, 2001, a group with extreme religious views placed an unwelcome burden on Zayed Yasin and many other Muslims as it attempted to drive fissures through not just buildings but American society itself. Terrorists hijacked four airliners: American Airlines flights 11 and 77, and United flights 175 and 93. Flights 11 and 175 crashed into the World Trade Center towers in Manhattan around nine a.m. and set in motion events that killed 2,749 people, including 343 firefighters, 23 NYPD officers, and 37 Port Authority police officers. Aboard Flight 93, which crashed in Pennsylvania, 40 people died. Another 184 perished when Flight 77 crashed into the Pentagon.

People of all faiths and creeds responded to the tragedies. On that September day, thousands of women and men demonstrated traits unbounded by religion: bravery, duty, and selflessness. They rushed to a still-dangerous Ground Zero as paramedics, doctors, and rescuers. They all thought little of their own safety and reacted almost on instinct. Among the first to respond was Scott Strauss.

SCOTT STRAUSS

TROOP 45, MINEOLA, NEW YORK

EAGLE SCOUT, 1981

The nighttime shift of September 10–11, 2001, had been an uneventful one, and at eight a.m., Tuesday the eleventh, Officer Scott Strauss put New York City behind him as he traveled home to his wife, Pat, and sons, Brian and Christopher, who were waiting for him on Long Island. Far from being a typical policeman, Scott served on the elite Emergency Services Unit of the New York Police Department. "In the Emergency Services Unit," he explained, "there is a saying; 'If a civilian needs help, they'll call the police. If the police need help, they call Emergency Services." The ESU handles hostage or terrorist situations, bomb jobs, building collapses, or any other dire circumstance. "You are the answer," he continued. "There is nobody to call. If you get there and you can't do the job, nobody is going to do it. You *have* to do it because there is nobody else. You are the last resort."

That morning Scott was riding the Long Island Railroad eastward toward his home in Mineola. He had been on duty since Monday morning and was reading the newspaper to stay awake. "I am reading the paper, finish reading Monday's paper, and I put my Walkman on and I am sitting on the train—the same train you took coming out here," he said referencing the train I had ridden to meet him on Long Island that evening. "I hear them talking about a plane that crashed into the Trade Center. I'm thinking it's a small plane. At first I thought it was a joke, and then you could tell that they were serious."

After arriving home, he and his wife Pat were watching the scene unfold on CNN when a second plane slammed into the south tower of the Trade Center. Scott stood up, and Pat asked, "Where are you going?"

"I'm going back to work," said her husband. Scott also served as a volunteer firefighter, and he jumped into the fire chief's truck with Pat crying and begging him to be careful. Then he raced back to the city. "I remember driving," he said, "but I couldn't tell you anything about the trip back into Manhattan. I am flying, and I have the chief's car, lights and sirens. I am just flying. All I can remember is staring at those towers burning."

When he reached his unit's headquarters, other off-duty officers were arriving and, together, they changed into their fatigues and began collecting vehicles, weapons, and rescue gear. Nobody knew what to expect. "So we are gearing up tactically and rescue wise," Scott explained, "and we go racing down there. We pull up just as the second tower is collapsing, and it is absolutely, absolutely incredible. The pictures that you saw on TV do *not* do that place justice. The devastation that the firemen, the cops, the rescue workers, and certainly the civilians had to deal with was incredible, absolutely incredible. The dust, the smoke—you couldn't see, you couldn't drive. We get down as close as we can, just a few blocks away, and we are getting out, and the second tower comes down. It was an incredible noise."

The officers assembled at the park surrounding City Hall, organized themselves, and ventured south down Vessey Street past Trinity Church. They walked into a war zone, carrying all the equipment they could. Cars and buildings were burning, people were scrambling away from the Trade Center, and the whole area was choked with smoke. They turned one corner and found ESU Truck No. 9 in flames. It seemed unreal.

"The dust is still blowing," he said, describing what they faced. "It was like snow, like a blizzard. You can't see anything; you are coughing and gagging. You are trying to work your way through everything, and then during the course of the day it is starting to settle. Not all of us had radios, so not all of us are up on what is going on . . . and we are hearing fighter jets coming over us. You can't see them because the buildings are so tall, and you look up and, even without the Trade Center, you can only see a small section of the sky. You hear fighter jets screaming back and forth, and you're like, 'I hope they're ours, and if they are, what else is going on here?' Are we expecting to see some foreign army come across Battery Park now and just overtake the city? It was absolutely incredible. You didn't know what to think.

"So we left that to the tactics guys, and we went searching for people. We couldn't find anybody. Just dead people . . . All day long we are searching and climbing down, getting here and trying to get in there, thinking and hoping that you are going to find a pocket of people somewhere and just be like, 'Come on out,' and pull out ten to twenty people at a time. None of that."

Search efforts lasted throughout the day. At dusk there was total devastation: Buildings were burning, buildings had collapsed, and mountains of rubble were on fire. After Building Seven collapsed, Scott's supervisor said, "Guys, pull back. Let's do a roll call to make sure we didn't lose anybody else." The ESU officers had already lost many of their fellow officers that day and did not want to lose more. After they assembled, one of Scott's sergeants suggested they check the buildings on the south side of Liberty Street for survivors. They set off and began climbing over twisted I beams and remnants of the building: "Pulverized desks and chairs, computers, rubble, chunks of cement, steel girders and I beams, rebar wires, you are just climbing over everything," Scott remembered. Then they heard news they'd been hoping for all day: Two officers were still alive in the rubble. Scott and his partner quickened their pace but soon found an NYFD officer blocking their path. "You can't come past here," he said. "This is a collapse zone."

"We kind of blew him off and just kept going," Scott said. Minutes later, Scott found a surviving Port Authority officer trapped deep in the quagmire. He realized the only way to reach him was to crawl under and around the officer through a tiny opening in an enormous pile of debris he described as a "mountain of pickup sticks."

To fit into the maze below him, which was burning and collapsing, he had to crawl through a tight hole. He took off his harness, his air pack, and lastly, his gun belt so he could fit. He knew he wouldn't need his gun but explained, "For a cop to give up his gun? A cop *never* gives up his gun. It is your last resort. When everything goes really bad and you are about to die, that is your last hope, and I was about to die and I just gave it up. Not that it could have helped me, but it was just 'I am completely naked now.' I give up my gun and climb down in this hole, and before I went down there I told my wife I loved her and told my kids, to myself, I said, 'Be good. I hope you do well in school,' because I didn't think I was coming out." Never did it occur to Scott Strauss *not* to go in. He knew he was the trapped officer's last resort and last hope. He had a duty, and he would do his best to carry it out.

Twenty feet below the surface of the rubble, Scott, Chuck Cerica, and Patrick McGee squeezed themselves through the dark maze, putting their hands through tiny openings and pulling themselves through crevices. All the while, a fire raged to their right and pieces of Building Five were toppling onto the rubble heap. They finally reached the trapped officer, Will Jimeno. "He was completely encased in debris," Scott remembered. "Not rocks and stuff, but pulverized concrete. He was just encased in it. All you could see was his head and his arm and part of his right leg." Scott and Chuck began scraping debris from around Will's body and passing it to "Paddy." At this point, Scott and Chuck were lying down face-to-face with barely enough room to pass the dirt through to the more open space behind them. At the same time, the fire was coming closer, choking them and stinging their eyes with smoke, and Building Five was growing increasingly unstable.

"The firemen are screaming, 'Get out! Get out! The building is coming down, get out . . . We can't control this fire anymore!' Will is like, 'Get out of here.' And I said, 'I am *not* leaving you.' How do you leave him? 'Oh, see ya later, you're on your own?' He can't do it; you gotta stay there. So I said, 'Will, I am *not* leaving you, we *will* get you out.' " Scott was an Eagle Scout and an Emergency Services officer; this was exactly what he was trained and prepared to do. He couldn't walk away.

They slowly dug away at the rubble encasing Will, making slow but important progress. They unearthed Will's oxygen tank and cut it off his back, dropping Will just enough for Scott to have a chance to free him. They slipped a harness around him and pulled, but his leg was trapped by a concrete slab and a metal bar. "Cut his leg off," called someone from the crowd above that had gathered over the unfolding drama below. "To get him out you are going to have to cut his leg off."

Scott was not about to do that. "Are you out of your mind?" he asked. "What am I going to do? Start hacking this guy's leg off? So Will is like, 'Cut my leg off! Cut my leg off! Get me out of here.' I said, 'Will, I'm *not* cutting your leg off. I *will* get you out of here in one piece.' "

They continued working on the trapped officer, using a chisel and later air bags in an attempt to free Will's leg. Neither worked. Time was growing short, according to the shouts from above. The conditions below were worsening. The spreading fire had now cut off the route Scott, Paddy, and Chuck had taken to reach Will. They would have to find a new way out, but that was a worry for the future. Fatigue was also beginning to set in. "This is probably seven or eight o'clock on Tuesday night, and I have been up since Monday morning and I am shot," remembered Scott. "We can't breathe; we can't see. Every time you took a deep breath you feel like there are glass shards in your lungs. It was painful to breathe. It was painful to blink because all the stuff is in your eyes, and the choking smoke was incredible from this fire."

Time was running low and debris still ensnared Will. Finally, Scott used the jaws of life, which had been passed to them from above. It was a last resort since using the device to pry the concrete off Will's leg could bring the pile of unstable rubble crashing down on top of them.

Mayor Michael Bloomberg about to present the NYPD Medal of Honor to Scott Strauss (middle officer) for his service on September 11, 2001 KRISTEN ARTZ/MAYOR'S OFFICE

"I said, 'Will, we are going to go with it.' I am operating the tool and stuff is starting to come down on it, and, again, I told my wife and my kids 'I love you' and all of that. I honestly thought I was going to die there. I thought I was going to be buried alive with this guy, and we would never get out. So I am spreading the jaws and the tool is working, but there is stuff falling down on us. The tool goes all the way open, and it is enough to pull his leg out. Nothing comes down on us and I yell, 'Yes!' I slide back out and say, 'Paddy, I think I have him, I think I have him.'" But a piece of rebar still had his foot trapped.

Scott crawled on top of Will—a tight squeeze—and cut his foot free. "Boom! He is coming out now," Scott said, still seeming to feel genuine relief as he recalled the moment years later. Scott, Paddy, Chuck, and Will all went home that night to unspeakably grateful families.

"Will's wife was pregnant at the time, and she had the baby on Will's birthday, the Monday after Thanksgiving," Scott said as he neared the story's end. "We went to the christening, and I talk to Will a couple times a month . . . He'll say, 'Scott, I am just sitting here with Bianca on my chest, and if it wasn't for you I wouldn't be here. Thank you so much.' He is just a real nice guy." It was a terrible day, but at least one good thing came out of it, Scott observed: Bianca would know her father.

"No doubt being a Boy Scout, an Eagle Scout, had its mark on me that day," he reflected when he finished his story. "I mean, do your best; do whatever you possibly can to help someone. Help other people at all times even if it is going to cost you your life. That is what you do."

For his courage on September 11, 2001, Scott Strauss received the NYPD's highest decoration, the Medal of Honor. "They usually give it to widows," a police veteran told Scott; he had been lucky. At a January ceremony attended by dignitaries, family, and fellow officers, Scott stood before another Eagle Scout who reached up and placed the green ribbon around his sizable neck. Scott was deeply honored to receive the medal from Mayor Bloomberg, and he was *particularly* thankful that he was there to receive the honor in person.

Three years after the disaster of 9-11, the same red Ford Expedition that carried Scott Strauss to the chaos of Ground Zero met me at the Mineola, New York, train station. The father of two had just come from an elementary school holiday concert put on by his sons and their classmates, but the boys were now asleep and he had reserved the remainder of the night for me. "I almost didn't call you back," he said in an unmistakable Long Island accent as I climbed into the chief's truck. "I've been so busy this week and have gotten tired of talking with reporters, but you were an Eagle Scout, so I couldn't say no. I told my wife I had to come talk with you." He grinned.

Scott, who had retired from the NYPD in the spring of 2004 but was now chief of the Mineola Fire Department, drove me through the streets of his hometown to the fire station, where a number of volunteers—mostly guys no older than twenty-five—were enjoying a late evening together. They offered their chief and me some of the chicken wings that had just arrived from a local restaurant. We accepted the offer and then retired to another section of the firehouse to talk. "A lot of those guys were junior firefighters, at least at one time," he told me as we walked through the hallway. "This is part of the Explorer post of the Boy Scouts." Scott had been a junior firefighter in this very Explorer post and had become the first junior firefighter to become chief of the department.

Scott's passion for Scouting surfaced quickly when our conversation began in earnest in a room just off the garage that housed the department's shining engines. All Eagles consider Scouting to be a valuable experience, but the depth of their love for the program and appreciation for its lessons varies from Scout to Scout. Some Eagles enjoyed Scouting and felt that the experience helped them in some important but indefinable way in their later years. Others had fun in the program, earned their Eagle, but never took it too seriously; it was just a part of growing up. Then there are those like Scott Strauss. By the night's end, I had watched this SWAT team veteran who was every bit the tough, muscular Long Islander grow emotional as he talked about Scouting. At one point, his intense eyes even grew misty. He loved Scouting as a boy, and as he grew up, he learned to appreciate the values it instilled in him. Today he still remains active in Scouting as a leader of Troop 45, where his sons are both members.

In 1981, Scott became the fiftieth Eagle Scout in Troop 45, chartered at the First Presbyterian Church in 1929. Just two decades after Scott was awarded the badge, Troop 45 was about to award its one hundredth Eagle. The Scouts of Troop 45 had also just celebrated their eighty-fifth anniversary, with former Scouts coming from as far away as Texas for a reunion. Clearly, others shared Scott's attachment to the old Mineola troop.

Scott followed his older brother into Cub Scouts and then into Troop 45, but his brother dropped out before earning his Eagle. When his brother left, Scott's father, who had been a longtime fixture on the Troop Committee, sat them both down and said, "You want to stay; that's great. If you want to quit, that's fine too. I'm not going to force you to do anything you don't want to do, but *I* am staying."

"So I stayed too, and I made Eagle. Like every other Eagle Scout, I had to be pushed. If it wasn't for Frank Pewarski, the Scoutmaster at the time, I probably wouldn't have made Eagle. He kept after me." Scott made sure to give his parents credit for encouraging him as well, but he acknowledged his mentality at the time, adding, "Being a kid sixteen or seventeen years old, you were like, 'Yeah Dad, see ya later.' Hearing it from somebody outside the family, that's what actually pushed me over the edge to get it. I mean, naturally, my father is my idol, but Frank is another great man. Absolutely great man."

The leadership of this great man brought together a diverse group of boys and made them a troop. Within Troop 45, friendships formed between boys who would have likely never known each other—or at least never become friends—were it not for Scouting.

"When I was in Boy Scouts it wasn't cool to be in Boy Scouts," Scott continued, acknowledging an image many people recognize, rightly or wrongly. "But you know what? I had my friends in Scouting and my friends outside of Scouting. And you know what? Sometimes they mixed and sometimes they didn't, but I did what I wanted to do. So I know that aside from doing the requirements to be an Eagle Scout, it wasn't the coolest thing to do. You had to go against peer pressure a lot of times, so that is important also. You are a leader; you are not a follower."

Then he laughed and added, "I'm a trained sniper for crying out loud! I kick in doors with machine guns. You know, that is the nonnerdiest thing. You think of a Boy Scout, a little kid with glasses—that is the image that is portrayed. Not somebody who does what I do for a living."

Perhaps ironically, Scott came to be a trained sniper directly because of his experience in Troop 45. It was his Scoutmaster, Frank Pewarski, who saw that this skilled young man might be adept at rappelling down buildings and rescuing hostages. Mr. Pewarski was an officer with the NYPD's Emergency Services Unit, and when Scott had been with the department for three years, Mr. Pewarski asked him if he wanted to join the ESU. Scott said, "Absolutely." He explained, "ESU is the cream of the crop. There are 40,000 police officers and there are only 350 Emergency Service cops, and it is very, very hard to get in." His former Scoutmaster couldn't secure him a job directly but did get him an interview.

"So here I am, nineteen eighty-seven," he began. "I'm a kid. I'm twenty-four years old, and I am sitting at this table in front of these three lieutenants, and I have my little suit on. I am nervous as I could be, and I've got these three grizzly lieutenants, these guys are battle-scarred veterans of the police department. Like I said, they are in the SWAT and rescue team. This one lieutenant, I could never answer a question right for him. He was riding me; it was incredible. And I am sitting here saying to myself, 'I'm finished. I am not getting into this unit.' If he asked, 'What color is the sky,' and I said, 'Blue,' he would say, 'You're wrong' and give me an attitude.

"So towards the end of the interview the lead lieutenant says, 'Does anybody else want to ask him any other questions?' The guy who is giving me the problem says, 'Yeah, I've got something for him.' Real sarcastic. He pulls out the résumé that I sent in. He says, 'I see on this résumé here that you wrote down at the bottom that you are an Eagle Scout. Do you think that means anything to any of us up here?'

"I'm sitting there; now I'm *boiling*. I am not getting in this unit anyway because I can't answer this guy's questions right, so I might as well just tell him exactly how I feel. I said, 'Yeah, it means something to me. I don't care if it means anything to you. I worked hard for that. It wasn't a homework assignment that the teacher gave me to do, and I had to do it. It was something that I *wanted* to do, and it took a lot of work and I am proud of it and that is why I put it on there.'

"So he sits back and says, 'Oh yeah? I'm an Eagle Scout too.' He was just breaking my shoes the entire interview to see if I would crack and break. Then he pulled this up just to see what I would say. That alone, he told me later, pushed me over the top and got me in the unit."

Part of Scott's job as an active ESU officer entailed tying knots and rappelling, skills he learned and came to love as a Scout. "That put me head and shoulders above the average emergency cop because I loved it and I enjoyed it. I was taught how to tie the bowline, square knot, the clove hitch, all in Boy Scouts. Don Franche, who is an Eagle Scout taught me how to rappel. My first time rappelling was at summer camp. We built a twenty-foot tower out of trees and branches and he taught me how to rappel. From that day forward I loved every second of it. I was rappelling out of helicopters, rappelling off of buildings and bridges, and he made me love it. He taught me how to enjoy it and how to do it properly, and I used that throughout my entire career.

"It's not only fun. You're learning things that you are going to take with you the rest of your life. You learn from Boy Scouts. You gain camaraderie and learn how to deal with a team and how to live as a team, work as a team, and survive as a team. And you also learn independence and how to have confidence in yourself, all through Boy Scouts. If you have a good program and you get involved in the troop and you have leaders who are willing to teach you what they know and guide you, there is no stopping you. There really isn't."

It was nearly one a.m. when Scott cranked up the Expedition and drove me back to the train station. He idled the truck beside the platform so I wouldn't have to brave the December cold that had settled on New York. As we waited for the westbound train, the conversation turned to his two sons. He cares deeply about them and believes that Scouting will be as valuable to them as it

Scott Strauss with sons Brian and Christopher
COURTESY OF THE STRAUSS FAMILY

was to him. "I try to instill those Boy Scout beliefs and the morals and the standards into my kids. Even if they don't want to be in Boy Scouts, that's okay. I'm going to try to keep them in it, but I'm not going to get into fights with them about it. I have those values because my parents instilled them in me, and certainly Frank Pewarski helped too. I try to instill them into my kids. It is very important. They are perfect values."

Then he continued, "If it wasn't for Frank and my parents, I wouldn't have been in the Emergency Service and I wouldn't have saved Will's life. You do your best, do your absolute best. If you fail, you can look yourself in the mirror and say, 'I did my best.'"

Turning to Scouting's other values, he said, "I stress this, especially to my kids: All you have is your word and your honor, and nobody can take that from you but you. So you have got to live by that, and if you say you are going to do something you have to do it . . . You make a promise, you got to make sure you keep it. Always do your best; nobody is going to fault you if you do your best and you fail. You fail when you don't try your hardest and it's obvious. I preach that to my kids. They have to do their best every time." Then, harking back to his trial at Ground Zero, he concluded, "You might need to do your best, and you have to be used to giving it your all." Apparently, Brian and Christopher had been a receptive congregation to his preaching that year, and Scott happily told me about the presents they would open the next week on Christmas morning. He just hoped our late-night conversation didn't damage his prospects for a good gift from his wife, Pat.

"This is your train," he said as he watched the headlamps on the approaching westbound train begin to light the platform. "You're okay once you get to Manhattan?"

I assured him I was. I climbed out of the truck, and as I started to close the door, he smiled warmly and said with that Long Island accent, "Hey, Alvin, Merry Christmas."

As I sat down on the Long Island Railway, I watched the Expedition's taillights hurrying toward Scott's wife and sleeping boys and thought about how fortunate his family would be to wake up together on Christmas morning. On September 11, he had come perilously close to never sharing another Christmas with Pat, Brian, and Christopher.

I eased back in my seat and watched suburb after suburb speed by in the night, then considered the risk Scott Strauss took that autumn day in 2001. I thought about the risks firefighters and police officers around the nation take every day as they do their job of protecting others, strangers they rarely knew before and will likely never see again. Their risk is one I've never had to take. It's a risk that most Americans don't have to take. We have that luxury because of the thousands of men and women who so unselfishly *do* take that chance.

———

When my flight left New York the next day, I looked down on the hole in lower Manhattan where the World Trade Center once stood. The wreckage through which Scott Strauss crawled to rescue his fellow officers had been removed, but the vacancy left behind served as a reminder of what happened there on September 11, 2001. In some ways, the attacks were ironic. Islamic terrorists invoked the name of God as they attacked the World Trade Center and the Pentagon. Americans of Islamic and myriad other faiths then prayed to the very same God as the tragedy unfolded. Those who focused on what divides us wrought the destruction and sadness of September 11 and its aftermath.

When I began traveling, I knew little about many American religions, and I didn't necessarily understand what principles unite them. Then as I met Buddhists, Muslims, Jews, Mormons, Baptists, Catholics, and others, I saw the unique passions as well as the common threads that exist in all faiths. Among those in the Scouting community, I found a refreshing sense of understanding. I found people who held firmly to their own beliefs yet respected the practices of others. They all followed the last point of the Scout Law: A Scout is Reverent.

Thousands of times each year, Scouts gather together in dining halls, before flagpoles, and around campfire rings for services. There they focus quietly on their shared beliefs. They remember that they share the same values, regardless of their particular religions. In that, I found hope for the future not only of America but of the world. As boys of faith become men of faith, I hope their grounding in common ideals will help create understanding where too little exists today.

HURRICANE KATRINA

Early on the morning of August 29, 2005, the house where Charlie Chapman lived with his mother lost power. That much, Charlie expected; he doubted power lines in his Ocean Springs, Mississippi, neighborhood could withstand a battering from the 150-mile-per-hour winds swirling around the eye of Hurricane Katrina. He did not, however, expect what happened next. Water from the nearby bayou found its way into his home at eight o'clock. By nine that morning, the water had climbed five feet up the family's walls, over the head of seventy-five-year-old Mrs. Chapman. At that point, gathering floodwaters forced open the front door and miraculously delivered a life jacket into the living room. Six-foot-three Charlie slipped the orange vest around his mother as the open door added howling winds to the chaos inside the house. Soon, the rising waters covered the doors and windows, trapping the Chapmans inside, although inside or outside they had no escape; the churning water from the bayou had turned the surrounding neighborhood into a lake.

Air began to run short inside the house as the rising storm surge pushed mother and son steadily toward the ceiling. Fortunately, Charlie found a flashlight and knocked a hole in the drywall above him. The debris-filled water floated the pair through the hole and into the attic, where they could again breathe freely. The surge mercifully crested at their ceiling—nearly thirty feet above sea level—then left them suspended by rafters for the next six hours. Ten hours after Katrina's waters first entered their home, the Chapmans walked outside to see the devastation left by one of history's most powerful storms. The storm had laid their neighborhood to waste, but the

Chapmans realized that in many ways they were more fortunate than others. The storm claimed more than 1,200 lives.

Nearly two months after the disaster, the floodwaters had subsided, but the storm had left greater than $50 billion in estimated damages. Typically, hurricanes leave frame skeletons or roofless homes in their wake; Katrina left concrete slabs. Along streets blocks away from the Gulf of Mexico, successions of driveways led to nothing but bare foundations: no garages, no walls, no appliances, no floors. Debris of every imaginable variety— splintered tree limbs, crumpled clothes, useless appliances—blanketed the ground like autumn leaves in every direction. An equal amount of debris hung high in the otherwise naked pines, left there by the storm surge. Uprooted trees still leaned upon useless telephone wires. Katrina had left coastal Mississippi in ruins and precious little had changed.

In Charlie Chapman's inland subdivision, rows of ranch homes remained solid, brick intact. Behind the exterior of the homes, however, lay the same devastation. The relatively gentle rise of inland floodwaters had left walls and foundations undisturbed but utterly ruined the interiors. It carried clothes and belongings outside and scattered them indiscriminately across neighboring yards. What the water did not carry away, it soaked, ruining many items outright. Other items, it left to slowly festering black mold.

When our team of thirty volunteers arrived at the Chapman home, we strapped on masks with air filters, slipped on work gloves, and proceeded to dismantle everything below the high-water mark, a dark line etched inches below the ceiling. We shoveled loads of ruined clothes, books, and other possessions into wheelbarrows that ran constant relays to the growing pile of debris along the curb. Eventually, the team removed all the drywall, cabinetry, tile, and flooring from the home, adding it to the pile that the State of Mississippi hauled away by the tractor trailer load. After the team killed the mold with bleach, Charlie could begin rebuilding from the bare concrete foundation and stark wood framing that remained.

As our crew carted away all his belongings, Charlie silently watched the wheelbarrows come and go. He seemed lost and forlorn. I spoke with him about his son, Jonathan, an Eagle Scout, and I think he forgot, for a moment, the havoc surrounding him. He continued watching the wheelbarrows roll by as he talked of Jonathan's experiences, then suddenly he broke his gaze and fished a Scout patch and Pine Burr Council coffee mug from a nearby pile of debris. He handed them to me and smiled, a human connection and spot of light amidst so much darkness.

Holding the patch, I discovered that it was still wet, weeks after the hurricane hit. That should not have surprised me; it was as if nothing had changed since Katrina struck. Lives were still in disarray, neighborhoods were still devastated, and mountains of work remained.

REBUILDING THE GULF COAST

TIM MEHNE, TROOP 1, VALHALLA, NEW YORK—EAGLE SCOUT, 1972

DANNY BOST, TROOP 942, SANFORD, NORTH CAROLINA—EAGLE SCOUT, 1971

TRAVIS CLARK, TROOP 6, JUNEAU, ALASKA—EAGLE SCOUT, 2001

JON SIMS, TROOP 463, CLINTON, INDIANA—EAGLE SCOUT, 1973

I crossed into Mississippi late on an October night. With each westward mile, the trees outside my window became more twisted, the billboards more shredded. Few cars traveled with me along the highway. The southernmost counties of the state remained thoroughly trounced and largely abandoned. The long day's drive finally ended at St. Paul's United Methodist Church in Ocean Springs. Volunteers from Houston, Texas, had convinced St. Paul's to donate their facilities shortly after Hurricane Katrina hit, and by the time I arrived, more than twenty large military tents covered the field behind the church. Trailers of every sort surrounded the tents, providing supplies and services to volunteers who came from states as far away as Maine. Inside the church, hallways overflowed with supplies, food filled the kitchen, and volunteers constantly circulated around the fellowship hall, which had become the permanent dining room for the 100 to 300 volunteers who made St. Paul's their home at any given time.

I did not travel to Mississippi to write—in fact, I had hoped for a break—but among the volunteers at St. Paul's, I found something telling. Just as I found a disproportionate number of Eagle Scouts in the U.S. Senate, I discovered that at least 8 out of the 110 men and women sharing the campsite with me held Scouting's highest rank. Statistically, I should have been the lone Eagle.

———

Tim Mehne, an Eagle Scout from Troop 1 in Valhalla, New York, managed the camp's guests, of which I had become one. When I arrived, his staff assigned me to tent B-2, a sixteen-cot green army tent where I laid out my sleeping bag and prepared for the coming days. Truthfully, I didn't have to prepare much; Tim and the camp staff had taken care of every detail in their weeks of planning and preparation.

Soon after Katrina hit, a pastor at Tim's church asked him to help start a relief camp. Tim, a gourmet chef, considered the possibility of leaving his family for ten weeks, then finally decided that people on the Gulf Coast needed his help. He drove east along Interstate 10 toward three months in which no paycheck was the lone certainty. During the trip, Tim passed through the destruction of Hurricane Rita, then that of Hurricane Katrina. "It just got worse and worse," he remembered of his eastward drive. "At times, I was in tears."

Once in Ocean Springs, he and others began preparing the base. Tim's job became caring for the volunteers who filtered through the camp, week after week. "I feel like a Scoutmaster," he said. "Not that the volunteers are like Scouts, but I have a commitment to everyone who comes into this camp, and as you know, it's a real camp!"

Like a real camp, St. Paul's had a mess hall. During the week I benefited from its cooking, Danny Bost ran the entire operation. When sounds of a stirring camp woke me at six a.m. on my first morning, Danny had already been in the kitchen for an hour. He stood over the silver griddle, wearing an apron, scrambling eggs, and gently directing other volunteers. His team from North Carolina lined up at seven a.m. sharp to fill our plates with eggs, pancakes, and crisp bacon. When we volunteers left for our worksites at eight o'clock, the staff cleaned the dining hall and kitchen. Once they finished cleaning, they began cooking for lunch. Then they cleaned again. At two p.m., Danny started to prepare for dinner, and his team rarely finished mopping the floors before nine p.m. The next morning, the North Carolinians would do it again.

After returning the last mop to the supply closet one evening, Danny sat with me and explained how he came to that kitchen in Ocean Springs. "I had some talents in the kitchen," he said. "Maybe some people would debate that," he laughed, "but I could give something more than just a donation. Of course, I didn't realize what I'd be doing until four thirty in the morning as we were leaving North Carolina to come here. I suddenly found out I'd be managing the kitchen for the entire week! It was a little overwhelming, but you know, this goes back to what you learn in Scouting: help out and do what's needed. Not to stand by but to step up."

He learned this lesson from Dan Jones, who served as Scoutmaster of Troop 942, where Danny earned his Eagle in 1971. "Dan Jones led by example," Danny remembered. "He did things because they were right, not because people were looking." Due largely to his Scoutmaster's example, Danny began serving as an Assistant Scoutmaster at age eighteen when he joined the power company as a lineman, a career track he has followed to this day. Now that two decades have passed, he and Dan Jones share a particular sense of satisfaction. "It's so rewarding to see Scouts fifteen years later and see how they held onto those values you tried to teach them."

I expect Dan Jones was proud of this Eagle Scout today. "I'm here because I learned that you should help your neighbor every chance you get," Danny explained. "It goes back to Scouting and what Scoutmaster Jones taught us. Yes, we're all individuals, but we have to respect and help everyone else."

When images of the hurricane first reached North Carolina, Danny and his wife bought a trailer and parked it at a local supermarket in Sanford. They asked their neighbors to donate food and water for the victims. In their modest community, donating food and water allowed those who could not write large checks to assist. Each small donation helped fill the trailer. Danny in turn donated some of their collected supplies to another organization; the remainder the Bosts hauled to Mississippi. "After seeing this place once, I had to come back and help," he explained.

Travis Clark, an Eagle Scout from Troop 6 in Juneau, Alaska, responded to the same sense of duty. Late one night, the tall, slender junior at Pfeiffer University left his friends to their board game and sat down with me to explain what called him to Ocean Springs. Many people his age spend fall break in the mountains or on a still-warm beach, but he chose a mission trip in Mississippi. The fruits of his choice included spending chilly nights in a sleeping bag, toiling and sweating all day, then showering off layers of grime in a makeshift trailer. "I'm here because I have a duty," he said simply enough. "When something this bad happens so close to home, I have to help.

Sure, it's not luxurious here at camp, but look at what we have compared to the people we're helping out."

Particularly for Travis, the camping aspect of our experience posed little problem. His two troops in Alaska—6 in Juneau and 76 in Fairbanks—both found themselves at the edge of the continent's greatest wilderness, where just *being* outside for several days in the winter months constituted a serious challenge. He loved the challenge and developed a taste for the winter adventure so abundant in Alaska. His leaders in Fairbanks came from nearby military bases, and these servicemen made sure the Scouts had experiences that others in their community never had. They drove dogsleds, spent hours ice fishing on frozen lakes, and canoed forty miles down the Chena River in early spring. On the canoe trip, Travis and two other Scouts accidentally flipped their canoe and found themselves in near-freezing water, ice floes bobbing around them. Their life preservers kept them afloat until they reached shore, but air temperatures of only fifty degrees still threatened the wet boys. It took a campfire to safely warm them up so they could finish the trek.

"Our leaders always made sure we were safe," Travis reflected. "But that didn't mean we didn't push the limits sometimes, like the canoe trip, which was one of my scariest but also best moments in Scouting. We learned this idea that you could be free and exciting and have fun but at the same time be responsible. You can get excited about something and still have self-control. Our leaders taught us that you don't have to be wild and crazy to do wild and crazy things.

"If I look at everything those leaders taught us, they really showed us what it meant to be a man: to be passionate but remain calm. That's what the Eagle rank means. I learned or at least became aware of all the qualities of being a man as he was intended to be. To be an Eagle Scout, to me, means even if I choose not to apply those lessons, I'm at least aware of the things that I need to practice in my life to fulfill my potential and make the greatest positive impact on the world around me. Being an Eagle Scout is less about knowing how to tie a square knot and more about being able to help those around us without expecting anything in return and do it competently."

After Danny Bost and his North Carolinians served us eggs and grits for breakfast the next morning, Travis and his group boarded one bus, and I boarded another. My bus soon arrived at the home of Margaret, one of the storm's victims. Margaret's house sat next to the Chapman home, and Katrina had visited upon this grandmother the same devastation it had upon the Chapmans. The owners of both homes had little if any flood insurance; their homes were not *in* flood zones. Like thousands of other Mississippi and Louisiana residents, Margaret faced the financial challenge of rebuilding without full insurance coverage after already undergoing the hardship of losing her home. Without the help of volunteers, neither Margaret nor Charlie could afford to rebuild.

When our crew arrived at the site, we scattered throughout the house and began dismantling it from the inside out. Soon the house would be reduced to brick walls, a roof, concrete floors, and wooden framing; nothing else would remain. During our first morning of work, Jon Sims heard about my project, and over boxed lunches he shared his Scouting background. Jon received his Eagle in Clinton, Indiana, in 1973 and clearly remembered his first experience with service work. His troop confronted its most challenging project in repainting the Clinton First Christian Church. With a smile, Jon noted, "The church provided the paint, someone provided music, and the Scouts provided the labor. Each of us spent at least forty hours painting, and the stereo kept playing the song "You're So Vain." Every time I hear that song, I still think of painting that church!"

Jon returned to Clinton First Christian Church not long ago and found the congregation still sponsoring Troop 463, where he earned Eagle. A fellow Eagle from 463 now served on the church's board of trustees, and together they walked through the church, recalling the most ambitious of their service projects. Jon asked, "Do you remember painting this church?"

"How could I ever forget," replied his friend, giving a knowing smile.

"We understood from the beginning that's what you were supposed to do: serve," Jon observed. "God intended us to live life in a community, and the Boy Scouts taught us that we were supposed to help others."

Shortly after Jon earned Eagle, he became more concerned with God's intent as he delivered his first sermon on Youth Sunday. The pastor came to see him at home afterward and told Jon that God was calling him to the ministry. Jon thought little on the matter until later that year when the local Scout council had each Eagle Scout in the class of 1973 choose a mentor in a field that interested them.

"Three guys from our troop earned Eagle that year," Jon explained. "One chose a dentist, and he eventually became a dentist. Another chose an engineer; he's now an engineer himself. I chose a minister, and here I am, in a pulpit every Sunday!

"I'm not in a pulpit down here in Mississippi," this United Methodist minister expounded, "but these people are part of our community. My job is to minister to them, and this is the type of ministry they need. What an amazing blessing to minister to Margaret. We grew a bond that I'll call 'intimate' because we were seeing her entire life spread across the house, yard, and neighborhood for that matter. These were many of her most personal and intimate things. In her case, I found a stack of love letters that her husband—who is deceased—had written years ago. We were about to throw them away, but for some reason, I looked at them closely and realized what I'd found."

"It was just an enormous connection I felt with her," he tried to explain. "Sharing with her what's most intimate, a person's loves and heart. Being a complete stranger and being able to give her that . . . indescribable. The look I saw on her face, the feelings and hugs exchanged were just amazing."

Jon observed that giving benefits the giver as well: something his career in ministry proved to him time and again. He explained, "When the opportunity arose to come here, we all wrestled with taking time off from work and leaving family, just as we do when any similar chance comes to us. But when you meet people like Margaret, the Chapmans, or other families, I always find the blessing that comes from that sense of helping neighbors and feeling at peace with yourself honestly gives you much more than you ever gave to the people you've helped."

Before the day ended, I learned that three others on our team had Scouting ties. One fifteen-year-old had just earned Eagle in Troy, Illinois. Another Troy native had recently finished a stint as president of the Trails West Boy Scout Council. And Tyler, a young Star Scout had clear designs to reach Eagle in the coming year. By the time Tyler boarded his bus home, Jon and I had extracted a promise from him to that end.

But, promise aside, I realized that during our work, we had all joined the perpetual cycle that is part of Scouting's legacy: Eagle Scouts remembering the lessons they learned and showing the next generation what being an Eagle means. In this case, I believe young Tyler learned that helping others is certainly part of that badge's meaning.

Late on my final evening in camp, Tim Mehne, the chef from Texas, and I sat together in St. Paul's empty fellowship hall, reflecting on scenes and lessons from the past week. Oddly, I felt as if I scarcely had done anything to help. I felt almost more helpless than I had watching news coverage at home in Atlanta. I now understood how much work remained. Because that work remained, Tim planned to man the camp throughout the fall, although he knew the people of Ocean Springs would need help long after he left at Thanksgiving.

As midnight approached, our conversation turned to the Eagle Scouts who came to the Gulf that particular weekend. I told him that at least 8 Eagles were among the 110 men and women sleeping in the village of army-issue tents outside. It did not surprise him. "In Scouting, we all learned values," he explained. "Scouting taught you to give. Now look who came down here to the Gulf Coast to help: Eagle Scouts."

As our lives grow steadily busier, our time for matters beyond our own careers and families grows shorter. During my travels, I found many people who saw this happening in their lives. They seemed to keep their priorities in mind, yet struggled to honor them. Often, they spoke of reaching the next goal: *Then* they would be able to change their ways; *then* they would be content. There was conflict between the goals and the lives of some Eagles I met. The training we receive as Scouts drives us to set and achieve goals. The same training tries to teach us about living life along the way, but sometimes I saw the goals becoming life itself.

In writing this book, I forgot that I was living life every day. Thousands of miles wore me down, and I reacted by focusing intently on finishing this trek. I had thrown myself, my heart, and all I had into this venture and slowly, the daily challenges and stress of the risk itself began to obscure the greater purpose. Consequently, I grew more self-consumed than I imagined I could be. I focused on myself and became selfish with my time and my energy, certainly not the traits of an Eagle Scout. Those lapses in perspective took a tremendous toll. I should have been adopting the outward-looking philosophy these Eagles were showing me, but I worried about my fast-disappearing bank account, arranging interviews, and telling this story well. I forgot the value of giving and caring for others first. I forgot that life was most definitely not about me.

Hurricanes can be very real; they can also be figurative. In Mississippi, I wasn't just mending damage from Katrina; I was also patching holes in my own life and regaining the perspective I had lost. My concerns and preoccupations quickly faded when I saw what others had suffered. I tied on work boots, slipped on old jeans, picked up a shovel, and sweated for someone else. I remembered what it meant to be thoughtful and to put others first. My soul gently fell back into its place as I returned to the ideals I'd learned years ago on countless Scout projects. Again, this journey reminded me about something terribly important I had forgotten.

✦

PART II

A Legacy for the Future

Were this book about history alone, it would end here, but this story concerns a timeless legacy that is far more than a history. While both reflect the past, a legacy also looks to the future. It is a heritage that inspires and shapes what will come.

The actions and virtues of America's Eagle Scouts are inextricably and undeniably woven into the great tapestry of American history, but their actions are also influencing the years ahead. In ways astoundingly diverse and numerous, Eagles are giving of themselves to create opportunities for others and enhance the future. They are serving as teachers and stewards, mentors and fathers. They are making sacrifices to sustain their tradition and carry their legacy to the next generation.

SERVICE

In 1965, the Boy Scouts of America instituted a new requirement for the Eagle Scout rank: the service project. While the ideal of service had always been at the core scouting, Boy Scouts of America decided to reinforce that value in each new Eagle Scout by requiring Life Scouts to "plan, develop, and give leadership to others in a service project. . . ." Before earning Scouting's, highest rank, they had to prove their dedication to others. In their projects, boys saw how their labor could make life better for their community. For many Scouts, service projects don't end when they receive their Eagle badge.

For his 1969 Eagle Scout project, Steve Herbets developed an entertainment program for cancer patients in a local hospital. Decades later and after surviving his own bout with cancer, he continues to serve patients, although many of his current patients have never seen the inside of a modern hospital. Once a month, Dr. Steve Herbets leaves his home in Southern California and flies to Mexico with a team of doctors from the Flying Samaritans or LIGA, two medical aid groups. The teams land and set up clinics in Mexico's poor, underserved communities. Throughout the weekend, they see patients of all stripes. The children and adults who come through the clinics have few other options for health care. They become the beneficiaries of Dr. Herbets' never-ending service project.

"I just love being a doctor and being able to help people who can't get help in any other way," he explained. "I put my patients first; they're like my extended family. Sometimes HMOs in the States want to get them in and out. That's partly why I got involved in volunteer work; I can be a real advocate for my patients down here. I can really take care of them and give them the time they need. It's just tremendously rewarding as a doctor and as a person."

He related a story from one past trip to Mexico that, to him, encapsulated the reason he became a doctor in the first place. "We were almost done for the day," he recalled. "A mom brings her kid in and says, 'There's not much you can probably do, but my son was told he has cancer and doesn't have long.' He didn't look that bad, so I started checking things out and said, 'I have a funny feeling you don't have leukemia.'

"We took a drop of his blood back to the States and checked it out. He had ITP, where platelets are low. Kids can get it from a virus. We came back to the clinic, said there was no indication of leukemia, and gave him some medicine. They thought we hung the moon. After that, they'd always bring me food and tacos! The people there are so grateful for any little thing we do."

Every day, America's doctors serve others. They commit themselves to a life of waking up early to make people better. They are servants and healers. In operating rooms and offices—and in tents pitched in poverty-stricken communities beyond U.S. borders—they embody the commitment to serving others that lies at Scouting's heart. Dr. Herbets thought about his profession, then added, "But it doesn't matter if you're a doctor or an Assistant Scoutmaster or a politician; serving others is exactly what Eagles should probably be doing and probably are doing."

Service of any type seems to natural for Eagles of every type. Eagle Scouts learn to help others and leave the world a little better than they found it. They carry that obligation into occupations and workplaces of all sorts. In the U.S. Congress, I discovered someone who did not have the same degree as Steve Herbets, M.D., but who certainly shared his passion for serving.

SANFORD BISHOP

TROOP 201, MOBILE, ALABAMA
EAGLE SCOUT, 1961

He was about to take another bite of fried fish when his vibrating phone distracted him. He reached inside his sport coat, produced a small silver phone, and answered simply, "Hello?" He listened for a moment. "Yes, this is Congressman Bishop." He smiled at me and gestured to indicate that he'd only be a minute.

We were enjoying a late lunch at one of Sanford Bishop's favorite haunts, Columbus, Georgia's Royal Café, and while he talked, I occupied myself with the southern fare remaining on my plastic plate. The food was simple—fried meat, corn bread, and vegetables—but this sixth-term congressman was at home. Under his jacket, he wore a dark T-shirt and the gentle confidence of a veteran public servant. Discarded were the trepidation and cautious wording of a rookie. In their place was a sense of calm that came from being secure in position and confident in purpose. The congressman had good reason to be secure; he had just won reelection two weeks earlier. But as I ate, I gathered that the present aim of the congressman across the table from me was that of helping a citizen of his district.

"Do you really give your cell phone number to constituents," I asked as he put the phone back under his coat several minutes later.

"Well, I really do," the congressman answered. "It's my job. That was Mr. Walker. His son's been working for a couple of years doing manual labor and things of that nature and finally realized he needed to get a better education. He couldn't qualify for financial aid—a Pell Grant in this case—because of a technicality, so we've been helping him.

"When people come to us, they've already gone everywhere else, so we're their last hope, and we do what we can for them. We're supposed to help them. That's why I got into public service; it's what I like to do."

Sanford Bishop first felt this passion for public service in Troop 201, the first black Scout troop in the Mobile, Alabama, area. There in Troop 201, Bishop earned his three Citizenship merit badges—Citizenship in the Home, Community, and Nation—which he still credits for sparking his interest in the political process. As he worked toward those badges, he remembers

Sanford D. Bishop, Jr., Eagle Scout and Brotherhood member of the Order of the Arrow
COURTESY OF CONGRESSMAN
SANFORD D. BISHOP, JR.

learning about his local, state, and national governments and his role as a citizen in each. He had to learn the minute details about government and citizenship since Mr. Booker Pinckney stood between Troop 201's Scouts and the Citizenship badges.

"Mr. Pinckney was a no-nonsense kind of guy," the congressman explained about his merit badge counselor. "And he was the kind of guy who expected you to master the material and then when you went for your review, he examined you on it, and if you didn't know the material, you wouldn't get the merit badge. Some got washed out in terms of getting the Citizenship merit badges by Mr. Pinckney."

But before running Mr. Pinckney's gauntlet, young Sanford Bishop earned another merit badge that gave him the skills, not just the knowledge, on which his future career would depend. The first merit badge he earned was Public Speaking. "I remember my first speech was on the meaning of the Scout Oath," he said. "It was supposed to be one minute—I think I went for fifteen—but I got the merit badge." Since he gave his first speech at the dining hall of Camp Leon Roberts, where he served as a counselor each summer from age twelve to age eighteen, his smooth, resonant voice has captivated thousands of people who have gathered to hear him speak.

From those beginnings, he continued earning other merit badges as he progressed toward Eagle and recalled that he was constantly challenged along the way. "The Scout leaders were always taunting you but encouraging you in a sense," he remembered. " 'Not everyone can be an Eagle,' they'd say. 'Are you one of those who can? Which ones of you are going to be the Eagles?' "

I had begun to wonder if that was true—that not everyone can be an Eagle—and if the Scouting program led boys to Eagle by training or if certain boys simply already had the traits they needed to reach the rank?

Several weeks before I met Sanford Bishop, I had hiked the crest of Toxaway Mountain in North Carolina with Robert Balentine, an Eagle Scout who started a nature preserve to showcase the native plants of the Great Smoky Mountains. As he turned up a switchback on the trail, Robert paused, leaned against a thick branch of mountain laurel, and turned the conversation from botany to Scouting. He mused, "You know, I wonder to what extent Eagle Scouts are a self-selecting group. Are certain types of people just naturally attracted to the challenge and are those the people who'll finish the job? Beyond that, the question becomes would people who go on to achieve significant ends have been equally successful, or successful in the same way, without Scouting?" Robert had defined one of the questions driving me along this quest.

I put Robert's question to the gentleman sitting across from me at the Royal Café. Congressman Bishop reflected on the matter, then in his evenly paced voice, he responded, "Whatever leadership skills I had, whatever potential for it I had, Scouting allowed me to develop it so that I was able to become a mentor for Cub Scouts when I became a Webelos. I was able to become a patrol leader, senior patrol leader, and camp staff member. . . . I think the experiences of Scouting prepared me for leadership and gave me the values that focused me on how to harness that leadership, 'cause leadership can be used in any number of ways. You can be leader of a mob, you can be a gang leader, a leader on the football team, a leader on the basketball team—any number of ways leadership can be harnessed—but I think the values of Scouting helped me to focus my leadership in a positive kind of way, in a helpful way."

Once he graduated from college, Sanford Bishop's bent toward positive leadership led him not to join in the exodus of educated African-Americans from the South; his leadership was needed at home. "I was going to get a useful skill and try and use it to make my community, my native South, what it ought to be," he explained. "To make real the noble principles of Scouting—a friend to all; a brother to every other Scout—not just to black Scouts or white Scouts but to every Scout, every human being.

"Those are basic values," he said, reflecting further on Scouting's principles. "The values that really form the culture of our nation are melded right there in Scouting. 'On my Honor,' " he said and began reciting the Scout Oath like a preacher dissecting a scripture passage. " 'To do my Best' means I'm going to give it everything I got. 'To do my Duty'—we all have responsibilities; wherever we are, we have a duty and responsibility to somebody. 'To God' first 'and my Country and to obey the Scout Law/To help *other* People'— not just myself and my folks—'at *all* times/To keep my*self* physically strong'— I have a sense of obligation to be fit—'*mentally* awake and *morally* straight.' "

He then discussed the twelve points of the Scout Law, which describe the personal characteristics a Scout, particularly an Eagle Scout, should exhibit. The congressman recalled troop ceremonies where he would light candles corresponding to the twelve points of the Law while defining the meaning of each. " 'A Scout is Trustworthy,' " he began to recite. "He is honest. He must not tell a lie. If he were to lie or cheat or not do a directly given task when trusted on his honor, he must be directed to hand over his Scout badge. 'A Scout is Loyal.' He is loyal to all whom loyalty is due. 'A Scout is Friendly.' He is a friend to all and a brother to every other Scout,' he concluded, having provided a glimpse of how much he cherished those twelve virtues.

"It was repetitive and sort of rote at the time," he observed, "but the more you live and the more you say it, the more it becomes a part of you. To me, it became part of the values that form the foundation of my character." His fellow Scouts noticed those values in all that he did in Troop 201. They elected him to Scouting's honor society, the Order of the Arrow.

Sanford Bishop and I hadn't known each other for more than thirty seconds when he leaned toward me and softly said, *"Wimachtendienk, Wingolauchsik, Witahemui,"* the Lenape Indian phrase for "brotherhood of cheerful service" and the original name of the Order of the Arrow. It was a test that I fortunately passed. We were both brotherhood members of the "OA," as the Order is often called.

Founded by E. Urner Goodman and Carroll A. Edson in 1915 at Treasure Island Scout Camp in the Delaware River, the Order of the Arrow became an official part of Scouting in 1934. The Order pays tribute to the customs of Native Americans while honoring Scouts and leaders who show a particular dedication to the ideals of Scouting. Its rites leave members with a deep appreciation for the virtues and ways of the first Americans.

Eagle Scout and longtime philosophy professor John Silber told me, "The OA was a way of preserving a significant part of Indian culture, of learning how to survive in the woods by learning the woodcrafts and the camping crafts and the other crafts of surviving out in Nature. And in all of this, they used the Indian as the ideal, which I thought was very helpful in overcoming racial intolerance. It certainly left us with the impression that to become an Indian brave and be a member of a tribe was a very lofty thing. Native Americans, as we interpreted them, had all the virtues of the Boy Scouts."

Today, 176,000 Scouts and adults are active members of this Scouting honor society, having been elected by their peers for their character and ability. Interestingly, only nonmembers can vote on new members to the brotherhood.

It has been years since I last took part in one of the OA's campfire ceremonies, conducted by members dressed in elaborate Native American costumes. The regalia of the leaders combined with roaring fires, mysterious rituals, and the quiet of the woods at night make the ceremonies unforgettable. But while I still held the memory, the legend behind the OA had escaped me. In the decades since he last played the ceremonial role of the Order's Chieftain, Allowat Sakima, Congressman Bishop had forgotten neither his lines nor the legend.

"As you know, it's a brotherhood of honor campers based on service and sacrifice, and it's called a brotherhood of cheerful service," he said of the Order of the Arrow. "I became a member of the Ordeal Team and served in every one of the positions—Nutiket, Kitchkinet, Meteu, and Allowat Sakima—all four." Then, to my astonishment he quoted the words I'd heard more than a decade ago when I was "tapped" for membership in the Order.

"That you my fellow campers," he began, assuming once again the commanding voice of a great chieftain, "have been selected by your companions to become members of our band reflects great credit upon you, and I congratulate you upon your election. You have impressed upon those who for the past few weeks have lived closest to you the sincerity of your purpose to live in accord with the high ideals of Scouting. Before you become a member of our band, you must pass an ordeal." He continued describing the initiation rites, but those shall remain secret as the Order's founders intended.

"The whole experience was symbolic and meaningful," he reflected, "particularly being part of the ceremonial team and going through it so many times and then having reflected on it later in life and you can see the real meaning of it. The Scouts in general, but the Order of the Arrow in particular, really plants a seed in the individual to serve others and to be self-*less*."

Then he recounted the legend behind the Order of the Arrow: the story of the Lenni Lenape Indian brave Uncas, who helped save his village by selflessly placing himself in danger for the sake of his tribe. The moral, Bishop pointed out, was "that we as individuals should look beyond self and sometimes sacrifice and be courageous in order to promote the greater good. That was, I think, one of the bases for my interest in public service."

The Order of the Arrow and Scouting prepared him for the life he would lead, giving him the basic values, skills, and direction that would serve him in the future. Then as a senior in high school, he saw Leroy Johnson speak, and his path materialized before him. Johnson had become the first black elected to the Georgia Senate since Reconstruction, and Bishop decided that if Johnson could be a senator, so could he. Following Johnson's path, Sanford Bishop attended Morehouse College, where he majored in political science and served as student body president before entering law school at Emory University. After working briefly in New York City, Bishop returned to Georgia and began a civil rights law practice in Columbus, a growing city on the Alabama-Georgia state line.

By this time, the late 1960s, the courts had declared that all Americans were entitled to equal rights, but that legal ideal too often was denied many poor blacks—and whites—in the rural South. Injustice and discrimination still existed even though the segregated lunch counters and buses of Percy Sutton's era were gone. Minorities and the poor battled to gain land rights, employment rights, and since they constituted a disproportionately high percentage of state inmates, they often fought hard for prison rights as well. One such issue came to Sanford Bishop's desk—a case against the state of Georgia. He filed suit to remedy the overcrowding and poor conditions in which many prison inmates lived, and in the late 1960s, he won a judgment that mandated the state make changes. But those changes would cost $110 million.

"So after four years of litigating," the congressman explained, "nothing was done to remedy the situation in spite of the judge ordering the state to do it. The Corrections Department kept coming back and saying, 'Well, the legislature hasn't appropriated the money.' So I got frustrated after the eighth status conference and their saying the legislature hadn't appropriated the money. I said, 'I'm in the wrong place. I need to go to the legislature to do right.'"

In 1972, Bishop won election to the Georgia House of Representatives, and he remembered, "After being there for six years, the state *finally* appropriated the money! But I realized that I could win a case and it would help my clients, but if I passed one good law, it'd help everyone in the state. I thought that was a really effective way of implementing social change. So, there I was, a state representative, in a position to provide service to not just my Scout troop or not just my immediate area but to everyone in the whole state.

"But my platform for the State House and for Congress has been essentially the same: improving quality of life for people I represent through service," he said, before nodding to the Scout Law and interjecting, "Helpful!"

As a U.S. congressman representing citizens in twenty-seven Southwest Georgia counties, Sanford Bishop has fought hard for the lives of his constituents, literally in one case. A seventeen-year-old Georgian needed a heart transplant, but by the time a suitable heart arrived at Duke University Hospital, the young man was eighteen, too old for the Medicaid coverage that would have paid for the transplant were he still seventeen. The family could not afford the operation themselves and government agencies and insurance companies turned them away. They had no connections, no recourse, so they turned to their congressman. Instead of running their case through the usual bureaucratic channels, Bishop got personally involved. He called Georgia Governor Zell Miller as soon as he heard about the problem; his ill constituent did not have the luxury of time. The governor had left his office for the day, but Bishop insisted on speaking with him. Minutes later, Bishop and Miller were talking via cell phone. Days later, the young man traveled to Duke University for the transplant, his insurance reinstated and his family grateful to their congressman for making sure their son had a chance at life. What could be a more basic civil right than that? It didn't involve segregated buses or voting discrimination, but to Congressman Bishop, issues such as access to health care are the modern battlegrounds of the civil rights struggle.

It could not have been clearer after our time together: Sanford Bishop serves as an advocate for the people he represents and for the people whose interests are often overlooked in the halls of power. Answering his cell phone and finding a constituent in need always energizes him. "You're able to do a good turn there to help other people at all times," he said, chuckling at his reference to the Scout Oath and the Scout Slogan ("Do a good turn daily"). "And whatever *I* do in politics, it has to be in the framework of morality and ethical rules. One, because there is a code of ethics. But two, because I'm a Scout."

Forty years after receiving his Eagle badge, he still considers himself a Scout. "I had the biggest fight with my congressional staff about what to put in my biography," he remembered. "They went through the biography and said it was too long, and they cut out this, that, and the other. And they cut out Eagle Scout. I said, 'Nope, that's got to go back in.' "

The staff protested, arguing, "Nobody cares about that. That was when you were a kid."

"I said, 'No, that goes back in.' " That met with renewed protest.

"No," the congressman said one last time in his smooth voice. "Case closed. Read my lips, 'It goes back in.' "

Several months after that discussion, a Georgia peanut farmer approached Bishop at a dinner and said, "I didn't know you when you first ran, but I read your biography and I saw that you're an Eagle Scout. I knew that if you were an Eagle Scout, you were the kind of person who would represent us well." That alone had won the farmer's vote.

Sanford Bishop preached the idea of service, of helping other people at all times, and as we wrapped up lunch together at the Royal Café, I began to think of what, exactly, service to others can accomplish. But Thanksgiving lay just two days away, and family plans soon pushed those thoughts to the rear of my mind. There they remained until a meeting with another Eagle Scout on the far side of the continent brought them back to the fore.

William H. Gates, or Bill Gates, Sr., stands six feet, six inches tall, and as he walked up to meet me, the speed and ease with which his long legs closed the distance between us amazed me. Seconds after I first saw him round the corner, this spry eighty-year-old gently shook my hand in the atrium of the

Bill and Melinda Gates Foundation headquarters. He seemed intrigued that I had come. The Class of 1941 Eagle Scout from Troop 511 in Bremerton, Washington, admitted he hadn't thought deeply about Scouting in some time.

Warm memories of Troop 511 flooded his mind as we began to talk, and I learned about a most ambitious Scout troop. The boys of his Cougar patrol helped convince the Bremerton Lion's Club to purchase a six-acre parcel of land on which the troop built their own camp. The Scouts felled, barked, and cut timber, made cedar shingles by hand, and constructed a lodge that became a source of immense pride for the boys. Judging by Mr. Gates's demeanor as he related the story, that pride has never dissipated. The boys also built a cable suspension bridge across a nearby river, and again appealed to the Lion's Club for funding, this time for a bus that later carried Bill and thirty other Troop 511 Scouts to Glacier and Yellowstone national parks. In 1941, Bill and seven fellow Scouts received their Eagle rank. Two years later, this Troop 511 Eagle enlisted in the U.S. Army to serve in World War II.

Scouting returned to his life in the 1960s, as he began guiding his son, Bill, to the rank of Life, but the future founder of Microsoft never reached Eagle. Bill, Sr., and I laughed: The younger Bill Gates seemed to do just fine without the badge. "His troop was not quite as active," Mr. Gates explained. "It didn't come within a mile of 511. I don't think anyone ever has!"

Regardless of his rank, Scouting's values remained with the young entrepreneur, and as Microsoft prospered, Bill Gates created a vision for philanthropy. He recruited his Eagle Scout father, a highly successful attorney in his own right, to manage his new foundation. From 1994 until 1999, Mr. Gates's basement served as the world headquarters of the Gates Foundation. By 2005, Mr. Gates was helping direct more than $1 billion in donations per year. With the $30 billion commitment businessman Warren Buffett made to the foundation in 2006, Mr. Gates, along with his fellow co-chairs, Bill and Melinda, now oversees $3 billion in annual philanthropic giving, primarily to causes related to global health and education.

Bill Sr. and I squared off at a conference table and began discussing his work in Asia and Africa, where the foundation has funded immunization programs that have vaccinated millions of children and adults. Being a writer, I pressed him for a poignant example of how his work saved a child's life. He paused thoughtfully before responding, "Well, I know what you want, Alvin. But I can't actually point to a child who our programs have saved or brought back from the brink of death. These children are just all alive."

That struck me. Because of his work, millions of children now have a future, whereas before, many would have died before realizing any of their potential. Nobody knows what these young people may one day accomplish for their family, country, or continent. Through them, the effects of the Gates Foundation's giving will multiply, and expand across place and time. In viewing power as the ability to influence lives and events, few hold more power than William H. Gates. He has saved millions of young lives, unleashing untold potential.

William H. Gates with orphans in India
COURTESY OF THE BILL AND MELINDA GATES FOUNDATION

"I can't imagine a society where giving to others wasn't a theme," he said, as he explained away his work as the obligation that comes with good fortune. "I've never thought about it just this way before, but that would really be a dark world. The fact of the matter is there's no issue of fault around so many of these people, just circumstances. Some people don't have the ability without some help from others."

Mr. Gates reminded me that anyone can wield enormous power when they help change the lives of others. Power such as this is not a power of position or control; rather, it is a power of influence, which by nature entails a great responsibility. As generous philanthropists or simply as parents or friends, people can use this influence to affect some portion of the world, large or small. The sum of their actions becomes unbelievably powerful.

❦

CONSERVATION

T hat's a double-crested cormorant," Sonny Bass said, gesturing to a dark
bird flying over the sun-washed wetlands before us. "Over there are drag-
onflies," he explained, turning his attention to a nearby patch of tall grass.
"Those smaller ones are damselflies. The variety of wildlife—big and small—
out here is unbelievable. We even have Florida panthers. There used to be
thousands of them. That animal was all over North America, and now, in the
East, the only place they're still found is here in Everglades National Park."

Sonny serves as a biologist for the National Park Service and cares for
panthers, birds, and all of the park's species, fifteen of which are officially
endangered. During Sonny's tenure at the park, he estimated the panther
populations had grown from numbers in the twenties to nearly one hundred.
He explained much of this as we walked along the Anhinga Trail, a boardwalk
winding across thickets and marshes of the eastern Everglades. We walked
over the shallow slew of water that feeds the wetlands as he explained the
fragile ecosystem that sustains life in the park and in all of South Florida.

The Everglades are 11,000 square miles of marshes and low-lying wood-
lands that cover most of South Florida. Naturally, they are a slow flowing
"river of grass" fifty miles wide but only three feet to six inches deep. The
fragile system, which supplies much of Florida's water, has been endangered
for decades. In fact, the Department of the Interior established the 1.5-
million-acre Everglades National Park in 1947 specifically for the protection
of the ecosystem. Since then, Florida's population has ballooned to more
than 16 million, and the state's water usage has grown from 900 million gallons per day in 1950 to nearly 20 billion gallons per day at present. At the

same time those demands were increasing, new suburbs consumed half of Florida's original wetlands, and pollution began tainting the water supply.

Today, the Everglades are vitally important to everyone in South Florida. But the preserve occupies a particularly special place in Sonny's heart. The chance to camp in the park first coaxed him into Homestead, Florida's Troop 445 in the late 1950s, and he became the troop's second Eagle Scout. His love of the area and his fascination with its complex systems have kept him in Florida for most of his life. As a member of the Everglades National Park staff, he has done his best to instill that same love in the youth who will become the park's next generation of caretakers. As a Scoutmaster, he also has instilled that responsibility in his son and the other Scouts of Troop 10.

At least once a month, the troop ventured into the Everglades to camp on the wooden platforms or the firm, pine islands that are interspersed among the park's marshes. Over the course of these trips, the troop earned the William T. Hornaday Award, which honors the famous American conservationist. The award recognizes extensive work in ecology and conservation, and Sonny led the troop through the series of merit badges that the award required, including Fish and Wildlife Management, Environmental Science, Soil and Water Conservation, Energy, and Forestry. The requirements for each badge taught the Scouts about their responsibility toward our natural lands. They weren't just learning to preserve them, however. They learned about our role in Nature.

Over the decades, Scouting programs have taught generations of youth the value of both preserving and responsibly managing the environment. Scouts have earned more than 2 million Environmental Science merit badges and nearly 2 million Forestry and Soil & Water Conservation merit badges. Four million Scouts have earned the Camping merit badge, and leaders have awarded millions of Nature, Wilderness Survival, and Hiking merit badges throughout the past century.

Beyond badges, the boys simply learn to appreciate Nature. Most Scouts go camping each year, and for thousands of parents, sending their sons on weekend expeditions becomes a monthly ritual. Scouts and leaders enjoy the outdoors while they learn about the science and ecology underlying the woods, swamps, and mountains around them. On hikes and camping trips, during summer camp sessions and Scout meetings, leaders always stress the value of Nature. The lessons seem to stick.

HANK PAULSON

TROOP 21, BARRINGTON, ILLINOIS

EAGLE SCOUT, 1959

Arriving at the top of 85 Broad Street, in the heart of the Manhattan financial district and only steps from the New York Stock Exchange, I found wildlife. Pictures of condors, foxes, wetlands, and forests streamed across the mammoth digital display dominating the executive suite of one of the world's premier finance firms, a company with nearly $30 billion in total revenues. The legendary 137-year-old firm was internationally renowned for its starched white shirts, top-tier clients, and mastery of finance, not for birds and trees. On the reception tables, I expected annual reports, financial statements, and investment literature. Instead, I found only one brochure, a square, six-page piece covered with a blue river meandering through a plain, with a snow-capped mountain as backdrop: a scene from the Tierra del Fuego wilderness area in Chile. The title read: "Goldman Sachs & the Wildlife Conservation Society: Partners in Conservation."

When Goldman Sachs acquired a particular portfolio of loans, they discovered one backed by land, 680,000 unspoiled acres of stunning Chilean land. As a business firm, Goldman Sachs typically would explore ways to develop the land for commercial profit, but this site was too precious. The firm's chief executive firmly believed that business had a higher purpose, one that income statements often fail to capture. This gold-standard Wall Street firm found itself in a position to make a contribution to global conservation, and it followed through. Joining with the Wildlife Conservation Society, whose business *is* the environment, Goldman Sachs formed a partnership that protects this southern corner of Chile for perpetuity and creates a wilderness area roughly the size of California's Yosemite National Park. The pictures continuously streaming across the display atop 85 Broad Street were of the lands and animals of Tierra del Fuego. Most Wall Street firms would never have considered such an endeavor or display, but then most Wall Street firms weren't run by Hank Paulson.

The then chairman and CEO of Goldman Sachs and future secretary of the treasury never outgrew his love of the outdoors and fascination with wildlife. Raised on a farm in rural Illinois, Hank Paulson lived his childhood outside,

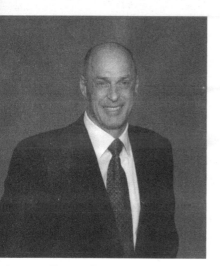

Treasury Secretary Hank Paulson former chairman of The Nature Conservancy and CEO of Goldman Sachs COURTESY OF GOLDMAN SACHS & CO.

and he became fascinated with the spaces and creatures around him. "Other kids were reading about Superman," he recalled after we had sat down together in his office. "I was drawing animal tracks and trying to figure out how I could go walk in the snow and tell a possum from a raccoon from a fox!" His parents indulged his interest, and before his tenth birthday, his family was taking long wilderness canoe trips to the Boundary Waters of northern Minnesota, where he learned to value those lonely woods and lakes for their majesty, purity, and wealth of life. By the time he entered Scouting, he already knew more than most about the woods and their wildlife.

So, for Hank, Scouting wasn't as much about developing an appreciation for Nature as it was for many boys of his generation. "Scouting has a different impact on Scouts or Eagle Scouts, depending on what their background is," he explained, his coat off and his tall, athletic frame slouched comfortably in an office chair. "For instance, I think a lot of Scouts is getting into the outdoors, camping, hiking, and all those kinds of experiences. And because I grew up in a rural area on a farm with a father who really made sure from a very young age that I was doing things like riding horses, hiking, going on wilderness canoe trips, and all of those kinds of things, a lot of those experiences that I had in Scouting were actually secondary to what I had in my family."

"For me," he emphasized, "the Scouting experience was more about working with others as part of a troop." And it was about working together with other boys from Troop 21 on projects larger than themselves.

"Before I was in Scouting," he reflected, "everything that I had done was with friends or with family, but was about pure enjoyment of the natural world—camping, being outdoors, working—the kind of work we did was work around the home, where there's a direct benefit to the family. Then I remember some of the Scout projects—service to the community or Order of the Arrow—doing work in public parks or building a bridge or those kinds of things. It wasn't any one project that was so important, but just the whole idea of *service* and working with others toward that end." He came to view the natural world with which he'd become so familiar in a different way. Nature did not exist solely for Hank's personal enjoyment. He learned to work with others to improve the environment, whether that was a local park in his Scouting days or an expansive tract of wilderness today.

Hank Paulson
COURTESY OF MARIANNA PAULSON

He relaxed and smiled as he recalled time spent at Scout camp in Wisconsin. "There's nothing glamorous about Camp Napowan," he added flatly. During several years of summer camp there, Hank scrubbed dishes in the mess hall and slept on the ground beneath canvas tents while working intently on merit badges during the day. Of all the badges he earned, this future All-East offensive lineman remembers Lifesaving most of all, thanks to the instructor who at that time was dealing with a Hank Paulson much smaller than the one with whom I sat in New York.

"I remember Lifesaving because this guy would hold you underwater and take you down," he explained. "The trick was not to fight. If you fight, you lose. If you just relax, they'll take you underwater and they'll let you go, and I remember I gave him a hard elbow to the solar plexus!"

Continuing to reflect on summer camp, Hank pointed out, "I signed up for as many merit badges as you could get. I forget what the number was, but nobody got more merit badges in those two weeks than me!"

The future CEO joined Scouting the moment he reached his twelfth birthday and proceeded to earn each new rank as soon as the requirements allowed. Nobody in Troop 21 reached Eagle in less time or earned more merit badges along the way. "It's called the gold star mentality," he added, enjoying a good laugh at his own expense. "That was clearly mine!" His mentality mirrored that of Sam Walton and Ross Perot, and I continued wondering to what extent the Eagle experience created leaders or if leaders just became Eagle Scouts. Hank addressed the question, observing, "Looking back on it, the three years or four years people are in Scouts from the time they join until they become an Eagle Scout isn't that long in the overall scheme of things, but at that stage of their life, it is. It can be very formative."

Soon after he became an Eagle Scout, Hank left Scouting. By the fall of his ninth-grade year, football and wrestling occupied his days and weekends. And years later, classes at Dartmouth and Harvard Business School consumed his time even moreso. Upon graduation from business school, he drifted into public service and worked in the Pentagon and the Nixon White House in the days leading up to the Watergate scandal.

"I had a ringside seat, and it really, really impressed one thing upon me," he observed with his loafers leisurely kicked up on the coffee table between us. "No one should be too impressed by rank. I saw people who one day looked like they were on top of the world, and the next day they were leaving in disgrace. . . . You need to always remind yourself of that. It's a good lesson in terms of how quickly things can change if someone loses their moral compass."

Through all his time in Washington, in school, and in his early days with Goldman Sachs, he never lost his passion for the environment. "I've always loved Nature and have a great affinity for wild places," he explained. "My personal involvement in conservation was triggered by the realization that some of the most precious parts of the world and the wildlife they support are increasingly endangered. It basically comes down to stewardship and the responsibility I believe each of us has to leave things better than we found them."

In the 1990s, Hank shouldered that responsibility and stepped onto the global stage as chairman of the Peregrine Fund, which protects birds of prey such as the American bald eagle and the peregrine falcon. He helped establish breeding centers in Idaho and Panama and oversaw raptor protection and reintroduction efforts in a host of other areas around the world. Perhaps most notably, he oversaw the continuance of a two-decades-long effort to reintroduce the peregrine falcon to the continental United States and saw the fund's work pay very real dividends. On August 20, 1999, three months after Hank assumed the top job at Goldman Sachs, the Department of the Interior removed the peregrine falcon from the endangered species list.

When we met, this future U.S. treasury secretary was serving his last full year as chairman and chief executive officer of Goldman Sachs, one of the world's most respected positions in business. In 2004, he had also assumed one of the world's most respected positions in conservation: He became chairman of The Nature Conservancy, an international conservation group that works with donors, governments, and private companies to protect natural lands and the wildlife those environments support. Since 1951, the Conservancy has helped to protect nearly 117 million acres of land, an area 13 million acres larger than the state of California.

Examples of the Conservancy's work are found on every continent. After Hank became chairman, The Nature Conservancy cofunded the purchase of 370,000 acres of at-risk tropical forests in Calakmul on Mexico's Yucatán Peninsula, an area serving as home to both endangered jaguars and ancient Mayan ruins that now falls under the protection of provisions included in the largest conservation land deal in Mexican history. In Brazil, the organization helped convert 148,000 acres of wetlands into private reserves to expand the size of the Pantanal National Park, forever protecting these forests and wetlands from the rampant development affecting other parts of Brazil. Two weeks before Hank and I met in New York, The Nature Conservancy announced that it had worked with the U.S. Fish and Wildlife Service, the Del-Mar-Va Council of the Boy Scouts of America, and the Maryland Department of Natural Resources to establish a conservation easement for the 1,485-acre Scout Camp Nanticoke, whose forests and wetlands are nesting grounds for bald eagles. Around the world, The Nature Conservancy constantly works with hundreds of governments, communities, private organizations, and corporations to protect and responsibly manage natural lands and oceans.

In an Eagle Scout project that perhaps tops all others, Hank had recently focused the Conservancy on the unprotected regions of Asia, China in particular. Why? To him, it's about going where a need exists. "There are *many* conservationists here," he pointed out, referring to the United States. "The impact of expanding populations and much of the industrial activity associated with supporting growth are, quite literally, destroying vital parts of our planet," he expounded. "I firmly believe that the overall impact of globalization is positive, but society needs to be better at assessing and addressing not just the impact on the lives of those affected but also the environmental impact of the policies and actions associated with globalization which ultimately affect the quality of life on Earth in very real and tangible ways."

His efforts in Asia represent the concept of service he carried away from Troop 2: The Asian project will benefit *others*, not him personally. In this venture, as in others, he leads by example and initiative. He began leading the Conservancy's new Asia-Pacific Council in the late 1990s and campaigned to give the area's needs greater attention. That campaigning included personally raising money from individuals, corporations, foundations, and governments all on his own time, in addition to managing a $30-billion public company and its 19,000 worldwide employees. Most recently, he worked with business executives and the Chinese government to protect land in southern China's Yunnan Province. The Yunnan Great Rivers Project energizes the seasoned executive more than any other topic.

"Yunnan is a very spectacular part of the world," he observed, assuming the authoritative air of a true naturalist. "There are four great rivers in China—the Yangtze, Salween, Irrawaddy, and Mekong—within fifty miles of each other. The land goes from subtropical rain forest to peaks over 20,000 feet. Tiger Leaping Gorge is 10,000 vertical feet. It's a spectacular area and there was a job to be done and there wasn't the same environmental focus, so I thought that being on the ground floor putting together this council to help focus The Nature Conservancy's efforts in China was a chance to do something that made a difference."

In addition to his efforts at sites around the world, Hank tapped his management background to help refine the corporate governance structure at The Nature Conservancy because he has always recognized the value of ethics and accountability, whether that accountability be to a young donor who makes a gift of one hundred hard-earned dollars to help protect a local watershed or to the board of directors of a *Fortune* 100 client, many of which Goldman Sachs has served during its long history.

Since the firm's founding in 1869, it has never merged or been acquired, becoming the only major firm on Wall Street to have successfully navigated such an independent course. And "Goldman" remained successful by smartly carving its own market niche as a top-quality investment bank, securities firm, and asset manager. Among its competitors are CitiGroup and JP Morgan Chase, financial behemoths offering every possible service to clients, continually posing a threat to the smaller Goldman Sachs, although calling a $30-billion enterprise "small" hardly seems accurate. But I think Hank Paulson liked that perception; it gave him an underdog mentality and played to his fiercely competitive nature. His intense eyes and steely features, combined with his strong six-foot-plus frame, are intimidating, but to those whom he leads, they reflect confidence and focus.

Leadership, as he sees it, should come from the top of an organization, but it should not come from a single person. "So much of leadership is the selection of the people you have around you, people you put in key jobs," he said. "That's among the most important decisions you make—very, very important. And CEOs get too much credit and too much blame. Goldman Sachs succeeds because we have very good people here, and so a lot of leadership is about, as I said, having the right people in the right seats, a strong sense of direction from the top, a culture which encourages teamwork and doing the right thing, having people really believe that the role you play in the world is a noble one and that you're a force for good. I'd say that the tone gets set at the top, at least at Goldman Sachs, and I think at the best-run companies, it's a team effort."

Wall Street is tough, but Hank led Goldman Sachs over the market's crests and through its troughs. He sat confidently in his office when we met as he'd just seen the firm through another strong year. In the terminology of the industry, gross revenues were up 26 percent to $29.8 billion (a $6.2-billion increase), while net earnings grew by 52 percent and the firm closed the year with $383 billion in assets under management.

As we continued to talk about the achievements with which he has been associated, he was careful to remind me of a very true point: "They've all been working with other people. That's the other thing Scouting teaches: There are no such things as individual successes."

He made sure he maintained effective teams at Goldman Sachs and at The Nature Conservancy by emphasizing ethics. As a business advisor, Goldman Sachs could not survive without its integrity, and their CEO understood that the questionable acts of a few could jeopardize the entire firm. When we first met, he had just launched the Chairman's Forum program, which took him around the world to meet with many of the firm's global leaders. Instead of sending a letter and a slide presentation to Goldman Sachs offices via e-mail, Paulson decided to meet the people of his firm face to face to *show* them his commitment to ethics and to talk with them personally about the choices they could face down the road.

He explained, "I just thought it was important to develop a course where I got to meet with our leaders, our managing directors, and talk about ethics, not about compliance and not about rules, but about doing the right things and about doing the right things in a complex world where there are not always the blacks and whites we knew in our Boy Scout days; there are various shades of gray."

The extraordinarily complex rules of the financial world have created many shades of gray, but Hank hoped that by concentrating on the *spirit* of the laws, the people of Goldman Sachs would make the right choices. His intense eyes met mine, and he said, "The longer I'm around in this world, the longer I look to principles and values as opposed to rules and laws. People always find their ways around rules and laws."

As he looks back on the Scout Oath and Law, he recognizes the first stirring of that philosophy in him, although he wasn't particularly aware of it at the time. In those creeds, he saw broad values, not a litany of rules. The principles of the Oath and Law became real as Troop 21 internalized them, night by night. "Some organizations will print their values and put them on the wall and have them in their annual report, but people don't really know them," he observed. "I remember standing up there before meetings, and, boy, you recited them!"

Today, Hank occasionally writes letters to young men who earn Eagle, typically sons of friends and family members who know he is an Eagle Scout. To these young men, he points out that achieving Eagle generally runs counter to popular culture. He commented, "If you wanted to just go along with the crowd, you wouldn't say, 'I want to be an Eagle Scout.' " In that, he sees the value of the rank. It tests a young man's perseverance that much more: Can he stick to a goal when currents of peer pressure run against him? Hank hopes that, perhaps later in life, that Eagle can stand against pressure to bend rules to close a deal or to inflate numbers to meet quarterly goals. Hopefully, that young man will have learned the value of working honestly and diligently toward a good end.

"We come from a short-term world," Hank observed. "People looking for instant gratification, wanting to judge success too quickly on everything there is. If it's a war in Iraq, on CNN every minute the commentator is telling you how it's going. If you're a corporation, it's corporate earnings on a quarterly basis. And yet the only things that are worth doing are things that take time and take effort. Happiness only comes from success where you need to work over a period of time." The process of reaching Eagle and *being* an Eagle, earning a starting slot on the football team, or attaining a seat in a corporate boardroom resembles a marathon more than a sprint.

"The world is filled with Eagle Scouts who are failures in addition to Eagle Scouts who are successes," this Illinois Scout mused. "The way you should look at this is to say, 'You can't rest on your laurels.' I get letters from Eagles who say, 'Paulson, would you look at hiring me at Goldman Sachs?' And their having that Eagle rank is a positive thing. Then I look and see if they've done anything *since* becoming an Eagle Scout. So the question is: 'Will you take the lessons you learned and go on and apply them in other areas?' "

Through his work at The Nature Conservancy and at Goldman Sachs, Hank Paulson continued proving he *is* an Eagle Scout. Not long after we met, he accepted the challenge of bringing those values to yet another arena. Like so many other Eagles, Hank answered the call of public service and accepted the presidential cabinet position of secretary of the treasury in 2006. It is rare to find someone so successful in vocation and avocation, but Hank is as exceptional as he is hard-working. He embraces his role as a steward of this world. He understands his obligation to care for natural lands while he is here so that future generations can enjoy and appreciate the Earth's forests, rivers, and oceans. He also understood his responsibility to the families who ultimately relied on his decisions as an executive, and now as treasury secretary, for their livelihood and their future. So whether he meets with government and business leaders to discuss making good choices or spends his evenings working to protect forests on other continents, he leads by example, remembering we all have obligations that transcend the financial balance sheets by which we too often judge success.

Along this journey, I found that nearly every Eagle I met still cherished the outdoors. We all talked fondly of our treks into the wilderness. We remembered being aware of threats to our natural lands and recalled our leaders reminding us to either "leave no trace" or "leave the woods better than we found them."

With various Eagles, I relived those days. Together we stomped through the Everglades in Florida, climbed the Bitterroot Range in Montana, camped beside the Jackson River in Virginia, and reflected on a common love of Nature in the Green Mountains of Vermont. When it came to the outdoors, I realized that many of us forever remained Boy Scouts, Hank Paulson included.

But after my meeting with Hank ended, I was surprised to find my thoughts drifting away from conservation. As my train left New York's Penn Station bound for Boston, I thought about how, like so many other Eagle Scouts, the CEO of Goldman Sachs and chairman of The Nature Conservancy was busy trying to re-create his Scout troop.

In my travels, I discovered that Eagles continually attempt to create environments shaped by the ideals they learned in Scouting. Ross Perot helped establish the honor code at the U.S. Naval Academy, and when I visited the academy's Annapolis, Maryland, campus I found Eagle Scout Colin Sullivan perpetuating the tradition by chairing the Honor Council. I also learned that a community of honor attracted Sandy Hooper and Kevin Batteh to Virginia's Washington and Lee University, an institution whose honor system dates to the 1870s. Both Eagles spent a year presiding over the group responsible for the system, and when we all served on the committee together, Eagle Scouts composed nearly one quarter of the committee's membership.

"Eagle Scouts have a genuine sense of duty," Sandy, a native of Brownsville, Tennessee, explained. "Whether that duty is to our school, our community, our job, or our family, the sense of commitment to others and to yourself that you take away from Scouting makes up a significant part of your personality. That character trait allows an Eagle Scout to gravitate to academic institutions with honor systems, where duty is paramount. And by achieving the status of Eagle Scout, they have already demonstrated that they believe in and practice concepts like honor, integrity, and trustworthiness. An Eagle Scout is likely to embrace an honor system as if it were his *own* system."

Kevin Batteh, who spent as much time kayaking the nearby Maury River as he did studying, reached back to Wilderness Survival merit badge to explain his interest in bringing Scouting's principles to his university. "For Wilderness Survival, I learned a set of skills and then applied them," he explained of his ordeal at Camp Daniel Boone. "For my test, I was alone in the woods. If I couldn't light my fire, I wouldn't eat. There wasn't a shelter from the rain unless I made one myself. But I had worked hard and learned those survival skills, and that paid off. I felt the same about my experience at Washington and Lee.

"Every grade we received was based strictly on how much work we put into our classes: no cheating, no outside help. Like my Wilderness Survival merit badge, when I earned my degrees at W&L, I knew I didn't just have the diplomas; I also had the skills that came with having put in the hard work to earn them. That sort of situation builds self-reliance and trust. I think Scouting, like living in a community with an honor system, necessitates hard work. If you've done the work honestly, you can survive. That's a model for excellence in school, business, and pretty much anything life throws at you. I've always gravitated to that type of environment, and I wanted to see it continue. Getting involved was doing my small part."

Beyond college campuses, I found Eagles in all arenas who, in ways large and small, had tried to re-create the atmosphere of trust and integrity they enjoyed within their Scout troop. I discovered that Mike Deimler, a Morehead Scholar at the University of North Carolina and leader of The Boston Consulting Group's venerated corporate strategy practice, places elements of the Scout Oath in every sales presentation he delivers. He believes talking about values sets him apart and gains his clients' trust. As proof, he consistently ranks among the international firm's leaders in sales.

I also found elements of Scouting in hospitals, governments, schools, and businesses from Costa Mesa, California, to New York, New York, where I witnessed Hank Paulson advocating for Nature and busily instilling the principles of the Scout Oath in the leaders of Goldman Sachs.

Along my path I did encounter several skeptics, people who wondered if programs such as Hank's Chairman's Forum were pointless. I had thought of those naysayers as I rode down New York City's Avenue of the Americas toward the Goldman Sachs office. I passed the former headquarters of Arthur Andersen LLP and Anderson Worldwide and remembered my trips to that building when I served as a staffer for one of the renowned firm's global executives. We came there in 2001 to develop and later unveil the firm's new strategy. It was a plan based on the principles of integrity and service for which the venerable firm was known around the world.

Several months after we released the new strategic plan, Andersen had found itself hopelessly embroiled in the Enron scandal. Questions surfaced about the accounting practices used by Andersen employees working with the Houston-based energy giant. A highly publicized court case ensued, and while the Supreme Court eventually ruled for Arthur Andersen, the damage was irreparable. No matter Andersen's long-standing reputation or its defense, just the perception of an ethical breach by a few doomed the entire firm. Within less than a year, an eighty-nine-year-old company disappeared, retirements evaporated, thousands of families were affected, and 85,000 people had to find new jobs. Hank Paulson is right: Ethics matter.

EDUCATION

Scouting has introduced millions of young men to teaching. Many taught merit badge courses during summer camp sessions; others simply helped younger Scouts learn to survive a backpacking expedition. At Scout meetings and on camping trips, learning is incessant, and, more often than not, Scouts themselves become the teachers.

"One of the most valuable things I got out of Scouting was my first exposure to teaching," reflected Larry Bacow of Pontiac, Michigan's Troop 7. The future president of Boston's Tufts University spent a week at Scout camp in Michigan before being recruited to teach merit badge courses for the remainder of the summer. "They needed someone to teach Cooking merit badge, and I didn't know a single thing about cooking other than I *had* Cooking merit badge! But it became an opportunity for me to teach for the first time, and I found I really enjoyed it." That experience shaped his career, and he spent many years as a professor at the Massachusetts Institute of Technology before coming to Tufts as president.

Larry mentioned something else of interest. "We've got three university presidents who are Eagles," he said. "John Silber at Boston University, Richard Freeland at Northeastern, and myself. Three of the six major universities in the Boston area were at one time headed by Eagle Scouts simultaneously." Likewise, the business school deans at both Harvard and MIT were Eagles. Distinguished professors in Boston who share the Eagle rank include a former governor, a Nobel Laureate, and a recipient of the Pulitzer Prize.

In total, thirty-six colleges and universities call Boston, Massachusetts, home, among them some of the most respected names in education. A scholarly air permeates the entire city, rising from the graceful reading rooms of the public library, the coffeehouses surrounding Harvard Square in Cambridge, tree-shaded campuses, and the 135,000 students who give a true and perpetually renewed vibrancy to the old New England city. Boston has some of the most prestigious colleges in the United States and thousands of young minds come to this historic city hoping to find answers, enrichment, and instruction. They find these in their teachers, and those in Boston are among the finest anywhere. Here, in what is perhaps the world's leading academic city, I found Eagles leading students and institutions. As in the U.S. Congress and in hurricane-stricken Mississippi, their presence was greater than their numbers should warrant, but their impact was what I had grown to expect.

A COMMUNITY OF TEACHERS

MICHAEL DUKAKIS, TROOP 7, CHESTNUT HILL, MASSACHUSETTS—
EAGLE SCOUT, 1949

KIM CLARK, TROOP 2023, SPOKANE, WASHINGTON—EAGLE SCOUT, 1964

EDWARD BENZ, TROOP 52, BETHLEHEM, PENNSYLVANIA—EAGLE SCOUT, 1960

"Tamara, what do you think?"

The dark-haired Northeastern University senior gave her answer, but it was not the precise response her public policy professor wanted.

"Jason, what about you?" A more satisfying response came from beneath Jason's dark blue baseball cap, and Professor Dukakis forged ahead to his lecture's next point. He spoke with the authority of a man who has experienced many times over the issues his students only face in books, articles, and in the memories of their professor. But Michael Dukakis stood before these thirty-five students to teach, not pontificate or relive moments from his thirty years as one of Massachusetts's leading politicians. In a distinctly Bostonian voice that truly surprised me with its strength and emotion, he again and again pressed his students to think beyond simple interpretations of the day's reading assignment.

"What's the main point, Jeff? Rachel, how would you handle the situation? Greg, what about you? How will this approach play in the media, Bill?" By the end of the hour-long class, this three-term governor of Massachusetts had solicited the opinions of almost every student in the class, by name.

"He really knows us," Tamara told me after class. "We can always go by to talk or we can e-mail him anytime, and when we give him our papers, we'll get back pages and pages of comments. He's a great teacher. His classes are always the hardest to get." This was Tamara's first course with Professor

Dukakis, and she'd registered for class over the telephone while in an airport to make sure she reserved a sought-after spot in Politics 307.

The discussion in Politics 307 on this particular day involved the reengineering of the New York City Police Department in the early 1990s, and on the chalkboard behind him, Dukakis listed seven key issues that historically plagued the NYPD. The last issue was *integrity*, a point he emphasized by clicking the chalk to the board loudly and drawing a circle around the term.

Michael Dukakis, professor of political science and public policy, Northeastern University and UCLA SAM OGDEN

Concocting an example based on his long career in Boston, he posed a question to the class. "Now, what do you do if you're Charlie Berry patrolling in a heavily Italian North End district when a restaurant owner invites you in for a plate of spaghetti," he asked. "Do you say, 'No, this is a violation of my status?' Or is it appropriate to do that because it's part of your job and makes you a much more effective community police officer? Well, you may decide that accepting the meal is okay, but that means that your organization and whoever your police commanders are have to help you define that in a way that is consistent with high standards of integrity and doesn't begin slipping into the kind of problems they had in the Thirtieth Precinct in New York.

"My view has always been to set high standards for yourself and people who work for you and make sure they're particularly reminded of those standards on a regular basis—this notion of in-service integrity and training which I think is very important. If you do that, you're not going to have problems." In his twelve years as governor, he always outlined his standards, and only two people in his administration ever crossed the line. His wife, Kitty, warned him about one. "Moral of *that* story is listen to First Ladies," he added.

As class ended with the rustle of papers being shuffled and backpacks being zipped shut, Professor Dukakis raised his voice over the din and reminded the rapidly departing students, "I'll be around every day this week people, so come at me. Drop by, e-mail, call, whatever, and I'll take a look at your papers. Remember they're due next week." It was a scene I'd seen many times: students leaving hurriedly with the professor trying to put in one last word. Leaning against the table at the front of the room in his plaid shirt and corduroy pants, he differed little in appearance from many professors I'd had in college. He knew his students, kept his door open for them, and was willing to help if they were willing to ask.

In teaching, Mike Dukakis found an extension of a long political career and an even longer interest in service. That interest began to form in Brookline, Massachusetts, when Dukakis was a Scout in Troop 7. "Today, we have community service requirements for high school students and this kind of stuff," he reflected, "but there was nothing like that at the time. [Scouting] was really one of the few organizations where you not only participated in an organized structured way, but you were expected to do community service."

After attending Swarthmore College and Harvard Law School, he entered public service in the early 1960s as a town meeting member. By 1975, he was governor of Massachusetts. Governor Dukakis neglected to heed one of Ross Perot's favorite maxims however: "A man is never more on trial than in the moment of excessive good fortune." He lost his bid for reelection in 1978. He remembered, "I won, and then I got beat four years later for reelection and I was 40 points ahead with five weeks to go in the polls. That was the year the Red Sox were fourteen games ahead at the All-Star break and [New York Yankee] Bucky Dent hit the famous home run that beat 'em in the playoffs. Both Dukakis and the Red Sox went down the tubes together for the same reason: much too much overconfidence in the ranks."

Humbled, he took stock of his career and realized, "I was a lousy listener and bad coalition builder. I knew what I wanted to do and 'Bingo! Here it is, and you guys pass it.' So when I came back [as governor again in 1982], I spent a lot more time bringing people into the process, listening, trying to constructively involve my legislature in what I was doing from the beginning, and there wasn't any question that I was a much better governor and much better public servant as a result of it."

In 1986, the National Governors Association named Dukakis America's Most Effective Governor for orchestrating the Massachusetts Miracle, a dramatic turnaround of the state's formerly struggling economy that included lowering the unemployment rate from 11 percent to 4 percent. His success led to his nomination as the Democratic Party's candidate for president of the United States in 1988. After the convention, he faced a campaign that surprised many—himself in particular—with its bitterness. In the '88 campaign there was an unusually large number of attack ads, and, looking back, Dukakis regretted not responding more aggressively.

"I think on the one hand, you don't want somebody to beat you with an attack campaign," he said. "But on the other hand, you also have to live with yourself. Can you do both? Yeah, I think you can do both. I could have done a much better job dealing with those attacks while remaining true to my basic principles and what is I hope a reasonably ethical approach to politics and public life." At the time, he had hoped that not responding in kind would allow him to remain on the moral high ground, but that course failed as a strategy. Dukakis and his running mate, Lloyd Bentsen, also an Eagle Scout, earned 46 percent of the popular vote and lost to Vice-President George H. W. Bush. After the election, Dukakis returned to Massachusetts to complete his term as governor, but the same desires still drove him.

As we sat across from each other in his warm, brick-walled office, he mused, "What is it about those of us who go into public life that drives us? I think it's fundamentally this sense that there are gaps between our expressed values and reality. The job of *all* of us, in whatever way we chose to do it, is to try to close and eliminate those gaps so we can create a society in which every single human being has the opportunity to be the best that they can be. With that goal in mind, Dukakis joined the faculty at Northeastern University with a very specific purpose: to continue in public service by inspiring the next generation of public servants.

"What can I do for these kids?" he asked about his political science students. "Encourage them and inspire them and try to at least begin to help them develop the kind of skills you need to be effective in what is a difficult enterprise, getting things done in a very contentious public sector where you got a zillion people out there, none of whom you control but all of whom want to be part of what you're doing. And then opening up doors for them, particularly through co-op so they can get the kind of experience to give them a real sense of what happens in the public sector, which invariably does hearten them, because what they discover is that it's nothing like what they're watching on television. You really have very good people working hard who care a lot about what they're doing.

"I've been at it for thirteen years and love what I'm doing," the still-energetic political veteran concluded. "One of my missions in life these days is to encourage young people to go into public service, and where can you do that better than teaching?"

A short subway ride from Northeastern's campus is Harvard Business School, which claims as its graduates some of the world's finest leaders and most influential figures, among them such Eagles as Michael Bloomberg, Hank Paulson, William Westmoreland, and Harvard Rector and former University of North Carolina President C. D. Spangler.

HBS has always aimed to educate leaders, but when Kim Clark assumed the helm in 1995, he made sure the school educated *principled* leaders, re-creating, like so many others, the values-based environment he enjoyed as a Scout. In a sense, the faculty and he distilled the Scout Oath and Law into three guiding virtues: integrity, personal accountability, and respect for other people. These three principles, this former Scoutmaster explained during his final year as dean, are essential to leadership and learning. "Those core values are small in number, but we think really fundamental and universal, so not culturally bound in any way, just fundamental values." With students from seventy different countries, the school needed explicit, unifying values. It's not much different than the philosophy behind Scouting, particularly on the international level, he noted.

"We have a strong commitment to these three core values because they're essential to effective leadership," Clark began, before dissecting his first principle. "Integrity includes being honest and telling the truth," he observed, "but it includes more than that. Integrity is a quality of the character of the individual. It's about the match between what individuals espouse or say and what they do. . . . My own sense is that an essential, critical function of a leader is to create confidence and trust in other people. That's very difficult, I believe, for a leader to do who does not walk the talk, who does not live by the values or the principles that leader espouses. People won't trust that individual if that individual doesn't really live and follow through on what they believe.

Moving to personal accountability, Clark observed, "My sense is that the very nature of the role requires leaders to take on responsibility. To be someone who is willing to assume all that goes with that responsibility. So leaders can't be effective, I believe, if their response is 'Oh, that's not my job.' Or 'Well I didn't do that. I'm not responsible for that.' Leaders are responsible. They're responsible for what happens, and they need therefore to have a sense of personal value that says, 'I'm willing to take personal responsibility.' "

Arriving at the third principle, he explained, "Respect for other people is your ability to listen, teach, motivate. If you don't respect other people, respect the dignity of other people, you are going to treat people in ways that will undercut your ability to enlist them in the enterprise, so I think those three things are essential to leadership.

Former Scoutmaster and Harvard Business School Dean Kim B. Clark, president of Brigham Young University-Idaho
BYU-IDAHO PHOTOGRAPH BY MICHAEL LEWIS

"Today," he said, moving to a larger point, "I think there's been an erosion of standards in our society and a tendency to downgrade and reduce in significance and visibility the values we talked about. We felt it was important to reaffirm our commitment to those standards and we've done that."

As dean, Kim Clark spent much of his time visiting the school's 65,000 alumni and managing the business of academia, not teaching as he did for seventeen years before assuming the top job. But in those seventeen previous years, he may not have found his most rewarding teaching experiences in Ivy League classrooms. He may have discovered them in Troop 66, chartered to a Cambridge ward of the Latter-Day Saints Church. Like many fathers, particularly those who hold the Eagle rank, Clark became Scoutmaster when his sons reached Scouting age. In this case, he succeeded former Scoutmasters Kent Bowen and Steve Wheelwright, both members of the HBS faculty.

During the day, Clark would spend hours lecturing to rooms full of focused Harvard students, then one evening each week, he would confront a room full of Scouts. He faced a very different scenario and had to learn a new method of teaching.

He remembered, "We tried to create situations where we could get the attention of the Scouts for concentrated periods, like twenty minutes!" He laughed. "Scouts at that age are full of beans, and they have all sorts of stuff going on, so you try to use the structure of the program to get kids in situations where they'll pay attention to something, and you try to make it really interesting. . . . I learned a lot about how to make it interesting to kids, so it wasn't like this was another school class, but there'd be something really fun and interesting going on."

Using the example of Troop 66's yearly snow-camping expedition, he said, "I learned to pick stuff that was bold, exciting, and challenging, then back out of it small chunks of learning that have a very clear purpose, so you're not just teaching them for fun; you're teaching them so they'd stay alive in a winter campout."

Then he told me about a project that will make every Scoutmaster I know terribly envious. An idea birthed by a leader in California wound its way across the country—Scoutmaster to Scoutmaster, Clark suspects—until it reached Steve Wheelwright, Clark's immediate predecessor. Thus started the troop's traditional kayak project.

For one month during the spring, Scouts and their fathers gathered on Saturday morning and built kayaks from plywood and canvas. I made the mistake of assuming these were small boats, not really fit for whitewater. Dean Clark corrected me: They were full-size boats, ten feet long, a yard wide, and watertight.

"You get to teach them how to do the gluing, how to do the assembly and get the fixtures right," he remembered of the process. "There are railings along the side that you have to screw in, so you get the kids and you teach them, and it's a lot about woodworking and a lot about gluing and assembly, then they have to paint them . . . and the kids learned a lot about different stuff: organizing, planning, executing. They learned some skills about using drills and screwdrivers, and then they had to learn how to kayak."

His conversational pace had quickened as he ceased being a dean and again became a Scoutmaster and father. With a beaming, satisfied smile he concluded, "It was a *ton* of work to do this, a *ton* of work. I mean, it took a lot of work, and you got the dads involved, Scouts doing stuff, then we took them up on the Saco River in Maine."

Although their methods differed, Scoutmaster Clark and Professor Clark taught the same lesson. Reflecting back on Troop 66's kayaks, Clark observed, "I think they learned a lot about their potential and their possibilities. And I *hope* they learned something about their limitations and how you need each other to make it work. You can't do everything all by yourself."

In Troop 52 of Bethlehem, Pennsylvania, Edward Benz learned similar lessons. In particular, he discovered his potential and how to realize it. He admitted he had little confidence as a boy, although nobody would guess the accomplished president of Harvard's renowned Dana-Farber Cancer Institute ever lacked self-assurance. "I was very tiny growing up," explained Doctor Benz. "I'm not exactly a giant right now. I was the smallest kid in my class and I was pretty good athletically, but because I was so small it was always a struggle." In Scouts, he discovered an environment in which he could achieve goals and become a leader.

"When I look back on my time in Scouts, that was the first place I could convince myself I could do things," he observed. "It was the first place where I ever held any leadership responsibility. I got to be a patrol leader, a senior patrol leader, a Junior Assistant Scoutmaster. I went into Scouting with no self-confidence and came out with some. And 'some' was a big deal. I would not have made it through my early years in high school if I couldn't have looked at experiences such as Scouting as evidence that I could succeed at something."

Edward J. Benz, Jr., M.D., set his sights on medicine early. Like many sons and daughters of doctors, he followed the family tradition established by his father and grandfather. In high school, he was an admittedly mediocre student, more interested in sports than academics. Then, he heard about new advances in biology regarding DNA. "The first thing that really turned me on was hearing about this thing that came to be called molecular biology, now called genomics in its third generation," he said. "That clinched it for me. I wanted to go to medical school, and I wanted to use [genomics] to study human disease problems, which people didn't think you could do in those days; now we know you can."

After finishing medical school at Harvard, this Eagle Scout spent his first postgraduate year in the laboratory, arduously attempting to prove his theory that genes and molecular biology could be used to attack diseases. He eventually made a breakthrough discovery that would help to change medical thought, but it didn't come quickly or easily.

"Laboratory research is like carrying your sled up the hill fifty times for one ride down," he joked. "The first year I devoted myself to research, fifty-two weeks. At the end of the forty-ninth week, I had nothing to show for it except one failed experiment after another. There was one key experiment in that progression, and I probably did it two hundred times before I got it to work. Then everything fell in place, and I got it all done in three weeks. So what launched my career in a sense was three weeks' work. But it was built on forty-nine weeks of frustration."

His weeks of frustration ended as he demonstrated the potential for genomics: He used gene DNA analysis to treat beta-thalassemia, a human blood-cell disease. He continued working to apply his research to cancer treatments while also heading the departments of medicine at the University of Pittsburgh and, later, Johns Hopkins University. In 2000, Benz joined the faculty at Harvard Medical School and assumed the presidency of the Dana-Farber Cancer Institute, which is ranked among the world's top cancer treatment and research centers.

"When I was growing up," he remembered, "[cancer] was the most dreaded word you could hear . . . so, curing cancer was something really great you could do. My wife likes to say that when we were dating, I'd say the two things I wanted to do were marry her and cure cancer." He ventured into hematology and helped gather the knowledge of genomics that would eventually lead to new cancer treatments. During all those years, however, he always hoped to return to the field of oncology and could not pass up the opportunity to work at Dana-Farber.

Learning in Boston is not restricted to students in college or graduate school classrooms. Dr. Benz now oversees an organization in which medical students, accomplished researchers, and veteran doctors learn from one another and from their patients as they work toward the institute's goal: reducing the burden of cancer on society. Encouraging interaction among his talented faculty has been among Dr. Benz's primary goals as president.

"Scientific discoveries proceed at an incredible pace," he explained, "but the translation of those discoveries into better clinical practices and better drugs and better diagnostic approaches occurs at a glacial pace. What has been missing is that process of connection and translation and supporting people so that they have the time to interact with each other. You need to have an environment where those people can interact." An observation one doctor makes in a patient might help a lab scientist understand a key aspect of a disease's behavior, and likewise, a breakthrough in the laboratory may lead a

Edward Benz, M.D., president of Dana-Farber Cancer Institute
COURTESY OF EDWARD BENZ

scientist and doctor to work together to test the discovery in humans, perhaps leading to a new drug or new treatment. Dr. Benz aims to ensure that Dana-Farber faculty have time to talk. Simple dialogue—this is how learning is perpetuated.

Eagle Scout John Elrod, who presented me with my diploma at Washington and Lee, boiled the essence of a university down to just that—personal interaction—when he said, "More and more, I've come to think of the university simply as a place where people have interesting conversations."

To sustain the dialogue, research, and patient care that are part of Dana-Farber, Dr. Benz must engage the talented staff and focus them on a single goal. The lessons he learned about leadership as a patrol leader in Bethlehem came back to him as he was confronted by the task of leading Dana-Farber.

"We are leading a group of very independent-minded people, whose

creativity and independence is a positive value," he noted. "You're not leading a company that's making products and pleasing shareholders. You're
leading a group of people who are in a sense—although people don't often
think of scientists in this way—in the creative arts industry. So you have to
think of yourself more as a conductor of a symphony or coach of an all-star
team than as a leader of a corporation. I think many people who have academic leadership jobs like mine who succeed, either implicitly or explicitly
understand that their job is much more steerage, persuasion, the power of
finding alignments, and much less trying to tell people, 'Here's the grand
vision, here's the grand strategy, here's the corporate policy; you fit into
them.' "

Boston nurtures an expansive community of learning and for that reason attracts scholars and teachers from around the world who bring with them lifelong passions for teaching others, advancing knowledge, and helping
younger generations lead a better life. Amidst this atmosphere, the values of
Scouting are palpable, seen in many but most of all in the Eagle Scouts who
lead so many of the city's foremost institutions. As Dr. Benz and I sat in his
Brookline Street office, we discussed the cadre of Eagles in Boston's higher-
education community. I mentioned his contemporaries who were Eagles.
The statistics momentarily surprised him. Then he mused, "But is that just
in Boston?"

To answer his question, it's not. I found Eagles disproportionately represented in leadership posts across the country. In explanation, Dr. Benz
concluded, "It's not easy to be an Eagle Scout. This may be one of the early
markers of people who are able to set goals and achieve them. So whether
that reflects talent, determination, or work ethic, or values, there is perseverance built in. And a quality that matters as much as anything in all those
positions is perseverance.

"You don't get to these things just by mounting one success after another. Every one of those people, including myself, at points in time either
failed or thought they were going to fail, or they got a comeuppance that could
have stopped them in their tracks or caused them to go do something else because it was easier.

"Plus you have the other things we talked about framing that," he said, referring to our afternoon's discussion of the values he derived from his years with Troop 52. "A focus on service and getting beyond yourself, the value of being honest, the value of delivering, the value of being collegial. Those are all built in implicitly or explicitly into what you're supposed to be if you're a Scout. Those who got to be Eagles presumably could actually walk the walk." And later in life, these ideals guided the steps of Boston's Eagle Scouts as they became leaders, servants, and, perhaps most importantly, teachers.

When I returned to Northeastern University's campus for my last visit to this community of Eagles, the spring sun had melted the snow through which Professor Dukakis and I had trudged to Politics 307 months earlier. Sandals and T-shirts had replaced the parkas and boots of winter, and the campus hummed with energy as Northeastern's 23,000 students swarmed the quadrangles and parks of the urban campus enjoying their first taste of spring. Richard Freeland, the university's president for nearly a decade, surveyed the scene from a sunny conference room where we sat together at one end of a long table.

I asked President Freeland, who was approaching the last year of his tenure, the same question I'd put to Dr. Benz: Why do Eagle Scouts fill the ranks of Boston's academic leaders? "I would say it doesn't surprise me because I would expect among high-achieving individuals to find a disproportionate representation of Eagle Scouts, at least on the male side of the equation," he responded. "Further, a thing that attracts people to university leadership and university work is that it's a values-driven organization. Fundamentally, this is an organization that is about trying to make lives better and make the world better. Scouting is a values-driven organization and inspires people for whom that concept resonates."

As the subway carried me away from Northeastern University one last time, I considered Dr. Freeland's comments and began to digest what I'd learned in Boston. I returned to something a professor told me when I visited Harvard Business School. He spoke of Kim Clark, now president of Brigham Young University-Idaho, commenting, "He always talks about integrity, honesty, and doing your duty. He behaves that way, in every way, and that's how he sets the standard for the students and faculty: he reminds them."

I realized those observations could apply far beyond Kim Clark. From my time in Boston, I learned that the Eagles leading the city's foremost institutions share more than a love of teaching and discovery. They share a lifestyle that in itself teaches others about principles. Teachers and leaders by example, they hope that in them, a younger generation will find lessons, hope, and inspiration.

❧

COACHES

I love this game," Mark Madsen mused as he looked around the now-empty arena where his Minnesota Timberwolves had lost the evening's game at the buzzer, 101–99. "The game of basketball has been great to me; the friendships I've made, the things I've learned and experienced, the places I've seen. I've been lucky."

The six-foot-nine forward's trademark intensity had subsided by the time we met courtside, but his passion for basketball remained unmistakable. Granted, the game has bestowed its blessings upon him. As an All-American, he led Stanford to the NCAA Final Four. Then the Los Angeles Lakers selected him in the first round of the NBA draft. As a Laker, he won two World Championship rings, playing alongside Shaquille O'Neal and Kobe Bryant. But despite his success, the difficult culture of the NBA, and the endless travel the sport demands, this thirty-year-old remains comfortably in his own skin. Part of that grounding stems from his years in Scouting, a rite of passage in the Madsen household whose four oldest brothers reached Eagle and whose youngest was well on his way.

"I took two lessons from Scouting," Mark explained. "First, I learned how to make good decisions. Second, I learned what to do when you make *bad* decisions. And I've certainly experienced both sides! Scouting gave me a framework that helped me make the good choices and it helped me be a man and deal with the bad ones."

"I learned those lessons from my Scout leaders," the Danville, California, native continued as he squeezed his sizable frame into an arena seat. "And also from my coaches. My Scout leaders and basketball coaches have one commonality: They were mentors. They helped me learn and grow. I'd like to turn around and help other young people in Scouting and in basketball grow as individuals. That's why we're all here: to help other people grow. I really want to give back to the game. One way to do that is to make it fun for young people and help kids take something positive from their experience on the court." To accomplish this, he became Coach Madsen.

The NBA season can run 230 days and sometimes longer. Just as this athlete used his high school summers to advance toward Eagle, he uses the brief off-time provided by his present summers to coach the game he loves. He started the Mark Madsen Minnesota Timberwolves Basketball Camp, where he helps seven- to fourteen-year-old players learn the game and its attendant lessons about character. By several accounts, the affable "Mad Dog" knew almost every camper by name. Like so many other Eagles, Mark had become a mentor.

Few adults influence the development of young people more than coaches. Like Scout leaders, coaches devote countless evenings, weekends, and often entire weeks at camp to the boys and girls on their teams. Rarely is the monetary reward substantial. Often, coaches receive no money at all. Their rewards seem far more personal, however, and often far greater than any paycheck. As sports become a mainstay of American youth, coaching becomes ever more important. More young people need to find role models and guidance on the sidelines. Many find those things in Eagle Scouts.

Eagles have coached championship hockey teams, struggling cross-country runners, and young soccer players who are just beginning to realize what they might one day achieve. Uniformly, these coaches would never list their highest goal as winning a championship. Instead, they would likely say they give their time to young athletes to help them grow into better people.

CHAN GAILEY

TROOP 21, AMERICUS, GEORGIA

EAGLE SCOUT, 1967

As he did every Saturday during the fall, Chan Gailey stood in a shadowy tunnel leading to the light and noise of a college football stadium. This particular Saturday he could be found in a tunnel at the University of Virginia in Charlottesville. In front of him were thirty-four young men, wearing white jerseys and gold helmets, all fidgeting with nervous energy. Beyond them lay the dim corridor's exit, a sunlit field, and 60,000 people who wished them only the worst.

There in the safety of the tunnel, they listened to spectators erupt as the Virginia Cavaliers poured onto the football field accompanied by the pomp of college football: an announcer's booming voice, cannon fire, and cheerleaders sprinting across the field carrying huge banners embroidered with great orange V's that matched the predominating color of the Virginia fans packed into Scott Stadium.

Then the Georgia Tech Yellow Jackets broke from their tunnel into the fall sunlight. Without losing any fervor, the cheers of the Virginia fans became a cascade of boos that washed over the Tech head coach and his players, who were moving toward the visitor's bench where I stood. The players congregated on the sidelines, yelling encouragement to each other over the crowd's roar. Then their coach, escorted by two Georgia State Troopers, jogged heavily to the fifty-yard line, where he donned his headset for kickoff. There, Head Coach Chan Gailey went to work, closely watched by an entire stadium, tens of thousands of television viewers, and armchair quarterbacks across the Southeast.

At high noon, emotions peaked, and the roller-coaster ride began with the opening kick. I had seen many football games from the stands and been part of the highs and lows of the fans, but I had never experienced a game from the sidelines. I had never felt the mass emotion and momentum swings that occur among the players on the field. From the opening kick, I was washed back and forth on the sidelines by waves of emotion, which sometimes swelled the entire bench to cheers and sometimes made players turn dejectedly from the game and shuffle slowly to the water cooler, where they hoped to forget about the most recent play. I quickly discovered that Gailey's job is not so much about football as it is about leadership.

Chan Gailey, head football coach, Georgia Tech
GEORGIA TECH/COLLEGIATE IMAGES

He spends each year preparing several dozen eighteen- to twenty-two-year-olds to focus on a single goal for over three hours. How a coach can motivate a young defense to play hard after a morale-crushing setback, I don't know, but I began wondering after Tech fumbled early in the game.

I thought back to an earlier conversation I'd had with Coach Gailey about his players. He'd told me, "First of all, you don't get to this level of academia if you don't have your life in order. You can't be a thug and get to this level of academics and this level of football. When I look at our kids, they all have high character, and the great ones have great character. And they all have self-discipline, but the great ones have the most self-discipline. So I think when you look at character and self-discipline and work ethic, that's what separates the good player from the great player, and that's not just at Georgia Tech; that's at every level of whatever you do."

A player's character and self-discipline show as he watches his team suffer failures, sees his chances of winning slip away, but still puts on a helmet and tries to win the ballgame. As the game wore on and Tech's hopes slipped away, I noticed Gailey's "great players"—team captains and leaders—walking the sidelines, continuing to rally others.

It's Chan Gailey's job to build the discipline of his team throughout the season and manage their emotions during a game. I watched him stalking the sidelines, focused intently on the game but always taking a minute to give a player a congratulatory pat on his way off the field if he deserved it. Or he would lend a player a few pointed words if he deserved that instead. But his purpose in those expressions was to help the team and help the players. While wins are important to Gailey, above all he hopes to make a difference in the lives of these young athletes. Fortunately, his words and leadership have helped amass a strong lifetime record of wins and of lives influenced. *Un*fortunately, on this day, his leadership was not enough; Tech fell to Virginia.

After the game, I walked up the steps through the Tech seating section, where the first comment I heard from a Tech fan was "This is all Chan Gailey's fault. Man, I hate that guy." Such criticism represents a part of the job that Chan Gailey understands too well. Over his thirty-year career, he has felt the love and loathing of college fans at Florida, the Air Force Academy, and Troy State, where he won the Division II National Championship in 1984. He has also worked NFL sidelines, coaching for the Denver Broncos and Pittsburg Steelers prior to Jerry Jones naming him the fourth head coach of the Dallas Cowboys in 1998. Gailey came to Dallas and saw the Cowboys claim the NFC Eastern Division title in his first year. But he was gone by the end of the next season; Dallas wanted a different kind of coach. And after Gailey's first seasons with Tech, some alumni were already calling for a change. Several strong showings had silenced those critics, but the loss at UVA would draw a fresh round of attacks. Gailey knows the game and its pitfalls well. He also knows how to remain constant through it all.

———

Several months earlier, I'd pulled into a small parking lot off Bobby Dodd Way on Georgia Tech's downtown Atlanta campus. I stepped from the car directly into the shadows of three industrial cranes that stretched into the spring sky, temporarily part of the city's ever-expanding skyline. Of even more note was the mammoth concrete-and-steel structure that served as the object of the cranes' attention. Towering above me were massive rust-colored steel beams reaching up to support tier upon tier of the concrete bleachers that were fast enclosing the end zone of the nation's oldest Division I football field. High expectations built this new addition, and I had come to meet the man whose shoulders bore those expectations.

I found Coach Gailey fixed before the big-screen television on his office wall. He stood entranced, his chin resting contemplatively on a burly fist and his brow furrowed as he reviewed a scene from a past game. When he noticed me step through his doorway, the lines on his forehead lifted, the game footage apparently forgotten. He smiled, then engulfed my right hand with his. With his handshake, he half-welcomed me and half-directed me to two chairs in which he'd probably fielded hundreds of Monday-morning questions about wins and losses alike. It was there that he put some perspective on the challenges of being a head coach and managing the pressure inherent in the job. For Gailey, that pressure started to mount one minute after he was announced as the new head coach.

"Chan Gailey is the right fit for Georgia Tech at this time," Tech's athletic director had commented upon the announcement of Gailey as head coach. "Besides all the great qualities he possesses as a football coach, he's an even better human being," he added, hinting at the ethical cloud that had gathered over the former coach. They were looking to their new coach to restore the program's integrity. Beyond ethics, however, many fans really wanted wins. Could Gailey beat Florida State and Georgia? One former Georgia Tech coach wrote an article posing that question.

As we sat there in his office, I handed Coach Gailey the article that coach Bill Curry wrote shortly after Gailey was hired. Curry's headline—"Chan Gailey must stifle his NFL gremlins"—introduced a dissertation about the challenges Gailey would face coaching at Georgia Tech. Curry wondered if Gailey, with his good nature and soft touch, could be a successful coach. He wondered, "Is Chan Gailey too good to be true?" As Curry posed the issue, it was apparent that he'd done less research than I had: "Gailey was *probably* an Eagle Scout," the punchline read.

Coach Gailey held the sheet of paper in one hand and, with the other large paw, donned a pair of delicate, very uncoachlike reading glasses. He mumbled about "his gremlins" before I focused him on the Eagle Scout quote. He read it, sighed quietly, then looked up from the article slowly and said, "It goes back to believing in what you are and who you are and what you stand for. And if what you believe you stand for is right, then you don't worry about what anybody else says; you can't. You just can't because if you try to please people and worry about what they say, you'll end up swaying with popular opinion or with what some writer says or what some interviewer asks you. You can't let that happen. If you're not strong enough to handle and do what you think is right, you won't be successful."

Pointing out an unfortunate reality, he continued, "Normally what happens in this game is, when you come in with my so-called image, if you're successful, everybody says, 'See there? That's exactly how you should do it. This was right all along, and this guy is a great guy.' And if you're not successful, they'll say, 'See there? He was too soft, too easygoing. He wasn't tough enough, mean enough to get the job done.'

"If you know going in that it's going to fall one of two ways, then you better not be too puffed up when you're successful because that's not all true, and don't get too down when you're *not* successful, because that's not true either. You're normally somewhere in the middle, trying to do what's right everyday and trying to be a good influence on young people and on people in general."

He said every word slowly, with an optimistic accent at the end of most sentences. And he said it all with a soft, distinctively Georgian accent reminiscent of the football coaches I knew growing up in the South. But he was trying to impress upon me that you must stay your course. He went on to point out that no trail is ever truly your own, as a host of other actors shape each person's path through life. In the rural town of Americus, Gailey's parents, church, and Scout troop set a young football player on *his* lifelong course.

He remembered his Scoutmaster warmly. "Charlie Hogg was his name," he recalled. "Great guy, great leader, really had an impact on a lot of kids throughout the years. He was organized, made it fun, but we worked, and it was something I really enjoyed. It wasn't all fun and games, but it wasn't all 'Salute,' 'Attention,' and going through steps; it was a great balance.

"There were two aspects of Scouting in Americus," he continued. "One was summer camp at Camp Chehaw down in Albany. That was a once-a-year thing, and you had the same cabin and you knew what you went for and it was fun. And then we had a big piece of property around our Scout hut, so everything took place inside that fence. We built our lean-tos, cooked. It was almost like our own club, our own private club. So everything took place in those two spots. We didn't do a lot of canoe trips; we didn't do a lot of those kinds of things. We had our land, and we had fun on that land."

Gailey also learned how to save a life, a skill which he took with him when he left the grounds of Camp Chehaw. One day in Americus, young Gailey happened across a snakebite victim, and his first-aid skills suddenly became important. Typically, he treats it nonchalantly. "They made a big deal out of it," he remembered. "A kid got bit; he was out in the swamp. We put a tourniquet on him to stop the blood flow, and we got him back up to where the doctors could get something done to him. I didn't do a lot. He was lucky. . . . A big deal was made of it, but it didn't seem like a big deal to me. It was just what you were supposed to do."

Enumerated or not, there was another aspect to Scouting in Americus that transcended the boundaries of the camp. It concerned the set of virtues that were so precisely articulated in the Scout Oath and Law. These two statements lay out a set of personal principles, unchanged for a century, that serve as the guiding "North Star" as Senator Gordon Smith of Oregon phrased it. Repeating those words every week for three years made an impression on Chan and the Scouts in his troop, just as their leaders knew it would.

"If you get told once a week every week for three years: 'Trustworthy, Loyal, Helpful, Friendly, Courteous, Kind, Obedient, Cheerful, Thrifty, Brave, Clean, and Reverent,' it sinks in," he observed, reciting the Scout Law. "And you see Scouters living it out. You see Scoutmasters and troop leaders living it out, and you look at it and you say, 'Okay, that makes sense. That's a part of what life's all about.' It starts to take root in your soul, it starts to take root in your spirit, and obviously it backed up all the things that my Dad taught, all the things I was hearing at church and from my teachers at school. You're hit with the same things everywhere you stop, and it starts to take root in your life."

Moving from the Scout Law to the Scout Oath, Gailey struck upon the opening phrase of the Oath: On my honor. "I was taught a long time ago that honor is important," he told me. "You have to have that aspect of your life, or you don't have anything. You can do all these other things, but if you do them without honor, it doesn't really count. If you win without honor and integrity, you're not really winning. So 'On my honor' was always really important to me. I learned that, I believe that, and I stick with that today."

Can he stick with that even in the world outside little Americus? Football and professional athletics are not the most gentle of environments. To be argumentative, I suggested that Scouting values might be slightly out of place in his world.

"I think those are interesting values if you take them into the business world too," he argued right back. "You have to decide who you are, and you have to believe in who you are; you have to take pride in who you are; you have to trust who you are as a person. And who you are is what you believe, what you stand for. And to me, you can't flip a switch and act one way in one place and another way in another place. . . . You don't change with the wind; you don't waver with popular opinion. You believe in and you stand for who you are."

Relating that to how he leads his players, he observed, "I try to do what's right. I don't want them to hear me say one thing, then see me do another. That's not good. If I stand up and give them the 'Teamwork, Unity, Trustworthy, Loyal' message, and then I go break rules, I'm sending them a mixed message. You can't do that. So I try to let them hear what's right *and* see what's right. And granted, it's what *I* deem as right, and kids today all will grow up with different standards, but right is still right. And so you're hoping they see right in you."

All of this helps him guide his team off the field so he can lead them on the field during draining games like the Virginia match. But it also helps him teach his young players something about life. Teaching virtues, not just football plays, has always been among his chief aims as a coach.

"I went to college, and my first major was accounting, and I realized that wasn't for me," he said. "Then I changed to marketing, and I stayed in that about a semester and finally realized my heart was in coaching. Because my high school coach had made such an impact on my life, I thought maybe I can have an impact on lives too and do something that I'd like and enjoy and be fairly successful at the same time.

"In life when you're growing up, you learn to be a giver or a taker," he elaborated. "I think Scouting and other avenues—church, your upbringing—teach you either to give something back or you're going to take your whole life and scrap for all you can get. Or you're going to give back to society and to young people. So I think you learn during your growing-up years to be a giver or a taker, and you have to choose what side you're going to fall on.

"When I die—and we all know the story—when you get to the Pearly Gates, Saint Peter asks you, 'Why should you be in here?' Not one time do I ever think I'll be asked 'What's your win-loss record? How many rings do you have? How many championships?' I probably *will* be asked 'Did you make a difference? Did you have an impact on lives?' And I want to be able to say that was the goal. That was what I was trying to get done: to make a difference while I was here."

So now he was at Georgia Tech, back in his home state, looking to make an impact. Thirty years out of Americus, and he was living in Atlanta's well-heeled Buckhead district, was known by name and face to thousands of people across the state and nation, and had coached some of the best-known teams in the country. But he essentially remains a humble quarterback from South Georgia. I wondered if he ever stopped to think about where he was and how far he'd traveled.

"I had no idea my coaching career would lead to where it is today and that I'd be able to experience all the things I've been able to experience to this point," he answered. "So I feel very fortunate, blessed in that respect. At one time, I thought if I could just find a small high school and coach there for the rest of my life, that'd be wonderful."

"At least then your fans might have been easier to deal with than Tech's fans," I joked.

"Not in Americus," he joked right back. Football is serious business in the Southeast, which is why there is so much pressure on Coach Gailey. Georgia Tech has a rich football history, and as the new stadium addition has hinted, the fans expect to see that history resurrected and continued. Looking out from the windows of his office onto the white chalk lines of historic

Grant Field, he sees a daily reminder of his challenge. "People don't realize it," he said as if he were sharing a well-kept secret, "but this field, this stadium, is the oldest Division I stadium still on its original site.

"The great players . . . ," he said, slightly drifting off in thought. Then he observed, "John Heisman coached right where I stand, and people don't realize that. That's a great honor to me to be on the same field."

But that's also a great challenge. He lives in the shadows of giants. Just like Dallas fans expected him to match the records of Tom Landry, their fedora-wearing icon, Georgia Tech alumni also remember past seasons under Bobby Dodd and John Heisman, and alumni want their new coach to bring back those winning days. Chan Gailey would like nothing better. But Gailey is experienced enough and grounded enough to know that he will make a difference in his own way, on his own terms.

"I know I'll never be another Bobby Dodd," he said, sliding forward in his chair and focusing intently on me. "I know I'll never be another John Heisman. I know I'll never be another Tom Landry. But I'm not trying to be! I'm trying to be the best *I* can be, right now, right here. I don't worry about how history will look on me. I don't worry about perception. I just try to do what's right every day, and that, to me, is all I can do."

"Chan Gailey was *probably* an Eagle Scout," Bill Curry had written. That raised a point. Many times along this trip, people would ask about the subject of this book. When I'd tell them, one or two things—and often both—would happen. First, they would tell me about their own Scouting experiences or the experience of a friend, son, nephew, or father who had reached Eagle. I always enjoyed hearing the stories, and it amazed me how Scouting has embedded itself in the American experience. Despite the political issues of today, I found that people saw the legacy of Scouting not in news reports about the national organization, court verdicts, or policy decisions, but in the virtues of the Eagles Scouts they knew. To them, the Eagle legacy was the high school letterman and class president who just finished a service project for a local charity, the local physician who looked after their family, or the Scoutmaster who taught their children about life in the outdoors.

Second, they would suggest other Eagles with whom I should meet, and more often than not, they'd suggest a person and say, "He was *probably* an Eagle Scout." Just like Bill Curry, the people with whom I spoke recognized the type of person who becomes an Eagle. The people they suggested were always leaders, parents, and community-minded men who were doing something for others. Those named were respected as sharp, hard working, and above all honest. They were "good folks," often representing the clean-cut image that Norman Rockwell cemented in the American psyche. Naturally, their friends just assumed they were Eagle Scouts.

I was walking along a downtown street with my friend Shelley one evening when the topic of conversation turned to Scouting. She had been involved in the co-ed Explorer program when she was a teenager in California and knew several Eagles quite well. She mentioned one in particular. After telling me about helping him with his Eagle project, she added, "He's a total Eagle Scout."

"What does that mean," I asked.

She laughed and then said coyly, "Oh, there's a type."

LEADERS

Shortly after earning Eagle at age fifteen, Robert Gates traveled from his home in Wichita, Kansas, to Philmont Scout Ranch in Cimaron, New Mexico, for a National Junior Leader Training Camp. Just several years earlier, he would never have imagined attending such a program. "When I got my Eagle at fifteen," he explained, "I was not a student leader. I was not an athlete. . . . Becoming an Eagle was the first time in my life that I believed I could lead others. My Scouting experience gave me the confidence to believe I could be a leader, and, incidentally, it also gave me the tools to do so.

"I've said before, only half in jest, that the course at Philmont was the only management course I ever had, and in some ways I never felt like I needed another one! In just a couple of weeks, I learned so much about leading others. It was because they gave you experience doing it. Each one of us would take a turn at being in charge and getting things done." From Philmont, Gates went on to earn his doctorate in Russian and Soviet history and then joined the Central Intelligence Agency, where he occasionally experienced a different type of leadership.

He explained, "Over the course of my career I've seen too many line supervisors who for the first time have a little authority over some other human being and decide to show it by making their lives miserable. I think someone who had been through the Scouting experience and who is an Eagle Scout is far more likely to have *positive* leadership skills that empower people and make them *want* to do things rather than coercing them into doing them."

Gates succeeded in navigating such relationships as he helped six presidents wage the Cold War, during which time he joined the inner circles of advisors to Presidents Reagan and Bush. Eventually, he became the first entry-level employee to become director of Central Intelligence. While serving his country in the CIA, he never forgot Scouting, and he became president of the National Eagle Scout Association after leaving government service.

By the time I caught up with him in College Station, Texas, he had put the national security business firmly in his past, having recently rebuffed an offer from President George W. Bush to serve as U.S. director of National Intelligence. Instead, he planned to remain at the post he'd held since 2002: president of Texas A&M University, a 44,000-student institution that places the same emphasis on honor and integrity as Scouting does. Under their new president's direction, the Aggies launched a program that specifically recruits high school seniors who have earned the rank of Eagle Scout or have achieved the Girl Scout Gold Award. Gates knows the types of people who will succeed at A&M and uphold the high standards of the community. The university, he believes, needs leaders.

Neither the Scout Oath nor the Scout Law specifically mentions leadership. Yet that quality remains at the program's heart. By their acts and examples, the Eagles I met taught me the many ways individuals can enlist others in a common cause. Some recognized they had become leaders; others never realized the role they were playing. In a seasoned leader who clearly recognized his role and his obligation, I learned quite directly about the concept and practice of leadership, one of Scouting's great aims. Surprisingly, it boiled down simply to caring.

BINNIE PEAY

TROOP 602, RICHMOND, VIRGINIA

EAGLE SCOUT, 1954

Four flights of balconies encircled me as I gazed upward from the courtyard of the Virginia Military Institute's barracks. The walls and railings rising around me obscured the late afternoon sunshine falling on Lexington, Virginia, but there appeared to be more activity on the pathways above than in the surrounding town of 7,000. The balconies and courtyard teemed with cadets in camouflage uniforms, class uniforms, dress uniforms, and standard-issue athletic uniforms, all engaged in a perpetual, dizzying pageant as they hurried along, entered and exited their small rooms, and shimmied up and down stairs, each looking decidedly purposeful and focused. First-year cadets, of whom 11 percent were Eagle Scouts, occupied the top flight. With their eyes straight ahead and chins pulled awkwardly into their necks, they clearly occupied the lowest rung of the Institute's ladder. On the bottom floor, first-classmen (seniors) moved with a noticeably more relaxed swagger, but they still maintained the focus ingrained by three years at Virginia's historic military college. Amidst the bustle, I stood witness to a scene few outside the Institute ever see. They passed me without notice, but each cadet sharply saluted the man to my left, General J. H. Binford Peay III, Class of 1962 and the fourteenth superintendent of VMI.

Presently the general and I turned and passed through a yawning archway, leaving the barracks that have housed cadets since 1839. We emerged into the afternoon sunlight and strolled along the edge of the 165-year-old drill field. General Peay surveyed the campus looking every bit the accomplished soldier he is: his hard-won decorations pinned on his uniform's chest pocket, his dark beret fixed just right, and his easy gaze constantly ob-

219

serving his final command. His sharp green eyes, coupled with his chiseled features, closely trimmed hair, and serious bearing would mark him as a military man even if he traded his starched greens for the casual jeans and shirts preferred by many others in Lexington.

We had chosen a particularly busy time to make our tour, so General Peay's right arm rarely had a chance to rest as he returned the snappy salute of each passing cadet. To spare them—and his right arm—we eventually took a less-traveled route along which he showed me the buildings where he had studied years ago as a VMI cadet. The Institute's alumni have since invested heavily in their *alma mater*, and nearly every building along the the parade field has had major renovations. Showing me his school's progress brought a smile to his serious face, and his carefully measured tone acquired a youthful enthusiasm despite his best efforts to maintain the stoic façade of a veteran commander.

As we walked, I wondered aloud about the purpose of the campus's rigid military system, and he graciously answered a question I expect he'd heard many times before. "It's just a very special place that has high standards," he responded. "You live that life for four years; you salute the flag every morn-ing and night. You lead that structured life. The *sine qua non* of that is devel-oping leaders for the state, the nation, in peace and war."

Our conversation then drifted to George C. Marshall, a VMI alumnus and truly a leader in peace and in war. The respected five-star general who served as President Franklin Roosevelt's chief-of-staff during World War II and was the architect of the Marshall Plan for reconstructing postwar Europe re-mains the only solider to ever win the Nobel Peace Prize. And that, General Peay observed, demonstrates the real purpose of a military education. Peay aspires to teach his cadets far more than structure and regimen. He hopes they adopt strong virtues, integrity, and a sense of patriotism. Using George Marshall's peacetime example, he noted that patriotism is not solely in-tended for the field of battle; patriots need not wave a flag. He pointed out that Scouting's charter includes the provision "to teach [Scouts] patriotism," and, he explained, "It is not a patriotism that one wears on one's sleeve, but a patriotism that one lives every day of one's life. It's internal to one's fabric. It is an abiding and deep love of country. It is a patriotism that includes the val-ues of 'caring and civility' in our daily lives." In a sense, he returned to an old

Scouting slogan: "Do a good turn daily." In his eyes, an act of patriotism can be as simple as helping a neighbor.

When we finally sat down in his office at the end of the parade ground, the general's bearing was easy and affable, a side of him I wondered if his 1,200 charges ever saw. There, sitting before great windows overlooking the post, he began to relate the structured world he now oversees to his experiences in Richmond, Virginia's Troops 2 and 602. Although J. H. Binford Peay, Jr., foreshadowed his son's path by earning his Eagle in 1923 with Richmond's Troop 6, graduating from VMI in 1929, and serving as a military officer, young Binnie Peay never intended to follow his father's footsteps *directly*. But family traditions are difficult to break, and now he chuckles at the realization that he followed in his father's footprints almost step for step. Another good laugh came as he pointed to pictures of two young soldiers bearing a strong resemblance to the man across from me. His sons, Jim and Ryan, had followed *his* footsteps, each earning his Eagle, graduating from VMI, and serving in the U.S. Army.

Looking back today, he sees the structure and preparation that subtly nudged him along the military path at each step. "Scouting is also a training experience because you lead in many ways a structured life," he said, "particularly when you go to summer camp. I wound up spending six or eight years at summer camp, and you lived that structured life: reveille every morning, you went to breakfast, merit badge classes, you went to lunch, you went to aquatics activities in the afternoon, you went to dinner and campfires at night. I did that all summer long."

General Peay spent two summers at Camp Shawondasse near Richmond, Virginia, as a camper before joining the staff as a dishwasher, making $3 per week plus room and board. Several years later, he became the waterfront director, following the path of John Knapp, a fellow Richmond Eagle Scout who later became the twelfth superintendent of VMI. Above all, Peay saw the value of young Scouts living by the right values on their own volition, away from the pressure or guidance of their parents. Those early tests become real indicators of a leader's future path.

Years later, when he entered Ranger School at Fort Benning as a second lieutenant, U.S. Army, he drew upon the skills and outdoor experience he gained during his years at Camp Shawondasse. "You live in the woods for nine to ten weeks," he said, explaining the first months of Ranger School. "It's very strenuous; you do rappelling, tie knots, go on long patrols—all under pressure. A lot of physical activity. Many of the Scouting skills fell right into that. That's the physical and mental piece, and clearly that carried over into combat as well, for me, in both Vietnam and in the First Gulf War."

In both theaters, Peay distinguished himself as a capable soldier and leader. He served two tours in Vietnam, commanding troops in combat and receiving the Purple Heart, Bronze Star, and the Silver Star during a tough three-month campaign on the Cambodian border. He progressed through the military ranks, and in 1989 he assumed command of the fabled 101st Airborne Division (Air Assault). As leader of this legendary group, he followed the footsteps of World War II commander Maxwell D. Taylor, a future chairman of the Joint Chiefs of Staff who led the paratroopers of the 101st into Normandy on D-Day in 1944. The division was later commanded by Eagle Scout William C. Westmoreland, who also served as superintendent of his *alma mater*, the U.S. Military Academy at West Point.

On January 17, 1991, General Peay perpetuated the tradition of the 101st as he led the unit into Iraq to open Operation Desert Strom. Peay's Airborne/Air Assault troops spearheaded the ground war. He deployed his men and women as planned, placing thousands of troops 150 miles inside enemy territory, a feat previously unmatched in scale or speed. Four days after the ground offensive opened, a cease-fire was declared. The 101st returned home several months later, their job well done.

After his success in the Gulf, Peay became a four-star general, the same rank held by Desert Storm commanders Norman Schwarzkopf and Colin Powell. Cadets at the nation's military academies rarely have leaders as accomplished as General Peay, and when he returned to VMI in July 2003, his four-star flag and résumé earned him instant respect among the corps of cadets and its alumni. But his values, which now must reflect the Institute's values, earned him their lasting trust.

"I think Scouting teaches you those values," he said, referring to the virtues cherished by VMI. Then he focused on the tenth point of the Scout Law: A Scout is Brave. "If you talk about a Scout is courageous or brave, what does that mean? There are all kinds of courage—courageous enough to live in the wilderness, courageous enough to jump in and save someone who is drowning—that's one piece of being courageous. The other piece is having the personal courage to speak up when things are wrong or take a strong position that you believe in even if it terminates your career.

"There's a value base—and I call that a bedrock—about the way you lead your life. I break this down simplistically. We've got all these forms of leadership and all these forms of management— behavioral theory and all that—but at the end of the day, just see what the Scout Oath and Law says, and there it is! It's that simple." Then this accomplished army general rattled off the Scout Law quickly and effortlessly. "Still got it," he said confidently.

But is leadership "that simple" as General Peay suggested? In capturing the Eagle legacy, I've struggled to understand how codes and values learned so long ago have affected individuals as adults when they live in places where the Scout Oath binds no one. I asked the question.

General Peay sat thoughtfully with his chin resting on his fists. He scowled momentarily and then returned us to his last years in the military. After commanding firing batteries in Vietnam and an entire division in Desert Storm, and after serv-

Gen. J. H. Binford Peay III.
U.S. Army (Ret.)
COURTESY OF
J. H. BINFORD PEAY III

ing on the U.S. Military Committee in the United Nations and as vice chief of staff for the U.S. Army, he had filled General Norman Schwarzkopf's Desert Storm post as commander-in-chief of U.S. Central Command, the military organization overseeing all U.S. forces in the Middle East, Africa, and South Asia.

During Peay's tenure at CENTCOM—a portent of things to come— America's forces in the Middle East suffered several terrorist attacks. The truck-bombing of the Khobar Towers facility in Saudi Arabia killed nineteen U.S. servicemen and injured hundreds of civilians from other countries. As a result of the attack, the secretary of defense and General Peay were called before the Senate Armed Services Committee, a group hungry for hard answers.

The committee soon focused its attention on an Air Force officer who served under General Peay and who perhaps became a scapegoat in the case. While Peay agreed there were errors in the protection of Khobar Towers, he also realized how difficult it was to provide total protection against unpredictable terrorist attacks and felt this officer was being treated unfairly. Congress felt pressured to take strong action, however, and General Peay shouldered the responsibility, remaining loyal to his subordinates in the face of pressure generously provided by television cameras, a cadre of reporters, and a panel of congressmen. He stood by his men but saw a shadow cast on the hard years of work done by his staff, work leveraged by CENTCOM commander Tommy Franks and others during the most recent Middle East conflicts. Even though he stood up for his besieged subordinate, he was saddened to see that officer's career effectively ended as a result of the hearings.

"That's life in the fast lane," he later reflected. "That's what goes on. I think Scouting told me there are certain right things you do. I could have cowered. I could have walked away from that, but I chose not to. So, I sleep fairly well." In the aftermath of the hearing, General Peay's tenure as commander of U.S. Central Command came to a close. He knows the price that can accompany a leader's principled stand.

In the Khobar Towers incident, Peay also saw the merits of his approach to discipline. It saddened him to watch a promising officer's career end because of one incident. Today, while he never shies from meting out strict penalties to his cadets, he remains mindful of the lessons young men need to learn. Punishment is important, he quickly noted—and I could imagine many tense scenes taking place between superintendent and cadet in the office where we sat—but, in the end, he wants to help youth become *more* successful in the years ahead. He tries his best to build their futures, not limit them.

He spoke to me about caring but not in the sense of concern, worry, or feelings. To General Peay, the value of caring is most important in another light. "Caring in this sense," he explained, "involves stewardship, custodianship, guidance, governance, responsibility, accountability, maintenance, sustenance, nurture, and provision," he said. "In this sense, caring is considerably more proactive and extends to taking responsibility for and guiding others whenever the circumstances call for it.

"The caring I am speaking about goes deep. I like to call it 'bone-deep caring,' and it is developed not as a rule of life or a regulation but as a way of life. You don't put it on like a suit of clothes; you embrace it. It's part of your fabric, and it changes all in your life."

From this perspective, caring can become discipline, which he always tries to exercise with restraint. This war-tested leader explained, "You always try, from the leader's perspective, to have enough leeway where young people can make mistakes and recover and then go on to be very successful. Our very best leaders have survived that way. I certainly did."

In January 1968, Captain Binnie Peay suddenly found himself atop Hill 1001 near Dac To, Vietnam, and in command of an artillery battery of the Fourth Infantry Division. The battle around the hill was intense, and thirty minutes after assuming command of the disorganized unit, one of the howitzers in his purview accidentally wounded several U.S. infantry soldiers in a forward position. The young commander was devastated. But as the result of the ensuing investigation, he received a letter of reprimand for his "field file," fortunately not his "official file" at the Pentagon. He explained, "The commander above me—from whom I've always drawn in the years since when I had to exercise discipline—was wise enough not to let that destroy my career, despite the pressure on him for perfection in his command. He made it a learning exercise, but he could have gone the other way. Later in my career, I handled a lot of junior officers the same way. And so I think that's part of leadership." It's also part of caring. In General Peay and others, I realized that effective leaders set out to raise the stature of those around them, not inflate their own reputations.

General Peay is too modest to mention another aspect of discipline: his own. Emory Thomas, one of the nation's preeminent Civil War historians, joined Troop 2 with Binnie Peay in Richmond at St. Thomas Church. "Our troop was big on camping and outdoor things, but our leaders didn't encourage advancement very much," Dr. Thomas recalled. "If you were going to advance, you had to take the initiative yourself. But that's what Binnie would do: focus on a goal and get it."

The friendship between Peay and Thomas continues to this day, but Emory left the troop before he earned his Eagle. "I always wished I'd earned it," he confided to me, echoing a sentiment I heard quite often during my travels; the sincere regret many men expressed for not reaching Eagle surprised me. "It's just such a great accomplishment, and you can only do it once, while you're young. You can't go back and get it. Of course, it never even occurred to Binnie not to get it."

General Peay remains proud of the rank he earned in Troop 602. "When you go in my study today, I have a little square case, and in it, I have my Cincinnatus Medal and I have my Eagle badge," he explained, indicating that he'd also received the Society of Cincinnatus Medal, the highest honor awarded to VMI cadets. The award, given for "excellence of character and efficiency of service," honors the ideal of the citizen-soldier—men who are leaders at home but who are able to lead men in battle when necessary—men like the society's first leader, George Washington.

"I consider those the two highest awards I've ever received, even higher than those I received in the military," he continued, "and I think when you get those types of awards, you have to be a role model for life. And you can't disfavor those awards. People know you've got them, and you have to emulate what they stand for. So, to me, as corny as it may sound, those two awards have always been in the back of my mind. If I were to do something improper, every one of my VMI classmates would know about it. It's like being an Eagle Scout. Everybody in your church knows you're an Eagle Scout."

Part of the formal "charge" given to each new Eagle as he receives his badge reads: "Your position, as you well know, is one of honor and responsibility. You are a marked man. As an Eagle Scout you have assumed a solemn obligation to do your duty to God, to country, to your fellow Scouts and to mankind in general. This is a great undertaking." No Eagle ever forgets the words *marked man*, and I can still remember Paul Lee, who served as Troop 103's Scoutmaster during my early Scouting days, reading the charge to Sean O'Brien and me as the audience listened intently. The trail to Eagle culminates at that very instant when, as an Eagle, you recognize and accept that you have a duty to the ideals of the badge you share with so many others.

General Peay believes Eagle Scouts are and always remain "marked men." Others recognize them as Eagles, and they must hold themselves to a higher standard, not only for their own sake but also for the sake of others who share their rank. They must make the right choices and bring honor to the badge. That is in part what he hopes to instill in the young men and women who graduate from VMI. He hopes the indoctrination that occurs in the barracks plus the gentle pressure that comes from leaders among the corps will guide his students to make the right decisions in the future. Honor, he hopes, will have become second nature.

"When times are challenging later in life," the general observed as we finished our conversation, "which they are for all of us at various times, whether you're very, very successful or not successful, there will be challenges in life, roads you've got to cross. My experience has been that Scouting takes you down the right path."

At the end of my afternoon with General Peay, I left the superintendent's office and returned to the warm fall sunlight that fell on the grassy parade ground. I glanced at the billowing flags, then turned, passed through the austere gates of VMI, and walked toward downtown Lexington. I mulled over my time with this commanding figure as I walked, and, before long, I found myself passing the church where I'd met that unknown gentleman years ago. It was he who first nudged me down this path by reminding me that neither he nor I had ever ceased being Eagle Scouts. I smiled to myself. I still hadn't found all the answers to the questions he prompted, but I had traveled many miles—literally and figuratively—since our encounter.

That particular day, Binnie Peay had provided yet another perspective. In his battle-tested, four-star persona, I expected to find a hard-nosed commander who cared more for outcomes than for individuals. I imagined him leading the 101st into battle across the Iraqi desert, fixated on his division's objectives and less concerned about those thousands of young soldiers in his charge. He proved me wrong. I had observed that many Eagles seem to sacrifice self for a larger ideal; I found that General Peay also sacrificed himself for other individuals. He cares for others in a genuine sense. They recognize his concern. They *see* his values.

The virtues General Peay does his best to exemplify flow from the codes he still remembers from his youth. Putting those values into practice, he became a leader. While Scouting's founders never articulated leadership as a value in the Oath or Law, they outlined the precise qualities young men would need to earn the trust and respect of others in the future. As Eagles develop those characteristics, they seem driven to stand up and lead others. Caring genuinely for those around them becomes not just a duty but a way of life.

COUNSELORS

Peter Huwe leapt over a friend, angling himself for a smooth entrance into the crowded pool. At the last instant, he swerved, going into a steep dive to avoid another swimmer. His head slammed into the bottom of the pool; his neck snapped. He knew exactly what had happened. Fully conscious but entirely paralyzed, he slid to the bottom. The nineteen-year-old Eagle Scout looked up, calmly waiting and hoping for one of his friends to take notice. Fortunately, William Dodd saw what happened and dove toward Peter.

"It seemed like forever," Peter remembered six months later, "but William went down and pulled me up. He knew what to do. I was talking with him the whole time, making sure he did things right, but I didn't have to correct him. He did a spinal-injury rescue just like I'd taught him at Camp Yocona."

Peter followed the lead of his three older brothers—all Eagle Scouts in Troop 123 and Vigil members of the Order of the Arrow—and spent five years on summer staff at Camp Yocona outside Pontotoc, Mississippi. A Red Cross lifeguard, Peter taught Lifesaving merit badge each summer. He made his Scouts practice rescuing a spinal-injury victim from the water by bracing the neck and spine. He often served as the victim.

"I remember William Dodd being in my class," Peter said of his fellow Eagle from Corinth, Mississippi. "I must have made him practice on me ten times before I signed him off. I made sure he got it perfect. As it turned out, that was a good thing."

Peter laughed, remembering how Scouts never thought they would use their CPR or lifesaving skills. His situation proved differently and, to Peter, the most rewarding part of serving as a counselor came from hearing how his former students had used their skills. He saved lives as a lifeguard, but his greatest rewards came from teaching others and later hearing how they had saved a life themselves.

"That's why I liked being a counselor," he reflected. "If I could teach more people lifesaving, how many more people can be saved? I'm really thankful the Scouts require that. There's no telling how many lives have been saved across the country."

For him, this training relates to being prepared and doing your best. Six months after his accident, he remains in a wheelchair. A rehabilitative stay at the renowned Shepherd Center helped him regain some use of his arms, and he can now care for himself—an important factor in returning to college and reclaiming his life.

"When I was in the hospital at Shepherd, all I could do was my best," the former cross-country runner explained. "I couldn't meet all the goals I set for myself—I'm not up and walking—but I did what I could. I did my best, and I'm thankful to be alive and have the abilities I *do* have."

Even though Peter himself can no longer dive into a lake to save someone, hundreds of former Scouts *can* save a life because Peter shared his knowledge with them while he worked the waterfront at Camp Yocoma. Thousands learn to save lives each summer at more than 600 Scout camps which cover half a million acres of the country's land. Nearly 700,000 Scouts and leaders attend summer camp, an almost essential part of the overall Scouting experience. Thousands of staff meet them there, becoming their teachers, counselors, and friends. These young men and women teach because they care about the campers and about the subjects. Skills like lifesaving, sailing, kayaking, and rock climbing—even academic topics like ecology, archaeology, and astronomy—all evoke real passions in teenage counselors and campers alike. At an early age these staffers realize the change they can spark by helping others.

JEFF ZAVATSKY

TROOP 121, ELKHART, INDIANA

EAGLE SCOUT, 1990

It can take Scouts several hours to paddle canoes across the strait separating Summerland Key from Munson Island. The twin engines of our boat carried Jeff Zavatsky and me across in less than fifteen minutes. We skimmed at full throttle over the crystal waters of the Florida Keys until we entered one of Munson Island's sheltered coves. Jeff cut the engines as we neared the beach, and we silently drifted toward the shore of the scrub-covered key. We jumped into the surf and waded ashore. Standing alone on the wet sand, we heard nothing but the steady lapping of waves and the hum of insects coming from the trees beyond the beach.

Jeff reached toward the sandy beach with a burly forearm and picked up a plastic bottle that had washed ashore. "You know, one of the things we try to teach our Scouts is that if you throw away trash in Florida or Iowa or wherever, it has to go somewhere, and it can end up on Munson Island."

As director of the Brinton Environmental Center, a division of the Boy Scouts of America's Florida National High Adventure Sea Base, Jeff oversees the hundred-acre wilderness that is Munson Island. He takes any disturbance or piece of litter quite personally. But that sensitivity comes from one desire: to give his Scouts an unforgettable experience.

Each summer, 3,000 guests drive down U.S. Route 1 to the Brinton Center, which sits on Summerland Key, fifty miles south of the main Florida Sea Base on Lower Matecumbe Key. The Florida Sea Base provides Scouts opportunities to sail fifty-foot sloops through the Keys, dive on coral reefs, and canoe through the Everglades. The 38,000 youth who annually participate in Scouting's National High Adventure programs also canoe the unspoiled lakes and rivers of the Northern Tier Bases in Minnesota and Canada, and 20,000 of these young men and women sojourn to Philmont Scout Ranch in Cimarron, New Mexico, where they backpack through the Rocky Mountains. The guides and counselors at each base help young men and women grow as they encourage Scouts to challenge their own limits. These staff members could spend their summers earning more money and living in quarters far more luxurious than those that are typical of Scout camps, but they all feel an obligation to pass along the care that someone had given them in the past.

A unique cast of counselors meets each group of teenagers who arrive at the Brinton Center for a week on Munson Island. The Scouts come seeking something they could experience nowhere else, and typically they find it. While the Summerland Key base lies just twenty-five miles northeast of Key West, it seems thousands of miles from anywhere. Munson Island seems even more removed. To reach the island, campers paddle outrigger canoes across a six-mile strait. When they finally pull their canoes onto the beach, they begin a week as castaways on the uninhabited spit of land. Under the guidance of eccentric counselors dubbed "island mates," many of whom are Eagle Scouts, the island's visitors fish the crystal waters of Munson's harbors for dinner, gather fuel for their cooking fires along its driftwood-lined beaches, and just survive.

"You've seen *Survivor* on television, right," one mate asked me. "That's what it's like on Munson. It's primitive." When I saw a photograph of a returning group of mates, all tanned and wearing tribal war paint, I understood. And each mate had his own story about the Scout leader who left base clean-cut and ghostly white, then returned from the island tanned, bearded, and with a new, wild look in his eye. "It changes people, Scouts and leaders," observed another island mate.

Back on Munson Island, Jeff explained how. "You rely on your whole crew for assistance," he observed as we meandered along the beach. "That is the one thing our counselors do well. We develop the crew, the team, the camaraderie. The experiences they gain strengthen them in the future. In tough times, if they are able to think back on their experiences on the island, then other things—passing a test, painting a house, doing something difficult—seem like nothing."

Jeff and I soon left the beach and its waterlogged debris and pushed through the thick mangroves that hide the salt plains and scrub of Munson's interior from the sea. The only two humans on the island, Jeff and I were joined under the canopy by several seafaring birds, legions of spiders and bugs, and several of the island's 30 Key deer, a tiny species of deer that rarely exceeds waist height. Only 800 remain in the world. Jeff was not only my companion here but even more important also my teacher, taking time to explain the workings of the island's ecosystem and dispensing his boundless knowledge of the island's flora and fauna. He began identifying species of flowers I'd never seen and showed me a hydralike gumbo limbo tree, its strong limbs twisting every way imaginable. He pointed to the tree's distinctive bark, joking, "You can always tell these trees because they look like a sunburned Florida tourist: red and peeling." From time to time, he gathered a seed, berry, or twig to add to his collection of native plants at the main base on Summerland Key. The facts he knew about each species belied a lifelong interest, and I gathered that the island—and what transpires here—had become Jeff's passions.

"This is just a fantastic proving ground," he said motioning to the woods around a primitive campsite. "The Scouts really have a changing experience and grow because of their week here. It doesn't matter how old you are or what rank you are. You learn to survive with others and do your part. Our mates are there to help."

To Jeff's point, a small silver Eagle badge or a Scoutmaster's patch has little value on the deserted island. The skills that should accompany those ranks, however, are absolutely vital. The skill to tie knots and lash together shelters, the knowledge of what berries and fruits are edible and how to prepare a fish, and the ability to lead others and work together to survive are all priceless.

"Nobody is going to survive out here alone," he observed, underscoring the bottom line. "When you're taking a canoe out to the island, if everyone paddles on the same side, you'll go around in circles. So we start you out right there working as a team. Either it's going to take you an hour and a half to get out to the island or it's going to take you five hours."

Long before Jeff ever heard of Munson Island, Don Arenz, Scoutmaster of Troop 121 in Elkhart, Indiana, gave the young Hoosier his first lesson in teamwork and responsibility. On his very first camping trip, Jeff was having a good time . . . at the expense of his duties. "Mr. A" pulled him aside and made him realize that there was a reason he was asked to do certain tasks, and although he was only a young Scout, people were counting on him to get those tasks accomplished.

"I thought, 'I got in trouble in Scouts. . . . Man, that's bad,'" he remembered. "He had me in tears. That little thing was an eye-opener. When they ask you to do something there is a reason why, and you need to get it done. That little coaching session he had with me began teaching me that people are counting on you, whether it's gathering firewood or counting how many matches you have. If we don't have firewood, we're not going to eat tonight." Whatever Mr. A told Jeff, it left an impression, and today he sees that lesson learned time and again on Munson Island.

When summer temperatures climb above ninety degrees and the humidity hovers near 100 percent on the island, people lose their motivation to do the tough chores. When that happens, the team either works together to fix the problem, or they'll go hungry, just like in Troop 121. These are the situations that truly test the character, leadership, and skill of an Eagle Scout. More often than not, Munson sees these Eagles rise to the challenge, teaching others and building their own abilities as well. Not only do these situations test the campers, they also test the ability of the mates to be guides, teachers, and, perhaps most important, counselors.

Jeff remembered two campers who arrived at the Brinton Center while their parents were involved in a particularly ugly divorce at home. "The parents were using the kids as ammunition," Jeff said sadly. "I told the staff what was happening and said, 'Watch these kids. They are the superstars this week. Make sure of that.' And at the end of the week at the closing campfire, the kids broke down. They lost it because they knew what they were going back to. You're giving these kids a unique experience, and you've got to be prepared for it. For a fourteen-year-old kid to break down in front of his friends—they don't do that; that's not a macho thing to do—but they've got that trust in the mate, and my mates help them through it. That's what mates have to be ready for. As counselors, we don't need to talk all the time; sometimes we just need to listen, then do whatever we can do to help them out."

Returning to the two campers, Jeff continued, "For the first time in a long time, the week we had them, those kids had a great time. Mom and Dad weren't even on their minds until they realized they had to go back home the next day and deal with that. But they confided in the mates. The mates are their friends. My mates get e-mails from crews from years and years ago. I get e-mails from crews years and years ago. We're with them the entire time. You trust each other.

"I still remember my staff member from Philmont in 1986, Nancy," he added. "She was an Explorer. Scouts open up to their staff, looking for advice on school trouble, friend trouble, problems at home. I've had staff come back year after year to be that role model and make that difference. I hire some that came through here as a Scout and say, 'The mate I had was awe-some. He kept me in Scouts. This is why I am here.' They want to put back into Scouts what they got out of it. These guys are the future leaders and the current role models. They are the ones you want with younger Scouts making a difference. If the younger guys can see older Scouts having fun, being safe, and being leaders, then maybe they'll become leaders too."

Jeff Zavatsky with a friend, 1989 COURTESY OF JEFF ZAVATSKY

Jeff sees being a counselor as part of an Eagle's ultimate responsibility: giving back to Scouting and proving that you *are* an Eagle each day by do-ing at least one thing to help some-one else, the proverbial daily good turn. For a mate, it may be counsel-ing a hurting Scout. For Jeff it started as a summer camp counselor who spent so much time helping others earn badges that he didn't finish his last re-quirements for Eagle until the day before his eighteenth birthday.

"Being an Eagle, people ask me why I don't have many merit badges. I was only a camper at summer camp for one year, then I became a counselor. I taught merit badges I didn't have. I was too busy at summer camps helping other kids get merit badges, teaching them how to swim, whereas it probably should've been me out there earning my Environmental Science at fifteen, not at seventeen, with the clock ticking away!" He laughed.

Then Jeff grew quiet and considered his career, which included serving as a sailboat captain for the Florida Sea Base, and its reflection of the Scout Oath's principles. He settled on the concept of helping other people at all times. "I've always lived by that," he said. "I've always tried to put others in front of myself. When it comes to the Scouts here, it's about serving the customers, making sure they're having a good time and making sure they're here for the right reasons. And as you can tell, I like teaching them a few things as well!"

To him, this is all part of being an Eagle Scout. "Scouting is really about opening doors," he reflected, noting how Scouting stirred his early interest in biology and Nature. "There are a lot of things I learned in it that I can apply and teach others to apply. It's kind of like the book *Everything I Needed to Know I Learned in Kindergarten*." In Scouting as in school, Jeff believes, you must prove what you've learned. While it clearly shows great dedication, being awarded the Eagle badge matters relatively little to Jeff. What an individual does once he has the badge matters much more: Does he use his knowledge? Does he give back to others?

"I hate to say 'Prove it,' but all Eagle Scouts need to prove they earned it," he said. "What have you done? Have you worked at a Scout camp? Are you an assistant Scoutmaster? Are you teaching a merit badge? Are you a counselor? Are you a teacher? Prove to me that you've earned this rank."

As Eagle Scouts, Jeff and his mates also teach campers about their duty. They want Scouts to know that Munson belongs to them and is thus their responsibility. Drawing a parallel to the larger world, he wants his campers to understand that when that plastic bottle washes up on Munson Island it affects them, regardless of where they live. "You and I own this island," he said. "You're a Scout. You own this island. It's yours. We go out and show them what the Scouts have given us and explain that it's up to us to take care of it."

His point: concern and accountability for this ecosystem should start far upstream. Although the Keys lie many miles south of the Everglades, the waters flowing from those wetlands into the Bay of Florida, which borders the Keys to the north, affect life in Florida's famous archipelago and beyond.

Ecosystems are connected to one another. If pollution from the mainland reaches the waters off the Keys, reefs are affected, fish are affected, and the hungry souls on Munson Island are affected.

"If we get bad water flowing down here from the Everglades, our islands and reefs won't live," Jeff said as he bent down to pick up a "sailor's heart" that had washed ashore. He handed me the seed that superstitious sailors keep for good luck and described in detail the vine it produces and its ability to float for decades on the sea. Then he reverted to ecology, explaining, "You get too much nitrogen and pollutants in the water, and you get huge dead zones in Florida Bay. Nothing can live there. And sea urchins? They keep the coral healthy, but they're dying, probably because of the same thing. If we lose our reefs, can you imagine the impact on this system? We'd lose the marine life here, and then where will people on Munson Island or in Miami get their fish?"

The staff at the Florida Sea Base's Brinton Center educates every camper about the delicate nature of this tropical environment not through textbooks or lectures, but through direct experience. Jeff believes that helping Scouts learn firsthand is one of a counselor's most important roles. He knows there are legions of people working to protect the seas, but he wonders how many lobbyists have ever seen one of the reefs for which they're advocating. He wonders how many water-quality advocates have ever seen an algae bloom choking out marine life. Jeff and his mates are ready to show them. "It's getting them out there and *showing* them why these things are important," he explained, "so when they go back home they may be the next person who is going to fight for what we have down here."

Each year, thousands of passionate counselors like Jeff serve the Scouts and leaders who attend Scout camps from Maine to Oregon. They teach Scouts lessons about Nature, their limits, and their duties. These teachers never escape the lasting culture of giving that Scouting fosters. They remain involved or become involved again just to help Scouts learn about leadership, skills, and themselves. To Jeff, that's just part of proving that you are, truly, an Eagle Scout.

It took just over half an hour for two of Jeff Zavatsky's island mates, James Agnor and Gary Heimbach, and me to cover the twenty-five miles from the southern tip of Summerland Key to downtown Key West. James drove us in his open-top Jeep, which shuddered if he pushed the aging engine past fifty-five miles per hour. The stars shone magnificently over the islands, and their lights danced on the dark water surrounding Route 1 as we headed south. I leaned back, closed my eyes, and enjoyed the warm wind swirling inside the Jeep. Then I smiled as I considered the Eagle Scouts with me.

In front of me sat James, who had just shaved his imposing head on a dare. He covered his new dome with a straw hat, his chin with a goatee. A one-piece mechanic's suit covered the remainder of his figure. Traces of stubble had begun to reclaim Gary's similarly scalped head, and we all wore beads saved from a past festival. Few observers in Key West would have believed either James or Gary were ever Boy Scouts, let alone Eagle Scouts and counselors at the Florida Sea Base. Those doubters knew only the stereotype: something akin to the caricature of Senator Richard Lugar run by the *Indianapolis Star*. While many of my encounters supported that popular image, they certainly failed to validate it entirely. If the stereotype always held true, my miles would have been significantly less entertaining. Eagles came in all varieties, some quite unexpected.

I recalled a trip to California, where I met Scott Rader, who, I expect, owned only one collared shirt when he was a teenager . . . and that was a part of his Scout uniform. The lead singer of a punk band, Scott sported a Mohawk haircut, several earrings, and three tattoos at his Eagle court of honor. "I was a walking embodiment of diversity," he admitted. "But no drugs or drinking."

I tried to imagine the confusion many parents felt when they discovered Scott patiently teaching their sons how to tie bowlines and pitch tents at Scout meetings. Then I thought, "Where else would boys get this interaction with such different personalities? What other group would have accepted someone like Scott Rader and allowed him to lead other boys and eventually award him their highest rank?"

The Mohawk has long since disappeared and Scott now cares for a growing family. He loves Scouting as much as anyone who has a closet full of starched button-downs. "It was camaraderie beyond the superficial," Scott reflected. "It felt real and gritty and idealistic."

I learned that Eagles from different backgrounds—who sometimes challenge stereotypes—help Scouts become more accepting of others. Seeing a Scout with a Mohawk, then hearing him recite the Scout Oath and embody those principles makes an impression. Being taught new skills by someone with a vastly different perspective gives young men a lesson in the value of diversity. Much like my friend Sean O'Brien and me, Eagle Scouts share something rare and fundamental in their hearts despite their outward differences. Those ties transcend the superficial.

Three a.m. had long since passed when James bounced the Jeep back onto the shell-and-gravel driveway of the Brinton Center on Summerland Key. No lights appeared in Jeff Zavatsky's quarters or anywhere else on the base. We trudged up the steps to the dormitory, where we crawled into our bunks and fell asleep after laughing about stories from our night in Key West.

I consider my trip to the Keys as one of my most important. I occasionally grew accustomed to meeting Eagles in office towers and government buildings, settings where everyone wore coats and ties. But those conversations were removed from the environments where everyone first experienced Scouting and learned its values. My days with the Sea Base staff shook up my routine and helped me take myself a bit less seriously. Summerland Key, along with the Scout meetings, camps, and jamborees I visited along my journey, reminded me about Scouting as I experienced it as a boy. I remembered the common interests and how they could bridge decades. I remembered the fun, the differences, and the adventure. I remembered why Eagles like James, Gary, and Jeff became counselors.

FATHERS

Years after he earned his Eagle in 1957, Wyoming Senator Mike Enzi had another opportunity to work on an Eagle project as his son Brad advanced toward Eagle himself. With the birth of Brad's first son, this proud grandfather already had dreams of another Eagle in the Enzi family. He envisioned a family tradition.

"From personal experience, I can tell you that Scouting families can be wonderful," I said as we sat together in Washington. Then I laughed and added, "Although, I don't recall that I had much choice in becoming an Eagle!"

"Brad would probably tell you he didn't have much of a choice either," the husky Wyoming native retorted, laughing heartily. "I remember being in a camping store, REI in Fort Collins, I believe. The guy waiting on us asked Brad if he was a Scout. Brad said, 'Yeah, I am.' And the guy said, 'I used to be. I was Life; I never got Eagle. Man, don't make that mistake.' And Brad turned to me and said, 'Okay, Dad, how much did you pay him to say that?' " Another laugh.

Fathers often provide the encouragement that pushes Scouts up the ladder of advancement. They remain focused on the next goal and understand how important achieving that rank or merit badge might be for their son, whether the son realizes it or not. Troops often recruit fathers to join the 1.2 million other registered adults that are active leaders at any given time. In fact, most of these leaders are fathers of Scouts and often serve as Assistant Scoutmasters. As such, they frequently have no less an impact on young men than the Scoutmaster himself. By virtue of participating in their son's troop, fathers can spend time with their own boys in particularly unique and meaningful ways. One of the most important aspects of Scouting is the opportunity for fathers and sons to spend time with one another on camping trips and outdoor expeditions.

"My dad was a reluctant leader, but he wound up as Scoutmaster for Troop 13 in La Verne, California," remembered architect Mike Riley. "At first, he wore a suit, not a uniform, but after his first week at Scout camp, he was in Class A uniform from head to toe! But the important thing about Dad as Scoutmaster was the time I spent with him. I had never spent a week alone with my father before our troop's trip to Mount Whitney. We were backpacking for a week in the Sierra Nevada range, and every morning, every night, and, more important, at every stop along the trail Dad was there. A lot of kids never get to spend that kind of time with their fathers."

When Mike Riley's own son reached Scouting age, he joked that he made the mistake of mentioning to other leaders that he had earned Eagle. "The next thing I knew, I was signed up and running things," he said, laughing. Laughter aside, Mike was just taking a step he knew he'd take since his own father became Scoutmaster. He was continuing the cycle of Scouting that seems to take root in families and is passed between generations of fathers and sons.

THE SESSIONS

TROOP 136, KEARNEY, NEBRASKA, 1947

TROOP 255, BETHESDA, MARYLAND, 1970

TROOP 890, DALLAS, TEXAS, 2005

A crowd of schoolchildren swarmed out of Pete Sessions's office, chattering excitedly about their meeting with the Texas congressman. "He was so nice; he was so young," they remarked as they flooded into the hallway of the Longworth House Office Building. As they poured from the office, none noticed the tall, white-haired gentleman who listened to their comments with a bemused smile across his face. The children were talking about his son.

"Well, it gives me a little chuckle," he said as we walked into his son's office, "and it's always nice to hear those things said about your children. But I'm proud of Pete and what he's accomplished. He fought to get it. He wasn't elected his first time out."

Seconds later, Pete met us at his conference table, a framed picture in hand. "This is 1969," he said pointing to the picture of his father and him atop Mount Baldy at Philmont Scout Ranch in New Mexico. "He's the director of the FBI and climbed all the way up there. We took him the first night to 6,000 feet, Camp Cimarroncito. This is 12,441."

"And a half," added the former director, Judge William S. Sessions.

The picture showed the director of the Federal Bureau of Investigation alongside his son, the scruffy Scoutmaster of Troop 88. They stood on Baldy's rocky summit wearing dusty boots, windbreakers, and shorts. The rugged Sangre de Cristo Range of the Rocky Mountains spread out magnificently behind them. Both Pete and his father had been to Philmont before, but this was their first trek together. They still relish the memory of climbing Philmont's highest peak and sharing the literal pinnacle of the Scouting experience.

241

A fast-talking politician in a good sense, Pete tends to fire off more words in a minute than most. In an astoundingly few seconds, he recited the campsites and itinerary from their 1989 expedition: "We went from 'Cito to Bench, Bench to Santa Claus, Santa Claus to Pueblano, Pueblano to Miranda, Miranda to Baldy Town and came back the northeast route; came over Ponil, Indian Writings, and out." He recited this all from memory; Pete loves that place.

The Sessions shared their experience on Baldy with the boys of Pete's New Jersey troop and, in a Philmont first, a detail of FBI agents. Armed and laden with communication equipment, the agents became part of the expedition, and the trip proved uneventful, save the two breaks the director took from the trail to speak with the president and secretary of state.

The photograph now before us recorded the second time the elder Sessions had stood on Baldy's summit. Pete prompted his father to recount the story of the first.

"It was 1945," the judge began in his calm, evenly paced voice, a remnant of thirteen years spent issuing carefully worded statements from the federal bench. "We went for a month: a week at Kit Carson, a week at Ponil, a week at Fish Camp, and a week at Cimarroncito," he said, naming several camps within Philmont's expansive 137,493 acres. "One hundred bucks for a full month. My deal was if I could raise $75, the family would contribute $25. So I raised the $75. I sold papers and tin cans and delivered my paper route and saved up that money."

"We made our own tents," he added. "Waterproof tents. We made our own backpacks. They were boards like the Indians carried, with stretched hide over the board frame: You packed them on, and you tied all your stuff on." He commandeered my notepad and meticulously diagrammed the packs, which were primitive compared to the advanced internal-frame packs the trails of Philmont regularly see today.

"When we got out there, it was just a dream, that's all," this son of the Nebraska plains reflected. "Here you were; you were *really* at Philmont. . . . It was just a dream. You had horses, and you walked, and you saw Indian writings. Then you went into the high mountains to Cimarroncito, and you went up to Baldy. The mountain was huge; I'd never seen anything like it."

Pete remembered the same. He recalled sleeping under a brilliant canopy of stars stretched between towering mountains that was unlike anything on the East Coast. The quiet power of the peaks moved him to consider life's unknowns as he hiked through the wilderness during his expeditions in 1971 and 1973. When the day's trek ended, he often found an isolated spot near the campsite where he would spend time just reflecting.

"I remember looking out down at Tent City and off into the distance," he said. "It was a beautiful clear night, and here I was fifteen years old, and it

FBI Director William Sessions and Scoutmaster Pete Sessions, Mt. Baldy, Philmont Scout Ranch, 1989
COURTESY OF PETE SESSIONS

was a religious experience. I contemplated the Earth and the stars, where we are, and what we are doing. What are we here for? What mission, what purpose does man have? Then your thoughts flow from there: What am I going to make of my life? What kind of pathway am I going to take? What kind of challenges do I want to accept? I think Scouting has been at every one of those decision points. At crossroads in my life, it sustained me. It provided me a results-oriented view of life that prepared me to accept that next challenge."

Pete never took his eye off Philmont, and as a congressman he worked with his colleagues to ensure that today's Scouts enjoy the same experience he did. In 1998 officials at nearby Dyess Air Force Base planned to designate Philmont's airspace a primary flight path for B-1 and B-52 bombers on training missions. Pete wouldn't stand for it. Along with a host of other congressmen, he petitioned the Joint Chiefs of Staff to block the action; otherwise, they threatened to pass legislation to prevent it. "Everybody's for the Boy Scouts," he explained with a grin of satisfaction. Their petition worked. Pete's coalition preserved Philmont's peaceful silence.

One morning, I stumbled across an anecdote that helped illustrate the experience Congressman Sessions sought to protect. When Judge Sessions trekked through Philmont in 1945, he traveled with nine Scouts from Kearney, Nebraska, and nine from Beaumont, Texas. These boys came from entirely different backgrounds, but on the trail they learned about Nature and they learned about each other.

Still, today, boys from different troops and different backgrounds often comprise trail crews. Jason Cox, a member of an affluent suburban troop, recalled hiking through Philmont with boys from an inner-city unit. "We learned what our differences were," recalled Jason, who earned his Eagle in 1990, "but we also learned how to get along. We learned that the color of our skin didn't matter. It's who you are as a person and how you get along as a *team*. I can remember being in a lightning storm one night, and we were camped on the edge of a meadow, and it was frightening. We all sat together in our tents and didn't cook that night; we just ate what we could. We were all huddled together and terrified. Huge lightning bolts were coming down all around us. Those things build bonds between you. Differences sort of erode away in situations like that. You're having to *survive* with people."

Pete Sessions has survived more Philmont expeditions than most, crossing over Baldy's summit and under the rustic entranceway to the ranch ten times. And since the ranch's founding in 1938, more than 700,000

Scouts and leaders have passed beneath the simple log crossbeam adorned with dangling pairs of worn-out boots that marks the entrance to the world's largest and most renowned Scout camp. In an average year, roughly 20,000 young men and leaders hike the reservation's 350 miles of trails, develop an appreciation for the wilderness, and perhaps find a new perspective.

This was the original vision of Lord Baden-Powell. Oklahoma oilman Waite Phillips shared the same vision, and in 1938 he stunned the country by donating 35,857 acres of land—one of the largest philanthropic gifts on record at the time—to the Boy Scouts of America. He and his wife, Genevieve, eventually donated 91,000 additional acres and a twenty-three-story Oklahoma City office tower that provided revenue to fund the operation of the ranch.

The words from Mr. Phillips's 1941 dedication struck me as important, for they capture not only his intentions but also something larger and more fundamental about the Scouting movement and those who sustain it. It reads: "These properties are donated and dedicated to the Boy Scouts of America for the purpose of perpetuating faith, self-reliance, integrity and freedom—principles used to build this great country by the American Pioneer. So that these future citizens may, through thoughtful adult guidance and by the inspiration of nature, visualize and form a code of living to diligently maintain these high ideals and our proper destiny."

The Scouts originally called their new camp "Philturn Rocky Mountain Scout Ranch," a name rooted in a combination of "Phillips" and the Scout slogan "Do a Good Turn Daily." The name later was changed to Philmont Scout Ranch, and the lasting effects of his gifts truly embody the philosophy underlying Mr. Phillips's good turn. "The only things we keep permanently," he often said, "are those we give away." The generosity of the Phillips family has affected hundreds of thousands of young lives, a legacy in itself.

Across the country, I found part of the Scouting legacy in the thousands of camps, programs, and troops that Eagle Scouts help support. "Everything we do takes resources," said Bob Mazzuca, an Eagle from Troop 28 in San Juan Bautista, California, who has spent over three decades raising funds for the Boy Scouts. "We cannot give kids these experiences without philanthropists, and the donor who provides logs to make benches for a camp chapel is every bit as much a philanthropist as Waite Phillips. We need a world of philanthropists, each in their own way."

Many donations have little to do with money. They come as time and talent. Each year, more than 1 million registered adults give those gifts. Many of those leaders are fathers, men just like William and Pete Sessions, who want to give something back to Scouting and to the country's youth.

"Let me tell you this, because I want Pete to hear it," Judge Sessions said as we sat huddled around Pete's office table. "When he got his Eagle, we had a little talk. I simply said, 'Pete, don't forget about the people who helped you get here. Make a commitment that at some time, you're going to pay it back.'

"He went out and he went to college," Judge Sessions continued in his still matter-of-fact voice. "He got out of college, went to work for Southwestern Bell. He went to St. Louis, and finally they were sending him to Bell Labs in New Jersey. And I stopped and had a little conversation with him again. I said, 'Pete . . .'"

"I was thirty," Pete interjected, letting me know not *too* much time had passed.

"'. . . Are you going to do it when you're a grandfather, or are you going to do it now?' Pete didn't get nasty, but he knew I was pushing him. He went to New Jersey and found a Methodist church troop that was dying—they were down to eight or ten boys—and Lord knows when they'd had their last Eagle. He took that troop, and for three years they went everywhere and did everything. And he got I don't know how many Eagles out of that troop!"

So it came to be that Pete fulfilled his obligation by serving as Scoutmaster of then-ailing Troop 88. He immersed himself in the troop and soon added a partner. When he came home late from his first meeting, his wife asked, "What's the deal?"

"Big Scout meeting," he explained, joking that at least his wife didn't have to worry that he'd been carousing around town.

"Next Monday, same thing," he said. "She came to the next one, and she became Assistant Scoutmaster. We decided if she could tie the knot with me then she could teach knots to anybody. So she became a mentor for these boys to teach them a lot of these skills. She knew I needed help. We were partners."

"I was thirty years old," he elaborated. "I became a Scoutmaster, and it was the greatest experience I've ever had in my life. I still keep up with a bunch of the guys. Thirteen Eagle Scouts. Wonderful boys."

Those thirteen Eagles didn't all enter Troop 88 as "wonderful boys," however. In some cases, that adjective now applies because of the changes Pete helped bring about. He remembered one particularly difficult case and recalled, "This one Scout was rough. He wanted to knock other boys down. He wanted to pick on them, he wanted to bully them . . . and I had a choice I had to make with him."

He pulled the Scout aside, and they talked. "You're gonna kick me out of the troop aren't you," the Scout asked.

"No, I'm going to require you to be here in a uniform every week and be here on time and to know that you learned a lesson," Pete answered. "Or I'm going to tell your parents, and then I *am* going to kick you out."

"He turned out to be one of my greatest Eagle Scouts," Pete concluded.

When I thought back on our conversation, I realized that the judge did not push Pete to serve as a Scoutmaster for his son's sake alone. The elder Sessions loves Scouting every bit as much as his son, but his career—as a U.S. attorney, a U.S. district judge, and director of the FBI—utterly consumed his personal time. Although he regrets not spending time working directly with Scouts beyond serving on a board of directors, he treasures his time in law enforcement.

"Tremendous challenge," he said of his tenure at the FBI, which began with a 1987 appointment from Ronald Reagan and lasted until 1993. "Very challenging, loved the agents, loved the agency. I did *not* like the constant pressure of the job. You're always attacked or criticized for one reason or another. But leading those men and women is a privilege. It's not leading them into battle, but it's close. It's an honor."

Judge Sessions never led Scouts on a campout or served as a Scoutmaster, however, and I sensed he sincerely regrets that. By encouraging Pete to serve as a Scoutmaster, he helped settle his score with the Boy Scouts.

The Scouting experience has always tied the Sessions family together. William A. Sessions, Jr., a preacher from Nebraska and father of the future director of the FBI, authored the first *God and Country* handbook, a guide for

Scouting's Protestant religious award. Since then, awards have appeared for most every religion, including Catholicism, Buddhism, and Islam. Like my grandfather, who was born on an Alabama farm in 1903 and orphaned shortly thereafter, Williams Sessions, Jr., never joined Scouting but received the Silver Beaver award for contributions to the program as an adult. I found that men such as William Sessions, Jr., and Alvin Townley, Sr., who never experienced Scouting as boys, seem to have a real and particular inspiration to ensure that others have the chance to benefit from the program.

When I first met with the Sessions family, Pete's son Bill stood several months shy of continuing the family tradition: He had almost earned Eagle. Bill's younger brother, Alex, who has Down syndrome, had recently become involved in Scouting as well. "Part of what I had was Scouting, and I want that for my boys," Pete reflected. Given the encouragement coming from Bill's father and grandfather, I expected he would reach Eagle soon. Otherwise, Pete told me, he wouldn't be driving! But Bill's original motivation came from something other than car keys. He found it in the person of his father, just like his father, Pete, found it in *his* father.

Pete still tells the story of how, like many sons of Eagles, his father's example started him down the trail. When his parents left him unattended, Pete occasionally rummaged through his father's sock drawer and retrieved a small hope chest.

"I'd open it up when he went out," Pete remembered, "and baby teeth were in there, a lock of hair—all from my older brother. They don't save yours when you're number two."

"You don't know if they're yours," his father protested.

"I asked," Pete shot back with a grin before listing the box's remaining contents: "his fraternity ring, his captain's bars from the Air Force, and also in there was his Eagle badge. And that became a symbol of what I wanted to be. I didn't know a thing about Scouting. I knew what my Dad was, and I knew what I wanted to be. I didn't pick the Air Force. I didn't pick a fraternity. I picked this thing which I felt best exemplified my Dad.

"One of the things which we in Scouting become is role models," he explained. "Sometimes good, sometimes not so good, but by and large we all have that same path of hard work and honesty and doing things in a way that will make our life better and life better for others. But I knew that I wanted to be an Eagle Scout as a result of my Dad. And that became a driving goal for me."

My own father's hope chest lived in the top left drawer of his dresser. Cufflinks and collar stays surrounded the small wooden chest and old bottles of English Leather and Old Spice cologne gave the drawer a scent I'll always remember. Inside the chest, red velvet padded fraternity pins, assorted trinkets, and a plastic case that held his Eagle Scout badge. That badge, and what it represented, always shaped my view of him.

When Senator Enzi and I joked that neither his son, Brad, nor I had much choice in becoming an Eagle, my laugh hid an element of truth. My father never *made* me join Scouting. He never *forced* me to earn Eagle, although at times, he did apply some strong—and in retrospect, needed—encouragement. Somewhat like Scoutmasters, fathers serve as our role models, and so, for me, I had little choice in earning the rank because the person I admired most happened to be an Eagle Scout. If I wanted to fill my father's shoes, I had to earn the badge. From the first time I opened the chest that held his Eagle medal, much of my choice in the matter vanished.

The Eagle legacy becomes a family legacy. Three generations of Perots earned Eagle; three generations of Honamans reached the rank. There were the Amerines, Yasins, and Huwes, three families of brothers who pulled—and egged—each other on toward Scouting's highest rank. There were the Grays in Texas, the Mullens in Virginia, and the Allens in Utah. I encountered an unending succession of Scouting families during my trips across the country. I wish I could tell each story because every one offered new clues that helped me better understand this timeless tradition of which all Eagles—and, by association, many mothers, sisters, uncles, and brothers—are part.

In addition to those born into Scouting, each year countless other young men become the first—but likely not the last—in their family to earn the rank of Eagle Scout. As Scoutmaster, Pete served as a role model for many such boys. By word and example, he helped them understand why they needed to spend their free time camping, tying knots, attending meetings, and reciting oaths just so they could earn a badge. I wondered how he encouraged them.

"I told them that I know of nothing that is more prestigious," he said.

"There's nothing that would be more of a challenge to them that they would carry through their whole life. In my obituary, they won't write down that I was president of the political science society of Southwestern University, and they won't write down that I was rush chairman of my fraternity. They won't write down that I was quarterback and captain of a team. They *will* write down that I was an Eagle Scout because that is something that we all identify with. It means honor and respect. I told them if they had the mettle to do it, they could achieve that."

Three Eagles: grandfather, father, and son at Bill Sessions's Eagle Scout Court of Honor
COURTESY OF PETE SESSIONS

He elaborated, saying, "It's honored; it's revered; it comes through hard work. It comes through taking that path less traveled. It comes through doing something that is a little bit different than all of the other guys. They say about eight out of one hundred boys are in Scouting, and then only 2 percent of those will make Eagle. Pretty steep odds, so you've got to really challenge yourself."

Then the judge jumped back into the fray at our conference table. "I take a great deal of pride in having been an Eagle," he said. "It's like being in the

presence of heroic people. . . . They do what they do because they feel compelled to do it, challenged to do it, responsible for doing it. Others needed
leadership, and they knew how to do that. And they knew they could be
trusted to do it and do it ethically, honestly, with honor, and according to the
Scout Oath and Law. They give it their best shot.

"It's very important to me to know that I'm with that caliber of people,
that group of men," he continued. "So much of it is built upon people who
give of themselves to help train young men and to be with them. They're just
like old shoes: They're there every Monday night for a troop meeting. That's
where they are, that's what they do. And they're heroes because they're the
people who made it possible for me or you or anybody else to achieve their
Eagle. And that's what I tell [new Eagles] in the letter I send to all these guys.
I say, 'Go thank your leaders for what they did for you and then make a commitment that you will pay it back.' That means you'll help Scouting wherever
you are.

"The driving force behind Scouting is those people who pay back," he
concluded. "Otherwise, it'd die. Who knows the wonderful experiences that
we've had, and if you don't pay back, how can other people have those same
experiences? How can they do it?"

They couldn't. Those who earn Eagle understand that, and they pass
along a sense of obligation to their sons and grandsons. Sometimes they pass
it along with encouraging words. In other instances, they perpetuate the
Scouting legacy simply by *showing* their children the meaning of the badge
that defines them. In their fathers, sons often see what they want to become,
and so it happens that every year, thousands of young men decide to walk a
familiar path and become Eagle Scouts.

The Scoutmaster of Troop 890 called the color guard forward. A crew of
Scouts trudged up the chapel aisle carrying the American and Troop flags.
They posted the colors, and the audience joined in the pledge of allegiance,
hands over their hearts. Then another call, this time to a cadre of four Eagles,
who escorted Bill Sessions and his parents to the stage. They looked out to an
audience of more than sixty people who had gathered to watch sixteen-year-
old Bill extend the family tradition.

Pete wore his Scout uniform. Around his neck hung his Distinguished

Eagle Scout Award, Woodbadge beads, and Silver Beaver. He was a congress-man and an accomplished Scouter, but on that warm afternoon, he stood there as a proud father. The beaming grandfather, Judge Sessions, sat nearby. I lost myself briefly, remembering my own Eagle ceremony: standing on stage alongside my father in his uniform and my grandfather in his red Scout jacket and slightly tattered garrison hat.

Bill's Scoutmaster returned my attention to the present as he summoned all Eagle Scouts in the audience to the front of the chapel. Roughly twenty of us formed a line, raised our right hands in the Scout sign, and repeated the Scout Oath. A warm feeling of comfort settled over me as we recited the words together, something I had not done in public for more than ten years. Repeating the familiar sentences, I thought back to Scouting, which meant I thought about my father and grandfather. I wondered how many of the Eagles beside me had similar thoughts. How many of them were part of a family tradition? Then I realized we all stood there as a family, a group of individuals united by a code that none of us will ever forget. We will always be moved by Scouting's pageantry and remain loyal to its oath and law. They will always remind us of the pure principles we learned as we worked toward Eagle.

Judge Sessions stood up and walked to the stage, parting a sea of khaki uniforms with his dark suit. He stood behind the podium, momentarily studied his audience, and began telling us how he charged Pete to remain active in Scouting, the story I'd heard several months before in Washington. Then he turned to his grandson and passed on the tradition. "Bill, you may think this is the reward," the white-haired judge said, referring to the day's ceremony. "Really, the reward is yet to come. It will come when you give back to Scouting as a man."

I witnessed the legacy handed down once more.

BROTHERS

Scouting does not just pass from one generation to the next. It also passes between members of the *same* generation, between brothers. Scouting becomes part of growing up for thousands of families that send brother after brother into the local troop, with the younger brothers often wearing hand-me-down uniforms from older siblings. To the best of my knowledge, no family has sent more brothers of one generation into Scouting than the Thomases of Las Vegas, Nevada, and no one mother has raised as many Eagle Scouts as Sherry Thomas.

When Rex Thomas received his Eagle in 2001 he became the eleventh—and last—Thomas brother to earn the rank, following a tradition begun in 1982 by DeCall, the oldest. Ten boys followed DeCall's example: twins Devon and Darren, Robert, Ralph, Gordon, Gilbert, Charles, Eddie, Harvey, and Rex. Only their sister Elaine never earned Eagle.

Like Bill Marriott and most other Eagle Scouts, DeCall quickly credited his mother with the family's record. He recalled her quiet persistence, but Mrs. Thomas deflected the accolades. "I don't think I really pushed them," she said. "They had good leaders. I did help with the planning, and I'd make things available for them, like inviting a merit badge counselor over for dinner. And for Personal Management merit badge, I'd take them to the bank and let them talk to the president. I put a lot of miles on the car driving them around!

"But once we got the first four Eagles, they were the ones who put the pressure on the younger brothers," she explained. "So I didn't have to do that anymore! Especially when we got to number ten and eleven, the older boys *really* put the pressure on the younger ones; they weren't going to let the tradition end! It was just expected of them. People will usually rise up to expectations."

I hadn't talked with Sherry Thomas long before I realized how she handled eleven boys: with her sweet laugh and gentle sense of humor. She shared a story about DeCall: "They went to the lake one summer. It was terrifically hot in the desert. DeCall didn't fill up his canteen before a hike, and he ended up drinking hotcake syrup he found in his backpack!" She laughed at the memory. "But whatever they go through, they learn. That doesn't mean I don't worry about them, but you can't hold them back. Boys have just got to experience campouts and getting away from home and things like that. It's hard for us mothers to cut those apron strings, but it's a tough world, and you've got to help them be prepared and then let them go. One of my sons is on a mission trip in Guatemala. He's in a third-world country on a two-year camping trip! I know he'll survive because he's an Eagle Scout."

Her boys' tenacity, however, makes Mrs. Thomas the most proud. "They've stuck with it," she said proudly. "They didn't say, 'The project's too hard,' and quit. They're finishers. It's rewarding to know that they stuck with it. When they achieve in one area they'll go on to achieve in other areas. I've got three that speak Japanese, one speaks Italian, and three others speak Spanish. They sing wonderfully together, and all play instruments. Scouting makes a person well rounded: My sons earned Music merit badge, Art, and Shotgun Shooting!"

"We're not a perfect family. I don't want you to think that," she added softly. "We have our problems, but our boys have that common link and have always been true brothers."

Sherry Thomas and her husband, Larry, together with the leaders of Troop 233, certainly prepared a generation of boys for life. As their Eagles grew older, many continued serving as Scout leaders, and all remained brothers in fact and in action, much like another band of young men I encountered on the other side of the Continental Divide.

THE AMERINES

TROOP 41, PARIS, ARKANSAS

It's often the small victories that sustain us, and they certainly sustained me from time to time as I pushed forward on this journey. At the outset, I never realized to what degree this venture would both exhaust me and energize me. I thought it would take several months. Originally, I had a job lined up that would start after my three-month hiatus. Then I found myself needing more answers. Nearly twelve months without a paycheck passed before I had simultaneously satisfied my quest and spent most of my savings. Thousands of miles of travel and the stress of having neither certainty nor income took its toll but also bestowed its gifts. I was alternately weary from traveling and buoyed by the wonderful stories I heard. But when I found myself spending more nights on the road than at home and when the sheer number of stories to hear overwhelmed me, the small things gave me the strength to continue.

One small personal victory along the way occurred on a windy day near the waterfront of Annapolis, Maryland. I had spent the past two months talking with Travis Amerine over the phone, having conversations about Scouting and about finding time to meet. Travis was a senior, a first-classman as they're called, at the U.S. Naval Academy, and nearly four years in that military environment had instilled in him any manners he might not have fully acquired in high school. He *always* called me "sir."

I was only seven years older than Travis, didn't wear a uniform, and never referred to myself as Mr. Townley, but that didn't seem to matter to Midshipman Amerine. Every time I heard the word *sir* slip from his mouth, I felt the chill of recognition that I was getting older. I had waged a two-month campaign to be "Alvin" with no luck, but when I called Travis as I walked through the Academy's gates, he answered his phone, "Alvin!" A laugh followed the salutation; he knew he'd given me the small victory I'd wanted all along.

That crack in his military façade continued to open as he walked me along the pathways that crisscross the historic 160-year-old campus. Far from being the stoic militarist I had originally expected the brigade commander to be, Travis had an energetic laugh that came easily and often. His eyes sparkled with optimism beneath the shiny black bill of his hat as we entered Tecumseh Court, where he led formations of the 4,400-person Brigade of Midshipmen throughout the fall. His peers and the staff at the Academy had appointed him brigade commander for his senior year. The position, the most prestigious a midshipman can hold, recognizes a young man's abilities as a leader and role model.

"He is the brigade commander," observed Captain T. R. Rains, the Academy's chief-of-staff and an Eagle Scout himself, "so he is someone who has obviously the leadership skills, the personality, and the personal integrity. Again, it is all those qualities that we see in Eagle Scouts which make it easy for him to step up to the plate and take charge of 4,400 midshipmen."

"Twenty-two years old, and he is in charge of 4,400 midshipmen," T. R. reiterated thoughtfully. "There is a brigade staff, two regiments, six battalions, and thirty companies. Being in a Scout troop where you have a troop and all the organization and leadership there, he has been in leadership positions before. That set him up to do what he is doing now."

The service academies all recognize that preparation, and their classes are comprised of disproportionately high numbers of Eagle Scouts as well as Girl Scouts who've earned the Gold Award. Eagles comprise roughly 12 percent of an entering Naval Academy class, and by graduation, they comprise an average of 14 percent of the class—a tribute to their ability to persevere.

It was Captain Rains who first told me about these statistics, and who also introduced me to the Amerines. As I visited with Captain and Mrs. Rains in their historic campus home several months earlier, the veteran F-18 Hornet commander mentioned a family from Paris, Arkansas. The Amerines, I discovered, had a storied tradition in Scouting and at the Naval Academy. Of the four brothers—Will, Lee, Travis, and Denver—three had attended the Academy, and all four had earned their Eagle rank.

So I had returned to Annapolis to meet Travis and his younger brother,

Denver, a third-classman. The older brother had met me just inside the Academy's Maryland Street gate and walked me through the campus toward the wide, stone-covered quadrangle that is Tecumseh Court. Then he ushered me through the gates of the world's largest dormitory, a mammoth yet graceful stone building bearing the name Bancroft Hall.

As we passed through the gates, I thought about the great leaders who, as young midshipmen, walked through those same doors, among them, World War II Admirals "Bull" Halsey and Chester Nimitz, President Jimmy Carter, Senator John McCain, legendary quarterback Roger Staubach, and NBA great David Robinson—all men known for their character as well as their ability.

Will, Denver, Travis, and Lee Amerine
COURTESY OF THE AMERINE FAMILY

Soon we met Travis's little, although taller, brother Denver. Their dark hair, tanned skin, and shining eyes immediately marked them as brothers, and on that windy afternoon, these Eagles taught me how far Scouting had carried the Amerine brothers and how they had also carried each other.

The Amerine home on Mt. Magazine in the Ozark Mountains sits fifteen minutes from downtown Paris, a town of 3,500. Their house, which mirrors the scale of Paris, has only two bedrooms, but in that small house, family ties grew strong.

"Our home is very, very small," said Travis after the three of us had sat down together in a room overlooking the central campus. "All four of us brothers, these guys were our best friends. We grew up in the same room. My dad wouldn't let us spend the night other places. The only time we spent the night away from the house was camping out at a Boy Scout campout. Dad said, 'Your brothers are your best friends, and you don't go anywhere else.' So we all grew up in one room, the four of us in bunk beds, one bathroom. Just an itty-bitty house in the middle of nowhere.

"Our parents' bedroom was on one side of the house; ours was on the other," Denver added after deferring to his older brother. "Mom was the only woman in the house with five men, and it was like that until Will went to college. At one point we were eighteen, sixteen, fourteen, and twelve. Dad had a purpose. He put us in that room for a purpose, and he knew by doing that he was going to lay the foundation for a bond between the four of us that would lead to where we are today being best friends."

Their father, Perry, believed Scouting provided another way to bring his family closer, and he involved Will, the oldest, in Scouts; the others followed. In Troop 41, the Amerine brothers found leaders like Scoutmaster Tom Spivey, Jim Shearer, and their father. Then there was Scoutmaster David Robberson, who also served as chief chef, and Travis and Denver couldn't recall ever eating better. "Give him a Dutch oven, and he could really cook," remembered Denver.

Perry Amerine served as an Assistant Scoutmaster and turned the troop into a merit badge factory. At every meeting, professionals he recruited from Paris and nearby towns would teach classes for several badges. The mayor taught Citizenship in the Community and Citizenship in the Nation; a local surgeon taught First Aid; and various high school coaches taught Athletics and Golf merit badges. These counselors, many former Scouts themselves, gave generously of their time to teach these boys lessons few classrooms offered. The entire village of Paris helped the Scouts of Troop 41 toward Eagle, and, with older citizens mentoring younger citizens, this small community grew stronger.

The Scouts also learned from each other as the older boys in 41 passed their skills, perspective, and knowledge to those behind them. Youth were teaching youth, learning to give their time to others for the good of the troop or the community. Sometimes I would think of the Eagle legacy in broad strokes, considering the marks particular Eagles have had on the nation, marks such as those left by Sam Walton or Percy Sutton. However, as I continued meeting Scouts who were not CEOs, astronauts, or senators, I realized that the legacy begins in the tradition young Eagles create in their troop. It starts with Scouts learning new skills and passing those skills on to others, not because they're required to or paid to but because they recognize something larger than themselves. They owe something to those who first helped them, and they owe something to their troop.

In those early days of Scouting, boys also begin building the foundations of their character as they, together with their fellow troop members, recite the Scout Oath and Law. "I'm thirteen years old, and I go into Scouts and start reciting this duty, honor, country, trustworthy, loyal, helpful, friendly—all that stuff," reflected Travis. "And these words, you start talking about them, and you would be hard pressed to find someone else at the age of thirteen that's thinking about these words and reciting them at a public forum and saying, 'These are my ideals.' So you start talking about these things at a young age. I'm not going to tell you that at thirteen I was really thinking about honor or the words; I didn't fully comprehend what those words meant. But by the time you're an Eagle, you figured it out. And your last project is your service project, and you're out there and you say, 'All right, I've got to do this for someone else.' That's what Scouts was about."

Service projects became a family affair, with Denver dutifully logging more hours than anyone else in the family since he participated in four projects. (Of course, as little brother, he had little choice.) For the first Amerine Eagle project, Lee's, the family and troop pitched in to build trailside tables and hiking signs on the paths that wove up Mt. Magazine. For Will's project, the brothers and the troop constructed a city park. They cut cedars in the nearby woods, hauled them to Paris, and built a fence and picnic tables for the community. Two years later, the brothers were hauling wood and posthole diggers up Mt. Magazine to build benches on the 2,753-foot summit for

Travis's project. Denver remembered, "I put a *lot* of work into Travis's project. Putting benches on the top of Mt. Magazine, digging through rock to put these benches in was just murder."

In his last years as a Scout, Denver became fascinated with aviation, and for the last of the family's Eagle projects he undertook the expansion of a small local runway. More akin to a construction project than a typical Eagle project, Denver oversaw bulldozers and work crews as they cleared trees, then he and his Scout volunteers leveled the fresh dirt and planted grass on what was to be the rural airstrip's new addition. In this project, as in all others, the Scouts learned about helping their communities and about helping each other. The boys elected to spend part of their weekends helping Denver work. They could have chosen to play sports, study, or relax at home. Instead, they turned out to shovel dirt, clear trees and brush, and help their brother Scout.

Several months later, older brother Lee would further explain, "Everyone who showed up for my Eagle project, when they had an Eagle project, I'd show up. They did it for me; I was going to be there for them. Every one of my brothers did that. And most everybody did that. You'd have guys you wouldn't see for two years, but if someone helped them with their Eagle project, they would pay it back."

The legacy of Scouts helping younger Scouts took hold in the Amerine household itself, and perhaps Denver, the youngest, felt it most of all. Just as Josh Morriss led Ross Perot to Eagle and then to the Naval Academy, so too did Will lead Lee, who led Travis, who in turn led Denver.

"In every instance, a brother read the Eagle Charge to the new Eagle," Travis said. "And Mom's on deck. Dad thought she was going to drown or dehydrate from crying so much. But I remember that being a significant moment, really kind of cool. Lee read the Charge to Will, then Will read mine, then I read Denver's."

"Did these brothers give you a hard time as you came along?" I asked the youngest.

"Oh, I got all *kinds* of stuff, Alvin," Denver said dramatically. "I was really viewed as the one who wasn't going to be an Eagle Scout. They were like, 'He's never going to get on the ball. He's never going to get his Eagle. He's way behind the power curve.' I had my brothers on my back for probably two years, starting when I was about fifteen, saying, 'You gotta get on this thing. You don't have many years left, and you're still First Class, so they really didn't think I was going to get my Eagle Scout, and when I got it, I really rubbed it in their face.

"There was some jawing between us," Denver restated. "Not so much between Will and Lee but with me and Travis. Will said it best. Will had Lee do his Eagle Charge to him. He made a comment that 'Lee is my younger brother, but he paved the way for me.' " But Lee would say Will paved the way for him.

"His leadership was something different," Lee said of Will several months later when we met at the Naval Air Station in Meridian, Mississippi. "What he did as an older brother was getting us through high school, and the support he's given us past that has been a lot and has really helped out the family. Here I was: I was the poster boy per se until Travis came along. I was this and that, all-state track, Naval Academy, battalion commander, and Will would always say, 'Way to be, Lee. Good job.' Then we'd be playing one-on-one basketball, and he'd be throwing elbows in my face, so I knew the rivalry was there! But I couldn't understand why he was so pro-Lee when I'm upstaging him."

"So then when all of a sudden Travis started doing real well, I'm like, 'Travis, way to be.' Then people started saying, 'Travis is going to be the *brigade* commander, and you were just a battalion commander. How does that make you feel?'

"I thought, 'That's awesome.' I was so *proud* that he was upstaging me."

Although Will never followed the military path, the oldest brother ushered his younger siblings along that course. Lee remembered the nicknames they each chose from their favorite movie: "Will was Maverick, I was Cougar, Travis was Iceman, Denver was Wolfman. We all had the same idea at the same time: 1986, *Top Gun*.

Several weeks after meeting Travis and Denver, I found Lee pursuing the collective boyhood dream of the Amerine boys and of every other boy who saw F-14 Tomcats thundering into the dawn sky during *Top Gun*'s opening scene. The navy's prestigious jet training program in Meridian, Mississippi, occupied his days—and many of his nights—but Lee didn't mind the long hours or dangers. Every day he was doing what he loved to do.

As he and I surveyed the rows of orange-and-white jets arranged on the airfield's sunlit tarmac, I noticed through his sunglasses the same sparkle of pride and excitement I had seen weeks earlier in his younger brother, Travis, the brigade commander. His gaze lingered on the planes, then he finally blinked, disengaged from the neatly parked jets, and began telling me about the first time he walked across the expansive flight deck of an aircraft carrier on which he would begin landing in just eighteen short months. The opportunity came at the 1993 National Scout Jamboree on board the *John F. Kennedy*. Standing on the carrier's four-acre flight deck, Lee promised himself, "The next time I'm on the *JFK*, it's going to be hook-down, catching that #3 wire in an F-18."

Aboard the *Kennedy* that day in 1993, Lee stood next to his older brother Will, reflecting the way that they approached Scouting, always at the other's side. Lee became the youngest Scout in Troop 41 by eight months and had no friends his age, but Will made sure the older Scouts adopted his younger brother. "I had an in with the big kids," Lee remembered. "I had my tent partner from day one, and I had a guy who knew how to do everything. Coming in at ten years of age, if I didn't have anyone, I'd have probably sunk. The transition and my ability to travel so fast through the ranks of Scouting was because of Will, because I had a home even though I had no peers."

Among the older Scouts who watched out for Lee were the Pickartz brothers, one a future submariner and the other a future Green Beret currently on duty in Afghanistan. They adopted Will's little brother as their own and helped Lee through his first years in the troop. During those early years in 41, Lee weighed in at half the size of many of the other Scouts but would never confess to the struggles that caused. He recalled, "If I was having a problem backpacking, I'd say, 'No, I'm fine. I'm fine.' Then all of a sudden my water's gone; some dude's carrying that. All of a sudden the tent poles are gone out of my bag and my pack is fifteen pounds lighter in a heartbeat, and there'd go the Pickartz boys hiking away with all my stuff!

"I was just a little ten-year-old, but that's what I learned, that unselfishness," he concluded. "That's why I liked the military so much, and I think that's why the bottom three boys are there."

In such a refreshingly honest manner, these brothers truly believe in the idea of service. Travis and Lee both talked at length about their attraction to the military and how much they enjoyed being able to serve others, serve their country, and live in a world where the traits they valued in Scouting still shape life around them.

"I'd like to think we've developed into honorable people who are service oriented and are loyal to something," Travis had said at Annapolis, "That's what the military is all about, that sense of patriotism that Scouts embeds in you. Saying the Pledge of Allegiance before a meeting, saluting the flag, you lay those foundations, and you want to continue to serve that. We're hopeless patriots."

Lee, a fellow hopeless patriot, loves the same concept. "Nobody's more important than the guy sitting next to you in your foxhole," he said, "or behind you or on your wing." And in the military, he found others who shared the same feeling. "It's just that group that makes Scouts so unique, those driven people looking for opportunities, the people who make the military unique. That middle-class group that comes in and just excels because they've got the drive, and they've just been looking for a chance to excel in something.

"The initial attraction is going Mach 2 with your hair on fire," he added candidly. "And it's a lot of fun so far. But then it's serving."

By this time, a low Mississippi moon had replaced the March sun, and Lee's wife, Jen, joined us at a picnic table where Lee and I were finishing dinner. Both twenty-four, they had married just six months earlier, slightly over a year since Lee "Pearl-Harbored" her, as she put it. Borrowing an idea from the film *Pearl Harbor*, Lee had made their second date a private sunset flight. His trick worked.

Growing more serious, albeit just slightly, Jen talked about the mark the Eagle rank left on her husband. "He is very self-motivated," she said, then paused, smiled, and added, "when it comes to something he's passionate about."

Lee reacted defensively: "What, I'm not passionate about the dishes?"

Jen just smiled and continued, "He gives me motivation. He knows what he wants to do and he goes for it and that's what I admire the most about him.

He always looks after other people." Modestly, Lee deflected her compliments by making a point about the way his parents and troop leaders raised the brothers.

"We were given that," Lee said. "You *care* about people. You don't judge them; you *care* about them."

The Amerines made friends with most everyone in their troop. Some were very poor, some ran in different social circles, but they all cared for their brother Scouts. Lee, a varsity athlete in high school, remembered eating lunch with one group but spending time with fellow Eagles who sat in different areas of the cafeteria. "We'd sit together, or I'd invite him to sit with me, and we would have genuine conversations about real-life stuff," he recalled.

Lee would then return to the conversation at the "jock table," as he called it. There, he remembered the conversation usually amounting to "Hey, that girl looks good over there!" He laughed at the memory and concluded, "It teaches you to value what's important, Scouting does. And that's what the Amerine boys do, and that's very simple. That's how we operate."

A significant part of Scouting in Paris involved understanding different types of people, a lesson lost on neither Lee nor Travis. "When you're out there camping and hanging around with these people, you just *talk*," Travis had observed. "I mean you really don't pick that up just by talking on the Internet or something. But when you're out there in the woods, you start to learn a little bit about everybody and your surroundings, and you appreciate the art of just speaking to someone and enjoying their company."

A majority of the conversations I had during this venture began with Scouting, then usually segued into other areas before inevitably returning to the subject of ethics. Unmistakably, Scouting leaves its boys with an acute sense of morality. That same grounding and preoccupation drew Lee back to ethics as the moon rose higher and the hour grew later. He returned to his older brother Will.

After college, Will worked as a coach for several years before entering business, where he quickly learned that the ethics driving Troop 41 do not mark every organization. He discovered his company's promises and practices didn't match.

Lee related the story, saying, "Will went back and said, 'You guys are lying to these people. This isn't how you do business. I'm out.' He went from a job making $55,000 to a job making $37,000 or $38,000. But he was like, 'It's not about this.' So, Will's applying our ethics in the business world, where it's not as cut and dried as it is here. If you back-stab someone in the military, you're done. They don't trust you; you're out. But Will's going to have a tougher time, whereas I'm still in Troop 41!"

I found Will settling into life as a businessman and a newlywed in Ohio, where he shared his thoughts about ethics and business while tending to the new puppy he and his wife, Meg, had just brought home. He pointed straight to the Scout Law. "I think if you listen to each of those twelve characteristics," he said, "you can almost apply that to anything you do in life, whether it be your marriage, your job, leading people, or even if you're just looking at yourself. I mean, if you can't respect yourself, how can you respect anybody else and have other people respect *you*? So, when you look at that Scout Law, those are twelve pretty powerful words that can be applied in any part of your life, and if you apply those, you'll be successful." Even though sometimes, being successful entails sacrificing a much-needed salary for a clean conscience.

It's about more than money, Will told me, adding that Scouting is also about more than ethics alone. To him, success begins and ends with leadership. From his first days in Troop 41, he learned the tactics as well as the ethics needed to work with others. "When I got started," he explained, "I was elected patrol leader, and you step back and you realize that people are expecting you to perform this duty and lead them and leadership is a great honor and you just didn't want to let them down."

From that first brush with responsibility forward, Will saw the leadership of Scouts make a tremendous difference in Troop 41 as they shouldered responsibility for running the troop, keeping in mind the adage "If it is to be, it is up to me." Like so many other future leaders, Will saw that results only come from action.

"I've preached this my whole life," he began. "I've seen it from sports teams to the classroom to my job. Whenever you have good leadership, things happen. We were lucky enough to have good leadership there in the Scouts, and the people you've interviewed—Bloomberg, Ross Perot, some of those other guys—they're great leaders, and the reason they're where they are right now is because of the leadership I *guarantee* you they started working on in the Boy Scouts.

"I think leadership is huge, and people say to me all the time, 'Will, how are you and your brothers the way you are? You guys have never met a stranger, you always stand up when somebody has to be the one to speak in front of a group, you four boys are the first ones to volunteer all the time. Why is that?'

"I think there's a combination," he said in answer. "Great parenting and then I think what we got from being involved in Scouting and being involved in athletic teams both put a heavy weight on leadership, and that's why you see Travis doing what he's doing now, Lee doing as great as he's doing, and Denver, even though he's still young, he comes over superimpressive when he wants to. I mean, he's got all the charisma in the world. I like to think I'm just holding my own with those three!"

The brothers share so much, but Will can never share the Navy experience, and I wondered if he regretted not applying to Annapolis after his days as Maverick. His answer came easily. "No," he said. "Because I met my wife in college, and I don't know if I'd have ever met her. I love her to death." Since their freshmen year at Hendrix College, Will and Meg have approached life together, and Meg had just learned that that would include Scouting.

Several weeks earlier, she suggested they work with a local charity, and, being a good husband, Will quickly agreed. But he added one stipulation. "If I do that," he said, "you have to get involved with me in Boy Scouts." When the three of us talked, he had her 75 percent committed.

"I got a love for kids," continued Will. "I always have, and I felt like Scouting did so much for me . . . I just wanted to see other kids have that same opportunity that I had." In becoming a volunteer leader, the older brother will again set the pace for the younger brothers. But they may not need his encouragement; they already have their own plans to become involved.

The Amerine brothers, all in their twenties, share a love of Scouting and a lifelong devotion to the program that I expected to find only in much older Scouts. As the brothers each spoke independently about the Boy Scouts and their aim to contribute as adults, their brown eyes shone with the same optimism and passion. They share a boundless faith in the value of Scouting and a firm belief that the lessons and virtues they learned in Troop 41 are truly timeless and form an inseparable thread in the nation's fabric.

Together, Travis, Denver, and I watched two U.S. Marines lower the colors at the Naval Academy as a bugler played *Retreat*, marking the day's end. As the pageant played itself out and the hauntingly familiar notes rolled across the quiet campus just as they roll across hundreds of Scout camps each summer, Travis turned our conversation to Scouting's future.

"It's worldwide, but it's a part of this country," he observed. "The image of a Scout escorting a grandmother across the road is part of this country. And as long as there are Eagle Scouts, there will be Scouting," he said confidently. "Look at us, I'm twenty-two years old. Denver is not even twenty yet . . ."

"Yeah, I am, Travis" Denver objected.

"Okay, he's twenty," Travis allowed. "And we're Eagle Scouts who have aspirations to go back and give to the program." Eagles give back to Scouting, they explained. The experience of every Eagle obligates them to ensure that others have the same opportunities. They are the next generation of Scoutmasters, Assistant Scoutmasters, parents, and merit badge counselors.

"Scouting is one of those things that's going to last forever," Travis concluded, confident that the Amerine brothers and thousands of other Eagles will ensure the tradition lasts. "It will always be part of the American landscape. Did you ever see *Field of Dreams*?"

I had, and Travis reminded me of a particular quote from the 1989 film about America and baseball. "The one constant through all the years, Ray, has been baseball," James Earl Jones said in his resonant voice. "America has rolled by like an army of steamrollers. It has been erased like a blackboard, rebuilt, and erased again, but baseball has marked the time. This field, this game, it's a part of our past, Ray. It reminds us of all that once was good and could be again."

So does Scouting, Travis explained. "If you look at the quote, you can exchange the word *Scouting* for *baseball*. It's enduring." Scouting has survived two world wars, the Great Depression, the upheaval of the 1960s, the challenges of the 1980s and 1990s, and the always changing culture of America's youth. It engaged young men who spent their days plowing fields in the early twentieth century, and it engages youth consumed by the pop culture of the twenty-first century. Scouts in and out of uniform have shaped our history at every turn and, I think, have always reminded others of all that remains good in America. At least, I know that I felt much better about our future having met Will, Lee, Travis, and Denver.

Unlike the Amerines, most young men do not enter Scouting as brothers. But many leave as such. The shared experiences Scouting affords have forged a genuine brotherhood among many friends. Scouts spend weeks together at camps, share experiences in the wilderness, and learn about life together. They see one another's vulnerabilities; they watch each other struggle to achieve goals. They often enter Scouts as strangers, yet once they leave, they remain brothers forever.

Along my way, I've discovered that few things enrich life more than friendships, particularly friendships that endure across decades. I spent one of the past year's most enjoyable afternoons being reminded of that lesson by two Eagle Scouts who have remained lifelong friends. The understanding that comes with familiarity cannot be replaced, and these two men are indeed rich in friendship.

Shortly after lunch, Bob Clement joined Ben Hagood and me on the porch of Ben's downtown Charleston, South Carolina, home. We sat under the shade of the roof, not far from First Scots Presbyterian Church, where both men had earned Eagle in Troop 50. Our conversation wound to their Order of the Arrow ordeals, and they described how they suffered through summertime nights in a damp Low Country field that hummed with mosquitoes.

"It was cruel and unusual punishment, that's what it was," Bob explained with a laugh.

"It was," Ben confirmed. "We didn't have anything to keep the mosquitoes off, and we were told to sleep *across* the plow furrows. It would have been unfair to lie down *in* the furrow, which would have been a little more comfortable. I just remember coming in at daybreak covered in mosquito bites from one end to the other!"

That was during World War II. Sixty years later, these two 1949 Citadel graduates still feel the bond that experiences such as their ordeals fostered. They also share a competitive spirit, and as they began talking about their Eagle badges, Ben proudly noted that he still knew exactly where to find his badge. Bob grinned and trumped his buddy: "Well, mine is right here in my pocket!"

Minutes later, Ben had retrieved his Eagle badge and Order of the Arrow pin from his upstairs bureau. Both men held their badges gently in their time-worn palms, studying the medals and, I think, remembering the early

Lifelong friends Bob Clement (left) and Ben Hagood, Charleston, South Carolina
AUTHOR'S COLLECTION

years of an enduring friendship. Bob broke the silence by pointedly attributing the rip in Ben's faded red, white, and blue ribbon to a fight, which Ben only halfheartedly denied. They both laughed.

Looking again at their medals, I noticed that the passing years had tarnished the silver pendants but that their badges still mirrored the one I received in 1993. And I was coming to realize they also bore the same meaning.

THE SCOUTMASTER

S coutmaster is the most distinguished title a man can have," observed Eagle Scout Jim Breedlove. "When I think of those people who have the opportunity to shape lives of individuals to produce an outcome that is relevant, the role of Scoutmaster does that better than any one position I can think of. Jack Langford's story is certainly one example."

As a superior court judge in Fulton County, Georgia, Jack Langford saw hundreds of young men in trouble pass before his bench, and he began to speculate that the experiences he enjoyed as a Scout in the Flint River Council might help boys from Atlanta's tough neighborhoods avoid appearances in his courtroom. Consequently, he developed a vision for a Boy Scout troop that catered to inner-city youth, a vision that would serve as the inspiration for a national program launched by the Boy Scouts.

After working with a suburban troop and guiding his own two sons to Eagle, Judge Langford accepted the challenge of becoming Scoutmaster of Troop 42 at All Saints Episcopal Church in downtown Atlanta. For ten years, Langford led a troop where half his boys attended Atlanta's finest private schools and half lived in the Techwood Homes housing project, just blocks away from the in-town church.

"They all found out, hey, the other guys are not too different from me," the white-haired judge said of his Scouts. "Some were underprivileged, and some were overprivileged. We worked our Scout troop so that didn't make a whole lot of difference. We had patrol equipment, and I had a trailer full of sleeping bags; the kids didn't have to own a lot of camping equipment to be a participating member of Troop 42. I had boys from Techwood Homes in downtown Atlanta go to Philmont and the Northern Tier Canoe Base."

Scouts from the violent Techwood neighborhood found a place to learn about the outdoors and about values they often didn't find in their neighborhood. Judge Langford recounted one particular story that remained with me. After Troop 42 staged a car wash, a young Scout named Billy Brown found a $20 bill while the Scouts were cleaning up the parking lot. Billy brought the bill to his Scoutmaster. Judge Langford knew how valuable $20 could be to Billy's family, and he said, "Billy, that ought to be yours."

Billy said, "That belongs to the troop."

The judge was thunderstruck. "Billy was just a little boy with no exposure to ethics other than being part of our Scout troop and talking the terminology that we talked and recited and wrote," Langford said. "Well, you never know when the things kids learn in Scouting are going to mean something. That would have been money that he or his family could have done a lot of things with."

During our meeting in his chambers, Judge Langford confided that he had recently received a Father's Day card from Billy, who became a U.S. Marine before starting a successful banking career. "I never had a father," Billy had written. "You were it."

On the other side of the equation, I learned how deeply these Scoutmasters cared for their boys. The job of Scoutmaster becomes a lifelong calling for many, as it did for Wilbert Bernshouse. I met Wilbert seventy-five years after he earned Eagle himself in Sumter, South Carolina's Troop 1, April 1930.

We visited under a perfect spring sky in his well-tended garden for some time before Mrs. Bernshouse called us inside for lunch. Her husband and I obeyed and walked into the simple whitewashed wood home the couple had shared since the 1950s. I found their legacy on the wood-paneled wall to my right. Hanging beneath a handsomely carved image of the Eagle badge were seventy-five polished wooden bars, each of which bore the name of an Eagle Scout from Troop 336, where Wilbert served as Scoutmaster from 1942 until 1986.

The Bernshouses viewed Scouting as a team endeavor, and they devoted themselves to the boys. They led simple lives, both working low-paying jobs at a local plant. Their joy came from being together and taking their Scouts camping in their slightly rusted station wagon. As she served us a home-cooked lunch, Mrs. Bernshouse explained, "We're simple people. We've never had fancy things. We just did our jobs so we could spend time with the boys."

"Scouting was not an avid part of his life; it was his life," observed Stan Brading, whose name hangs below the Eagle carving in Wilbert's home. "His success and character is not only measured in terms of merit badges and ranks earned by his Scouts—which probably ranks with anyone else in history—but more importantly, by the success and character he built in those of us lucky enough to call him Scoutmaster. He truly sacrificed having material things in his life so he could devote his entire existence to bettering the kids in his Scout troop, many of whom he personally recruited from 'the wrong side of town.' It is rare to find that individual who honestly lives for the betterment of others, with little personal regard other than knowing he's made a difference in a young man's life, a young man he didn't know before and may not know again."

Scoutmasters are the heart of the Scouting program; without them, Scouting would not exist. They volunteer untold hours to instill the values of the Oath and Law in their boys. Many become second fathers to their Scouts, and few Eagles forget the role their Scoutmaster played in their life. Stan Brading, now an accomplished attorney, still remembers the impact Wilbert Bernshouse had on him at the age Stan felt it mattered most. He had not seen his Scoutmaster in thirty years but said, "I have more respect and admiration for Wilbert Bernshouse than literally anyone else I know. I'm just regretful that I don't have a better ability to capture in words the incredible spirit of that great man."

Stan and I have the same regret.

ALVIN TOWNLEY, JR.

TROOP 84, ATLANTA, GEORGIA

EAGLE SCOUT, 1961

Sometimes, journeys end where they begin. As our car rolled onto Boy Scout Road outside Covington, Georgia, I think my father and I both sensed that we were driving the final leg of my 40,000-mile trek. We soon passed beneath the archway of heavy wooden beams that marked the entrance to Bert Adams Scout Reservation. We drove between thickets of East Georgia pines and grassy fields peppered with hills of irrepressible fire ants. We passed trails leading to the Order of the Arrow campfire ring and campsites named Sioux, Seminole, and Arapahoe, before we finally parked beside the old, familiar A-frame of Woodruff Dining Hall.

We stepped out of my Explorer and inhaled the rare, fleeting air that comes to the South at a time of year no longer summer yet not quite fall. The hush that marks camps after the summer season ends surrounded us. We stood practically alone.

Just to the east of the dining hall, a Chinese chestnut tree still grew where it had been planted four decades ago by my grandfather, Alvin Townley, Sr. Touching the smooth bark of its trunk was like finally reaching home plate after a long trip around the baseball diamond. For me, Scouting began with that tree. I trace my earliest memories of Scouting to Bert Adams, where my father and grandfather brought me to see this tree and this camp they both loved. Ultimately, the Scoutmaster who planted the chestnut bore responsibility for the two Eagle Scouts who now stood before it.

"This is a great returning point for us, to come down here to Bert Adams," said my father, Alvin Jr., as he stood beside me. "It's great to remember how much Dad loved Scouting and how enthusiastic he was about Eagle Scouts."

Like me, my father had become the son of a Scoutmaster. The Troop Committee at Haygood Memorial United Methodist Church asked my grandfather to serve as Scoutmaster of Troop 84 in 1960. Although he had never been a Scout himself, Scouting had always fascinated him, and he accepted the post. As the Troop Committee chairman, I suspect he had little choice. I think if I could ask him today, he would say that many of his warmest memories came from experiences in the Scout hut that still sits across the parking lot from the church sanctuary.

"He'd grown up in the country without the benefit of a Scouting program," my father observed of our namesake. "He saw what a wonderful opportunity Scouting was and how many skills it could develop in a young man, and I think he was able to see that had he been in a situation where there was a Scout troop, he certainly would have wanted to take advantage of that. I think he imparted that to me and later to you because he realized how Scouting gave you the opportunity to be a leader, how it gave you an opportunity to gain skills that would stay with you all your life.

"There's a country song out about wanting to be somebody," he continued. "I remember that was a phrase he used often. He wanted you to be somebody. He didn't write a song about it, but you knew by just being around him that he expected you to reach that goal of Eagle Scout. That was an important thing. It would please him. Whether *I* fully understood at the time how important it was for me, it was that constant encouragement that he gave me that got me to Eagle. He tied that idea of being somebody right into earning Eagle. For him, those two ideas went hand in hand."

My father reveled in nostalgia as we walked along the wide dirt trails that meandered through empty campsites and led to the silent waterfront. He began to recall his time with Troop 84 at this very camp, doing "buddy checks" and mile-swims in the same lake. As his mind drifted, he spoke about the older boys who pulled him through Scouting. For him, and for many other young Scouts, seeing a polished young man with real leadership skills motivated him more than a Scoutmaster's words ever could have.

Pulled along by the older boys in Atlanta's close-knit Morningside neighborhood, my father earned his Eagle in October 1961 at the age of fourteen. He went on to the University of Georgia and then joined the insurance agency his father started from scratch in 1946. He never forgot his debt to Scouting—I'm sure my grandfather never gave him the chance—and always remained a volunteer, serving as chairman of Atlanta's National Eagle Scout Association chapter. Like so many fathers, his involvement increased when I joined Scouting. He served as Cubmaster of Cub Scout Pack 577 before becoming Scoutmaster of Troop 103 several years later.

Neither of us could remember whether we discussed him taking the job, but he distinctly remembered talking over the idea with my mother, Holly, a Curved Bar (now Gold Award) Girl Scout. Having achieved the highest rank in the Girl Scouts of America, my mother understood the role of adult leaders well, which I expect helped my father's case. As Cubmaster, he already gave several hours each week to Pack 577. That was time away from home, his wife, and my brother and sister. The job of Scoutmaster would require much more time: monthly camping trips, summer camps, and the more complicated problems of adolescent young men. I still don't know what promises were made between my parents, but in 1988, I became the son of a Scoutmaster.

Alvin Townley, Jr., beneath a Chinese chestnut tree. Bert Adams Scout Reservation

"The Scoutmaster wives over the years have certainly made a great contribution in giving up their husbands for weekends, Scout meeting nights, and summer camp weeks," he observed. Then considering my brother and sister, he elaborated, "We were a Scouting family. Rob was there at the Pinewood Derby races as a young child, and Tressa was there spending time with siblings of other Scouts and with mothers whose husbands were either on the Troop Committee or involved in being an Assistant Scoutmaster. It's a family affair in many ways. You need the support of the entire family."

The job of Scoutmaster also required the support of other adults, the volunteers who served on the Troop Committee and as Assistant Scoutmasters. These men are no less important than Scoutmasters; without them, troops wouldn't exist. And in the case of John Kilpatrick, an Eagle himself, our troop wouldn't have eaten nearly so well on campouts. Nobody from Troop 103 will ever forget devouring Mr. Kilpatrick's Dutch-oven peach cobbler late at night under the light of softly hissing Coleman lanterns.

Alvin Townley, Jr., cover photograph for a 1960 National Jamboree program BOY SCOUTS OF AMERICA/COURTESY OF ALVIN TOWNLEY, JR.

"Not only did John have a merit badge sash that went over the shoulder and down the back a bit," my father said, "but he has been the glue that has held Troop 103 together through many Scoutmasters. If we hadn't had John on the Troop Committee, running so many aspects of the program and keeping up relations with our church sponsor, and if so many other dads hadn't been Assistant Scoutmasters, our troop couldn't have functioned. And I wouldn't have had as much fun on campouts, either!

"Part of being an Eagle Scout is giving back to Scouting by attempting to become a Scout leader of some type and helping other Scouts along the trail become an Eagle or achieve as many benefits as they can out of the Scouting program. That, to me, completes the process. You realize you never can give back as much as you have received from Scouting, but there is a great satisfaction in being able to help other Scouts achieve a measure of success."

As Scoutmaster, Alvin Townley, Jr., took two things seriously: safety and his Scoutmaster Conferences. He always proclaimed "A Scout is Safe" as the unwritten thirteenth point of the Scout Law. Until this particular trip to Bert

Adams Scout Reservation, however, I hadn't understood the root of his pre-occupation with safety.

The summer before I entered ninth grade, Peter McCarthy of nearby Troop 77 died in a car accident en route to Philmont. It shook our community badly. I remember my mother hugging me the morning after the news reached Atlanta, and I can still see my father, red-eyed, walking through the door that same morning in his Scout uniform; the community's Scout leaders had stayed with Peter's family during the night.

Peter's death deeply affected my father and every parent in our community. Every time the National Eagle Scout Association newsletter arrived in the mail, the number of Eagle Scouts listed as killed in automobile accidents struck him. When he received an offer from the National Safety Council for training as a defensive driving instructor, he accepted. "That's something I've done that helped make the community a little safer. I've thoroughly enjoyed doing it, and I think that was an outgrowth of having been Peter's Cubmaster and having pinned his Bobcat on him, his Wolf, his Bear, and his Webelos."

That explained all the Saturday mornings and Monday nights that he would leave home with a stack of papers and binders to teach groups of teenagers, parents, and grandparents how to drive with more care. I had never known the reason.

My father's other primary concern was the Scoutmaster conference. Before a boy could advance from one rank to the next, he had to prove his skills and knowledge to his Scoutmaster. Then he and the Scoutmaster discussed his personal goals and challenges, not only those related to Scouting but also those related to other aspects of his life. To this Scoutmaster, the primary aim of Scouting in general, and the conference in particular, was to teach boys how to make good decisions.

"In the Scoutmaster conference," he explained, "I'd try to use a little decision tree thought process with them, saying that if you made a bad decision, you now had a chance to make a good decision. In any of those Scoutmaster conferences with a young man who maybe had made a bad decision and was perhaps getting involved in things he shouldn't be getting involved in, sitting down with an adult—his Scoutmaster—and having an open and frank discussion about the fact that you were not doomed to continue making bad decisions became important. You had the *power* to make a good decision and continue making good decisions and reach the goals you'd set for yourself.

"In Troop 103 and in Eagle ceremonies at other troops across the United States," he expounded, "they use the phrase 'marked man.' Indeed Eagles are 'marked men' from there on out. And I think it's good for us to be reminded that we are, so if we find ourselves in a situation where we reach points on

Alvin Townley, Jr., (back row, far left) and Scoutmaster Alvin Townley, Sr., with Troop 84. COURTESY OF ALVIN TOWNLEY, JR.

that decision tree where we can either make a good or a bad choice, we will try to remember to make that good choice. The term *Eagle Scout*, is another phrase for 'making good choices.'"

My first memory of Scouting was the Chinese chestnut tree. The second was of the great buffalo trophy hanging over the stone fireplace in the Woodruff Dining Hall. After we had walked through several campsites, along the waterfront, and across the main field, we found a pair of rocking chairs in the empty dining hall and sat talking under the buffalo. We stayed there for some time, enjoying the shade and easy rhythm of the rockers.

I sat with the person who had encouraged me to complete my first Eagle project and ultimately earn the rank. I sat with the person who also had walked next to me ever since I started pursuing this journey, which became my second Eagle Scout project. From my first steps along this trail, my father encouraged me and challenged me. Although he no longer wore a uniform and his broad-brimmed campaign hat, he remained the Scoutmaster, helping me complete this project just as he helped me reach Eagle. He counseled me in making good decisions and always supported me when I felt like the journey had become too difficult. When I found myself feeling negative or discouraged, I always counted on the phone call that came as he commuted home from a day at work. Inevitably, he would have discovered a new Scouting story that he knew would lift my spirits. He encouraged me at every step, keeping me focused on my goal and on an ideal greater than myself. I in turn shared each of my stories with him, but I had yet to ask him about the legacy he saw in those accounts.

Turning to the Eagles I'd met during my travels, he observed, "Whether the Eagle Scouts you have met with are famous or only known by the Scouts from their troop and the families there, they all share a *love* for Scouting. I know in so many of the interviews you've had, the Eagle Scout you're interviewing, even though they may have a *huge* demand on their time, have difficulty pulling away once they start talking about Scouting because they begin to remember, I think, what a valuable experience it was. They remember their friendships. They begin to reflect on how important it was in their life. So from what you've discovered, I've learned how much people genuinely love their Scouting experience. And even the young Scouts—the Amerine brothers for example—they're all dedicated to passing on the ideals of Scouting to others.

"Those values of service to others, leadership, courage, excellence, dedication, and integrity—in short, honor—will never die out because that passion is there and every Scout passes those values on to the next generation, each in his own way. It happens in classrooms and communities. It happens in corporate boardrooms and in hospitals. It happens countless times every week in Scout meetings. It happens at summer camps and at jamborees and at world jamborees. It's an eternal cycle. That is the legacy of Scouting."

Our steps echoed across the empty floor as we walked through the dining hall beneath flags from old Scout troops and banners from jamborees of the past. We pushed through the screen doors that keep the Georgia gnats at bay during meals and emerged into the shade of ancient trees that had seen thousands of Scouts pass beneath their limbs during the past half century. The Scouts and their uniforms had changed over the generations, but the trees witnessed boys learning the same lessons year after year. In the dining hall behind them, the oaks heard one Oath taken in unison again and again. They heard the same songs. They listened to the same blessings recited over dinner. They saw the same cycle of giving and receiving between generations of Scouts.

My father and I looked out onto the expansive field separating the dining hall and the lake. The constant rattle and hum of crickets carried across the thick air that had settled over the sunlit grass. Nothing moved but the halyards on the three vacant flagpoles, which clanked gently against the metal poles with each warm breeze. The occasional gusts rustled the still-green leaves of the old oaks overhead and stirred those of a solitary Chinese chestnut tree behind us. The journey was over.

EPILOGUE

Near the end of the long trail that led to the shady trees of Bert Adams Scout Reservation, I stopped in St. Helena, California. I had come to meet Jeff Mathy, an Eagle Scout from Troop 93 in Orange County. Jeff and I chose hamburgers and Coca-Colas at Taylor's Refresher on Main Street over sauvignon blanc and hors d'oeuvres at one of the surrounding vineyards. We ate outdoors watching traffic pass up and down Napa Valley's main thorough-fare. We were roughly the same age and quickly discovered we were both travelers, or maybe *dreamers* is the better term. Soon, we were talking about dragons and journeys.

When he graduated from UC–Davis, Jeff set out to become the youngest climber to scale the world's Seven Summits, the highest peak on each conti-nent. He summited six before falling 400 meters short on Mt. Everest in 2003. He explained, "In the mountains, especially above 8,000 meters, if you don't feel 100 percent, you turn around and save it for another day. That's how mountaineers live to climb more mountains." His twenty-six-year-old life wasn't worth the risk.

There on the ridge leading to Everest's 29,035 foot summit, he realized that his quest was over. "It wasn't about finding success at the top of a moun-tain," he said. "The success came in overcoming what had challenged me to that point. It almost surprised me because the reward was everything else, and I didn't need the summit—to touch the top—to feel like I'd climbed Ever-est.

"I had to work so hard to get there. When it comes down to it, I'm an am-ateur climber. I'm somebody who doesn't have a lot of climbing skill. I found my way to the top of this mountain having at the beginning no skill, no money, and no experience. I had no starting point really other than Boy Scouts. I always say I blame the Boy Scouts for setting me on this path. I chuckle about it, but to tie it back to something like that is easy to do. Scouting gave me the tools I needed." I could certainly relate.

In Jeff's mind, he had completed his journey, finally answered what questions he had. "My ex-girlfriend's mother told me that all young men have a dragon they have to slay," he confided. "Once we do that, she said we could then come home and be normal again. I slew my dragon. I hope you've finally slain yours."

I hadn't thought of it like that. I contemplated Jeff's observation quietly as he finished his fries. For many, many months, I had been consumed by my questions, which in the end were equally about Scouting and my own heart. The wear of travel, the pressure to carry this project forward, and the challenge of telling these stories surprised me with their intensity. The experience of learning so much about so many things so quickly also shocked me. Taking a leap of faith and leaving work for a year, combined with attempting to digest the lessons these amazing people had taught me, stirred a level of introspection I'd never anticipated. That introspection, accentuated by days on the road and time alone with my thoughts, in some ways tore me down before it began building me back up. But at last, after many difficult and sometimes lonely miles, feelings of certainty and satisfaction began slowly warming me from inside. My deepest questions were finding answers. My dragon was in its death throes.

I knew this journey would never truly end; there are just too many perspectives for any one man, or any hundred men, to record. But I felt that I was nearing my last summit. I had been far more fortunate than I deserved. Wonderful people had welcomed me into their lives and homes. They openly shared their memories and experiences. They each helped me answer the questions with which I started, and they also put to rest questions that arose along the way. As my father and I drove away from the dining hall at Bert Adams, I knew it was time to stop and reflect on what I had learned.

When I began this trek, I didn't know what answers I would find or who might provide them. I did, however, have my hunches. Accordingly, I sought out the high-profile men universally recognized as Eagle Scouts, and I succeeded in meeting many of them. I began to suspect that the commonly held image was accurate: Eagles are conservative, clean-cut, and unflaggingly responsible. I thought Scouting produced Eagle Scouts who fit the same image, who were straight arrows and successful in traditional fields in conventional ways. But eventually, I discovered that the first steps along any trail rarely prove the most enlightening. The more Eagles I met, the more the old image began to morph. I did meet with polished businessmen and politicians, but I also spent time with Eagles from coast to coast who would shatter the predominant stereotype. I found some things I expected, many things I did not. By the end of this trip, my experiences had broadened my perspective and disproved many of my presumptions.

In the end, the individuals I encountered mirrored the diversity of America herself. Yet, irrespective of their politics, heritage, occupation, or interests, every one of these Eagles still tried to live life according to the principles of the Scout Oath and Law, both of which most still knew by heart.

That point brings me back to Sean O'Brien, my friend and frequent tent mate throughout our time in Troop 103. I can never say Sean was right or wrong when he decided to return his Eagle badge to National, but truthfully, I'm glad the idea struck him. He prompted me to ask important questions and seek out answers. When I began this search, I had wondered if there were a legacy and tradition of which Sean and I had a right to be proud. I wondered if Scouting has mattered. I found the answers in the lives of these Eagle Scouts and their shared belief in the concept of honor.

The initial words of the Scout Oath, "On my honor," constitute the first phrase recited by each young man when he joins Scouting. Over time, more than 110 million boys have stood before their fellow Scouts and taken the Oath, their right arm at a ninety-degree angle and their hand making the Scout sign. They pledge their honor to a set of ideals and a way of life. During the course of a Scouting career, that phrase—"On my honor"—is probably repeated more often than any other, and the term itself seemed especially important to this journey. But while I asked hundreds of Eagles about honor, I found no singular meaning. One eloquently described honor as "building the best part of yourself every day and sharing it with other human beings."

Others called it "keeping your word" or "being trustworthy." But few ideas of honor were the same.

Upon hearing the words my father used at Bert Adams Scout Reservation, I finally realized that honor goes beyond any blanket definition. It means the courage Freedom Rider Percy Sutton showed as he held his head high while he walked through crowds that despised him. It means the drive for excellence that always burned in Bill Marriott. Honor is, in part, the integrity about which Kim Clark spoke at Harvard Business School; in part, it is also the duty to others that marked Scott Strauss's actions on September 11. Honor is the sense of service that guides William H. Gates as he creates new futures for the world's children. It is the leadership of Travis Amerine, as a brigade commander and a brother.

As I came to understand the facets of this ideal, I gradually realized the concept of honor forms a framework in which millions of people have found a context for their lives. During their younger years, they learned to excel and attain great heights, but, more important, they learned to achieve—and live— significantly. Their parents and leaders trained them to consider goals and accomplishments in a broader context. They grew to understand that ability and success in turn entail duty and responsibility.

I considered this framework and began to understand one of my journey's great lessons. I grew to believe that, in the end, our only truly worthwhile actions are those we perform for others and that it matters little whether those acts are for millions of constituents, thousands of patients, several friends, your children, your spouse, or one stranger. Over time, the only marks we leave will be those seen in the lives of others.

In this sense, honor can become quite personal, a point conveyed to me one night in South Carolina. I recall standing beside Donnie Boyd as he slowly rifled through the top drawer of his dresser. He soon closed the drawer and turned to me, holding four black cases in his hands. He had me open each in turn. He smiled gently as I opened the first three medals and read aloud the inscription penciled into each case. Written in the hand of a young teenager, they read: "To Donnie Boyd, for Marksmanship, Camp Barstow." They were dated 1939, 1940, and 1941.

Then Mr. Boyd had me open the last case, which held his Eagle badge. As we stood looking at the worn medal, his wife, Susan, walked into the bedroom, her still-young eyes sparkling. "The real reason he's a good Eagle

Scout," she said, wrapping her arms around her husband, "is that he's taken good care of me for fifty years!"

No matter the venue, whether it be home, Wall Street, or Congress, those who adopted the virtues represented by the Eagle rank have lived for others. They live the same values whether they are wilderness guides who spend days on rivers and trails, teaching the values of the backcountry; businessmen who travel from state to state building companies and earning a living; or physicians who tend to patients every day, then return home to be with family each night. Most every individual I met had found his or her own way of making a mark, of leaving the world better for their having lived here. They also felt an obligation to lead others toward those ends, and, again, it mattered not if they led by position, example, or word; as a general, Scoutmaster, volunteer, or teacher.

In a broader sense, the world depends upon people each doing their best to make their mark. It is the sum of many actions rather than several solitary deeds that will ultimately shape history. The individuals I met are Eagle Scouts, but their legacy is not Scouting's alone. Their stories are part of our American legacy. Their actions, values, and character represent those things all citizens cherish and aspire to live up to. With millions of similar personal acts of courage, kindness, and duty, people bound by common virtues will create our future.

Lord Baden-Powell understood that reality a century ago when he founded the Scouting movement. By instilling common values in Britain's—and later the world's young men, Baden-Powell truly influenced the path of world events. One Scout might become prime minister, but Scouting's founder knew the legacy of his movement would largely be reflected in thousands of small, unheralded deeds and decisions that would collectively shape what was to come.

To extend Scouting to other nations, Baden-Powell designed a program with a foundation supported by individuals as diverse as the world itself. He had to distill virtues equally respected in imperial Britain and its far-flung colonies, mainland Europe, the Americas, and the nations of Asia. The founders of Scouting in the United States had to overcome a similar challenge. I found their success in the variety of Eagles I met: stalwart liberals from the South and stubborn conservatives from the Northeast, a Muslim in Massachusetts and a Mormon in Utah, a soldier serving in Iraq and a teacher

speaking out against the war. They believe in living honestly, working diligently, and caring for others. They share fundamental values and experiences
that remind all of us—Scouts or not—that, at heart, we aren't so different
from each other. In a world that seems to be drifting toward polarization, that
may be Scouting's most valuable contribution of all.

So, having traveled these miles and having met a portion of America's Eagle
Scouts, how do I answer my good friend Sean? As POW George Coker explained, I discovered that Scouting is not an organization, although a large
infrastructure supports it. In truth, a century after it began, it remains a
movement and a program in which millions of youth in thousands of unique
Scout troops participate. Scouting truly happens in more than 53,000 individual troops, each sponsored by a different institution and each with a different group of volunteer leaders. Yet the remarkable thing is this: The young
men these thousands of diverse troops produce all learn the same basic lessons. They learn to set goals and reach them; to help Scouts in their troop and
citizens in their community; to lead others and to meet challenges. They become outdoorsmen and conservationists; they discover new passions and
possibilities. They come to understand one another and carry away something fundamental about honesty, loyalty, reverence, and duty.

Like Sean, most Eagles forever carry a sense of responsibility to the
ideals of the Scouting program. Sean planned to return his badge because he
still cared about the program years after he left it. He took a stand and did
what he thought was right. I would tell him, however, that I found Scouting to
be much larger than the policies and politics of the present day, but that I respect his views. I would share the amazing ways dedicated Scoutmasters in
troops large and small change millions of young lives for the better. I would
let him know that I found a real and vibrant legacy comprised of millions of
individual acts of which we can both always be proud.

As I considered what I had learned and what I wanted to share, I realized that
perhaps one last section of this trail remained. Sean and I walked it together
at Notre Dame. Crossing the historic university's campus beneath canopies
of shady trees, Sean, now a professor of Irish literature, patiently listened to

me reflect on my time with these Eagle Scouts. Then he shared his own perspectives.

"Your journey has been my journey in many ways," observed Sean. "I was there with you along the way, and this journey kept our friendship steady during a time when there were lots of reasons not to keep in touch: Life moves pretty fast after college, and it only gets faster. Friends tend to drift apart. But you kept me thinking about Scouting—and thinking about more than the politics involved—although you know I still take issue with the same policies. Scouting and the values we learned there and the experiences we had together—you and me—are just a part of who I am, and, indirectly, you kept reminding me of that."

Then Sean took a deep breath. "So here's the thing," he said. "I never sent my Eagle badge back to National."

Silence.

Quickly filling the void, Sean explained, "I never felt I could abandon Scouting like that. Ever since I first told you I was going to send back my Eagle, I've really intended to follow through. My brother Kevin and I kept planning to send ours back together, but we never did it. We just had too many mixed feelings. I always meant to return it, but I just couldn't do it. Scouting is too much a part of me. I hope that doesn't ruin your story."

I thought for a moment about what my old friend had told me, and I considered the many miles I'd traveled thinking he *had* abandoned Scouting. I contemplated the journey he prompted me to take. I thought about what I had wanted to discover, what I *did* discover, and what I had shared with him along the way. I smiled. He had answered my last question.

"That doesn't ruin the story, Sean," I said. "That completes it."

IN REMEMBRANCE

Alvin M. Townley, Sr.

1903–1996

Alvin Townley, Sr., presenting the Eagle Scout rank to the author, Alvin Townley III

ACKNOWLEDGMENTS

One of the most valuable pieces of advice I received along these miles came from a professor I met in Boston who told me, "Alvin, remember three things: First, there are millions of stories, and you can't hear them all. Second, you can't tell all the stories you *do* hear. Third, if something is really worth doing, it's worth doing imperfectly. So you have to do your best, then make yourself finish."

At first, I didn't anticipate the challenges that professor knew I would eventually face. Soon after I began exploring the legacy of Scouting, however, I began to understand the enormity and, in some senses, the impossibility of what I'd started. More than 110 million people of every conceivable type have experienced Scouting in units from Florida to Texas to California. The leaders, experiences, and values of the program have shaped each Scout in a different way. I quickly realized that my journey would leave millions of worthy stories unheard, many important subjects unexplained. But in the time I had, I did my best to capture accounts of Scouting and of life from Eagles young and old, from the West Coast and the East Coast, from middle-class families and from those of the most humble backgrounds. My chief regret will always be that I could never hear every story and that I could not tell each story that I did hear. But each person kind enough to share his time with me has in some way shaped the pages of *Legacy of Honor*.

When this journey became a book, I was both honored and challenged to explain in writing how deeply one set of ideals has affected so many in so many ways. Telling this story has been a privilege and, truly, a labor of love. I just hope I have not failed these virtues or the individuals who have lived them.

An old Blue Ridge Mountains maxim says, "If you see a turtle on top of a fence post, you know it didn't get there by itself." I feel like that turtle. Without the time, counsel, and help of so many individuals, I could never have told these stories.

This adventure really began years ago when I became a Scout myself. I will always remember the leaders—adults and Scouts alike—who helped me through the ranks in Troop 103 and in the Egwa Tawa Dee Lodge. I'm forever in the debt of my teachers at Lakeside, who made me hungry to learn. My professors and deans at Washington and Lee University taught me to ask questions and challenge myself; they continued teaching me long after I graduated. My extended families at Washington and Lee, Haygood, Paces Valley, Reach for Excellence, and Marist School in Atlanta always supported me and helped me learn about character and life. I am also thankful for the many members of the Scouting family who have assisted and encouraged me along the way.

Innumerable people have helped me arrange interviews, obtain information and long-lost photographs, and make contact with certain Eagles; I'm in their debt as well. And what can I say to the Eagle Scouts who made time amidst busy lives to talk with me about life, Scouting, and character? In a very real sense, this is your book, and I'm forever appreciative.

In New York, my agent, Jack Scovil, stuck with the book until we found the perfect home, and he always tempered the impulsive whims of this first-time writer. Pete Wolverton at Thomas Dunne Books believed in the book from the instant he saw it, as did my patient editor, Peter Joseph, who helped shape the manuscript and guide this project as only an Eagle Scout could.

In Atlanta, many talented and patient individuals contributed their thoughts to the manuscript, reading (and rereading) innumerable chapters along the way. This story is immeasurably better for your insights. And a special thanks to my cousin Mary Ellen Wiggins who did Wellesley proud by contributing her perspectives during the final stretch.

When I first began this long journey, I found only encouragement in those who knew me well and even in those whom I had just met. Their support never wavered. They never seemed to doubt me, even when I took a quite unconventional leap into total uncertainty and spent a year immersed in writing this book. I could never have afforded hotel rooms for all the nights I spent on the road, so I will always be indebted to the many friends who opened their homes to me and who, in a very real way, sustained me. Many of my best memories from the past months come from the time I spent with hosts across the country: walking through the surf before dinner in San Diego, being picked up time and again from the Boston Public Library after a day of writing, having breakfast with the Entrepreneurship Merit Badge team at the National Jamboree, playing bocce in the evenings behind the Wasatch Mountains. These friends became family, and I'm grateful for their enthusiasm. Without them, this book would not have been completed.

I'm particularly blessed with a wonderful circle of close friends and family to whom and for whom I'm very thankful. There are so many people who supported and encouraged me along the way and I wish I could list each one herein, but that would be a chapter unto itself. You know who you are. Thank you. Specifically, however, I do want to thank Stephen Thomas and Chris Baldwin, who never let me lose focus. My brother and sister, Rob and Tressa, along with my brother-in-law, Marty, always kept my perspective light. My parents always believed in me. Their constant example, support, and love have meant everything.

In the end, I've written a story about others, and I hope I've done them justice. I want those who read these pages to share their own stories of character and service, for each is part of this legacy. I also hope they will remember the value that comes from putting others first. And I wish all those who hear this story will forever bear in mind those common values that make our country a nation.

BIBLIOGRAPHY

Ashman, Fred and Liener Temerlin. 2004 Eisenhower Award Honoring Ross Perot. Multi Image Productions, Inc., San Diego, California, 2004.

Bloomberg, Michael. *Bloomberg by Bloomberg*. New York: John Wiley & Sons, 2001.

Boy Scouts of America, *Annual Report, 2005*.

Boy Scouts of America, "Fact Sheet: Scouting Around the World."

Boy Scouts of America, *Historical Highlights*, 2004 printing.

Boy Scouts of America, National Council African-American Scouting presentation, 2006.

Boy Scouts of America, "Research Report on Eagle Scouts," 2006.

CNN, "Remembering September 11, 2001." Saturday, September 11, 2004.

Covington, Howard and Marian A. Ellis. *Terry Sanford: Politics, Progress, and Outrageous Ambition*. Durham, N.C.: Duke University Press, 1999.

Fox News, Interview with U.S. Senator Richard G. Lugar, September 2001.

Gergen, David. "A Conscience with Bite." *U.S. News & World Report*, May 4, 1998.

Gergen, David. "Putting Country First." *Cigar Aficionado*. March/April 2002.

Hillcourt, William. *Baden-Powell: The Two Lives of a Hero*. Boy Scouts of America, 1981.

Laackman, Blair. *Gerald Ford's Scouting Years*. Grand Rapids: West Michigan Shores Council, Boy Scouts of America, 1982.

Lovell, Jim and Jeffrey Kluger. *Apollo 13*. New York: Houghton Mifflin, 2000.

Marriott, J. W., Jr., and Kathi Ann Brown. *The Spirit to Serve: Marriott's Way*. New York: HarperBusiness, 1997.

McLaughlin, Elliott. "No More Hurricane Katrinas." *CNN*, Friday, April 7, 2006.

Posner, Gerald. *Citizen Perot*. New York: Random House, 1996.

Robinson, Phil Alden. *Field of Dreams*. Universal Studios, Hollywood, 1989.

Scott, Robert L., Jr. *God Is My Co-Pilot*. New York: Scribners, 1943.

Scott, Robert L., Jr. *The Day I Owned the Sky*. New York: Bantam, 1988.

Troop 354, Dundalk, Maryland. "Troop 354 Helps Create Artificial Reef in Chesapeake Bay," February 2006, http://www.troop354.org.

Walton, Sam and John Huey. *Sam Walton: Made in America*. New York: Doubleday, 1992.

U.S. Congress. Federal Charter, Boy Scouts of America, June 15, 1916.

INDEX